God's Prayer Book showcases the
read, lived, and prayed deeply. Ben Patterson has a marvelous gift of being able to engage the seasoned disciple of Christ while also ably tutoring those just beginning the journey. This book is a deeply affecting, gentle, and practical guide to the art and relationship of prayer.

GARY THOMAS
Author of *The Beautiful Fight*

Ben Patterson has written a wise book about a tough topic. He helps us not only *understand* the Psalms but *pray* them—so that our fractured souls can embrace the fullness of God.

MARK GALLI
Senior managing editor of *Christianity Today*; author of *Jesus Mean and Wild: The Unexpected Love of an Untamable God*

If you are like me, you find yourself often drawn to prayer, and at other times, utterly incapable of it. Using the Psalms as a lighted path, Patterson guides us, with great freedom, to prayers that unlock our souls and cause us to experience a compelling vision of God. These pages are by my bedside table, my nighttime companion in my conversations with God.

NANCY ORTBERG
Founding partner of Teamworx2; author of *Looking for God: An Unexpected Journey Through Tattoos, Tofu, and Pronouns*

The Psalms are the prayer book of the people of God, but his wonderful resource of communion with God is foreign to many Christians today. Ben Patterson masterfully opens up the riches of the Psalms in a way that will deepen and enliven the prayer life of his readers.

TREMPER LONGMAN III
Robert H. Gundry Professor of Biblical Studies, Westmont College; author of *How to Read the Psalms*

In this wise, thoughtful, and engaging introduction and reflections on the Psalms, Patterson invites us to a fresh and deeper life of prayer in response to God and in communion with God's people throughout the centuries and around the world. This is a helpful resource for beginners and beyond.

THE REV. DR. ROBERTA HESTENES
Educator, speaker, and author of *Using the Bible in Groups*

THE POWER
AND PLEASURE OF
PRAYING THE PSALMS

GOD'S PRAYER BOOK

BEN PATTERSON

SALTRIVER®

An Imprint of Tyndale House Publishers, Inc.,
Carol Stream, Illinois

Visit Tyndale's exciting Web site at www.tyndale.com

TYNDALE is a registered trademark of Tyndale House Publishers, Inc.

SaltRiver and the SaltRiver logo are registered trademarks of Tyndale House Publishers, Inc.

God's Prayer Book: The Power and Pleasure of Praying the Psalms

Designed by Beth Sparkman

Published in association with the literary agency of Credo Communications, LLC, Grand Rapids, MI 49525; www.credocommunications.net.

Library of Congress Cataloging-in-Publication Data

Patterson, Ben, date.
God's prayer book : the power and pleasure of praying the psalms / Ben Patterson.
p. cm.
Includes bibliographical references and index.
ISBN-13: 978-1-4143-1665-9 (sc)
ISBN-10: 1-4143-1665-8 (sc)
1. Bible. O.T. Psalms—Criticism, interpretation, etc. 2. Prayer—Christianity. I. Title.
BS1430.52.P38 2008
223'.2077—dc22 2008021253

Printed in the United States of America

14 13 12 11 10 09 08
7 6 5 4 3 2 1

DEDICATION

To Lauretta, my dearest, my wife, my prayer companion, my wise editor, and fountain of insights into the Psalms. You have prayed with me through these psalms every step of the way, and through a marriage whose grace, richness, and hilarity I could not have imagined when we began this pilgrimage together thirty-seven years ago. In his light we have seen light.

To the good folks at Santa Barbara Community Church and to the finest pastors I know: Reed, Steve, Kelly, and Mike. You great people have met with me weekly every Tuesday morning at 6:45 for six years to learn prayer! This is your book too.

SOLI DEO GLORIA.

CONTENTS

PSALMS AND DEVOTIONALS

THE PSALMS: MUSIC TO GOD'S EARS

James Boice said learning to pray is a little like learning to play the violin with the virtuosos. No instrument sounds worse in the beginning stages of learning; it's all screech and scratch. But if the student is determined to play well, he checks the program guide for the classical music station and notes when the violin concertos will be aired. He buys the music score for each concerto and does his best to play along with the orchestra. At first he sounds terrible. As time passes, however, he begins little by little to sound more and more like the orchestra. But all along, as he groans on his instrument, the orchestra plays the music beautifully—his poor performance is caught up and completed in the music of the masters. So it is with us and prayer: By praying the Psalms back to God, we learn to pray in tune with the Father, Son, and Holy Spirit.[1]

It is no accident that the great prayers of the book of Psalms are also songs. They are the sheet music, the score and libretto of prayer. They are the building blocks for the music of eternity. Better than the things we ask God for in prayer is the God we pray to—and *with*—and the sweet music we make as we do.

I am learning to pray in harmony with the Psalms, but I must admit I got off to a slow start. I became a Christian at age ten, but it wasn't until decades later that the Psalms began to teach me to pray. So although I'm now well into adulthood, you are reading the words of a new convert. I'm still wide eyed and breathless and maybe a little over the top with enthusiasm when I talk about their value. If I succeed with this book, you will be too.

There is no better place in all of Scripture than the Psalms to learn to be with God and to see with the eyes of faith the face of the One who longs to form us fully in his image. But the Psalms can be hard; they often stretch and perplex as they teach. How could it be otherwise? The Psalms are *God's* prayer book, and they teach us to talk to God in his own language.

Learning to pray is, in fact, like learning language. Most babies come into the world full of some very strong desires and feelings. They are quite capable of expressing them in grunts, gurgles, squeals, and sobs. But it's a stretch to call their utterances language. It would be tragic if, at age eighteen, these noises were still all they knew about communication. And it would be worse than tragic if at age eighteen they were still asking for the things they wanted at three months, if their desires had not expanded and matured as they learned to speak.

The process of learning language is complex and wonderful; it begins with a child listening to his or her parents, then mimicking and copying what he or she hears. But a child is not a parrot, and very quickly mimicry turns to meaning. Words and ideas and desires match up with each other and are woven together in syntax and grammar. With language comes a culture and a way of understanding the world and other people. It's marvelous what happens when we learn language: We are taken out of ourselves to what is beyond ourselves. It's not just our informing the world who we are; it's the world informing us who it is. It's not just our telling others what we want; it's others telling us what they want. Language changes us, making us more than we were when we were merely trying to express ourselves.

Prayer, like language, begins with being able to hear. Prayer starts not when we speak to God but when God speaks to us. In the beginning was the Word; God's word, not ours. Before all time, before you and I were, was the Word; the Light that gives light and life to everyone.[2] There would be no speech if God had not first spoken. We would have nothing to say if God had not first said something to us. Ultimately then, all our prayers are answers to God's prayer—his gracious Word of love to us! We love, and we pray, because he first loved us.[3] That's what Dietrich Bonhoeffer was referring to when he wrote, "The richness of the Word of God ought to determine our prayer, not the poverty of our heart."[4] The Bible, the written Word of God, tells us what God wants, and more important, what God is like. It expresses his will and reveals his character. The relationship between the Bible and prayer is profound. This is especially true when it comes to the Psalms.

Picture it this way: Children and other novices to the Scriptures have long been told that the best way to find the book of Psalms, the longest book in the Bible, is to put their fingers in the middle of the Bible—in its heart, so to speak. What is the book of Psalms? It is a book of prayers. And the longest prayer in this longest book is Psalm 119, a prayer about God's Word, the Scriptures. Prayer is at the heart of the Bible, and the Bible is in the heart of prayer.

But that's just a picture, an illustration of the relationship between the Psalms and prayer. Better is a demonstration—the prayer life of our Lord Jesus Christ. At the end of his life, as he hung dying on the cross, he went to the Scriptures for his prayers—more specifically, to the Psalms. "My God, my God, why have you abandoned me?" (Matthew 27:46) is a quotation from Psalm 22:1. "Father, I entrust my spirit into your hands!" (Luke 23:46) comes from Psalm 31:5. At the point of his greatest anguish and extremity, Jesus turned to the Bible for his prayers. Charles Spurgeon reminds us that, when he most needed to pray, Jesus, the grand original thinker, saw no need to be original or extemporaneous. "How instructive is this great truth that the Incarnate Word lived on the Inspired Word! It was food to him, as it is to us; and . . . if Christ thus lived upon the Word of God, should not you and I do the same? . . . I think it well worthy of your constant remembrance that, even in death, our blessed Master showed the ruling passion of his spirit, so that his last words were a quotation from Scripture."[5]

As a devout Jew, Jesus considered the Psalms to be his prayer book. A close look at the Psalms shows the Lord's Prayer—the prayer Jesus taught us to pray—to be a summary and distillation of all the prayers that are to be found in the heart of the Bible. It's all there in the Psalms: prayer that God's name be hallowed, that his rule be supreme and his will be done, that our needs be met and our sins forgiven, that we be kept safe from all danger to soul and body.

Martin Luther loved the Psalms. He called them "a little Bible," because they contain, "set out in the briefest and most beautiful form, all that is to be found in the Bible."

Sizing Up the Psalms

The psalms that first got my attention were the psalms that always seem to be the right thing to pray, no matter the mood or situation. I call them the "one size fits all" psalms, like the band on my adjustable baseball hat. These psalms can be expanded or contracted to fit any situation. For example, Psalm 103 is always the right thing to pray—always true, always fitting, in every time and place:

Let all that I am praise the LORD;
with my whole heart, I will praise his holy name.
Let all that I am praise the LORD;
may I never forget the good things he does for me.
He forgives all my sins
and heals all my diseases.
He redeems me from death
and crowns me with love and tender mercies.
He fills my life with good things.
My youth is renewed like the eagle's!

Next came the psalms that seemed to fit my mood, that helped me say what I felt in the moment. I call them the "this size fits some" psalms. For instance, when I was feeling guilty, speechless with remorse, Psalm 51 was a perfect fit. No matter how mute guilt had made me, I could open my Bible and my mouth and say, "Have mercy on me, O God, because of your unfailing love. Because of your great compassion, blot out the stain of my sins." Same with Psalm 130: "LORD, if you kept a record of our sins, who, O Lord, could ever survive? But you offer forgiveness, that we might learn to fear you." I literally couldn't have said it better myself. If God held my sins against me, I'd be toast, dead meat, on the ash heap. But he forgives them all! Therefore I bow in abject, broken, and joyful reverence. Psalms like these gave me confidence to speak to God when I least felt that I could. They still do.

Adding up the psalms in the two categories I could relate to—the "this size fits some" psalms, or the mood psalms; and the "one size fits all" psalms—I didn't know what to do with all the rest, which was most of them. The most obvious example is Psalm 137, with its chilling last line: "Happy is the one who takes your babies and smashes them against the rocks!" But that's an extreme example. There were plenty of psalms that seemed too remote from my experience to have much to do with my prayer life. Psalm 87 has a good line or two if I was preaching a sermon that needed to reference ancient Jewish attitudes toward Jerusalem, but otherwise I didn't know how I could meaningfully pray personally,

On the holy mountain
stands the city founded by the LORD.

He loves the city of Jerusalem
        more than any other city in Israel.
O city of God,
        what glorious things are said of you!

I was really at a loss with psalms like Psalm 88. It doesn't have one happy thing to say about God or life and ends with, "You have taken away my companions and loved ones. Darkness is my closest friend." Those lines do not describe anything I have ever felt. Maybe they will someday, but so far, so good. But most problematic was Psalm 22, which Jesus quoted on the cross. I could preach this psalm as a meditation on the sufferings of Christ, but I couldn't get myself to pray, "My God, my God, why have you abandoned me? Why are you so far away when I groan for help?" Would it not be blasphemous for me, Ben Patterson, to pray what only Jesus could pray?

My enemies surround me like a pack of dogs;
        an evil gang closes in on me.
        They have pierced my hands and feet.
I can count all my bones.
        My enemies stare at me and gloat.
They divide my garments among themselves
        and throw dice for my clothing.

So there were a lot of psalms that seemed either alien or off limits. Most of them, actually. My slim psalm repertoire was a picture of the thinness of my prayer life—and my heart.

It was also a picture of my shallow sense of Christian identity. I was what someone called a "yearbook Christian." I came to the Psalms like I came to my twenty-year high school reunion—thumbing through the index of my old yearbook, looking only for the page numbers of the pictures of me and my friends, and ignoring the rest.

Not Much in My Heart to Pour Out

My sophomore year in college, my friends and I decided to spend two hours in prayer for the salvation of the unsaved high school students we were working with. We purposed to storm heaven and bring down the blessings of God for these kids. One of us had a part-time job in a church, so he asked the pastor if we could meet for prayer in the church building, a logical place to pray, one would think. The pastor told us just to show up some evening, any evening, and since my friend had a key to the building, we could pray anywhere we wanted. But the night we came to pray the church was bustling with activity, as various committee meetings, youth programs, and choir practice were spread throughout the facility. It was busier and more full of distraction than our homes and dorm rooms. The only free space was a large janitor's closet that smelled strongly of detergent and disinfectant.

So we gathered in that closet to pour out our hearts to God. We had two hours to do nothing but stand before the Lord's throne and plead for the salvation of souls. We prayed every which way we knew: We praised God and confessed our sins and lifted up the names of all the students we could think of. Then we praised and confessed and interceded some more. When we had prayed for everything and in every way we could think of, over and over, I looked at my watch to see if we had any time left. Just fifteen minutes had passed! The next one hour and forty-five minutes of prayer were the longest and slowest I had ever experienced.

I came to pour out my heart to God and discovered that there wasn't much in my heart to pour out. It would be years before I understood why I saw prayer in the same way I saw the Psalms—only as a tool to help me ask God for what I wanted. The problem was that I wanted so little! What I didn't understand was that learning to pray was learning to desire the things God wants to give, and then asking him for them.

The greatest enemy of prayer is not asking for too much of God but for too little. We're like Bontsha the Silent in the Yiddish writer Isaac Peretz's sad tale. All his life he had been denied, passed over, oppressed, and forgotten. Chronic disappointment had robbed him of the ability even to dream or desire; he had come to expect nothing and want nothing. He was Bontsha the Silent.

When he died he found himself standing before God in the court of heaven. God smiled tenderly at Bontsha and said, "My son, all your joyless life you had nothing. You lived without hope. But now, here in my presence, there is the fullness of joy, eternal pleasures at my right hand. Only ask, and you shall receive. Anything, anything you want, shall be yours."

The little man with a shrunken soul squinted his eyes and pondered the offer. "Anything? Anything at all?" he asked suspiciously.

"Yes," said the Almighty. "Anything you want."

After a long pause, he said to the Almighty, "I would like a freshly baked roll, with real butter."

Heaven wept.[6] The greater tragedy of Bontsha's life was not what he had been denied, but what he had ceased to desire. God had been reduced to the size of a loaf of bread and butter. This man had become far too easily pleased.

It wasn't—and isn't—that Bontsha's desires or ours are unworthy to express to God in prayer. He is our loving and compassionate Father, and he listens to all we say with a kind and wise heart. But he knows better than we do what we need—and better yet, he desires things for us that we may not even desire for ourselves.

More than a Tool for Self-Expression

Prayer is more than a tool for self-expression, a means to get God to give us what we want. It is a means he uses to give us what he wants,[7] and to teach us to want what he wants. Holy Scripture in general, and the Psalms in particular, teach us who God is and what he wants to give.

When the members of his synagogue complained that the words of the liturgy did not express what they felt, Abraham Heschel, the great philosopher of religion, replied wisely and very biblically. He told them that the liturgy wasn't supposed to express what they felt; they were supposed to feel what the liturgy expressed. To be taught by the Bible to pray is to learn to want and feel what the Bible expresses—to say what it means and mean what it says.

Those who have practiced this kind of prayer over time make a surprising discovery: As they learn to feel what the Psalms express, their hearts and desires are enlarged. They find that what they once regarded as strong desires were really weak, puerile little wishes, debased inklings of what is good. Of course! Would not the God who made us in his own image understand better than we ever could what we really need? And shouldn't we ask him for it? As C. S. Lewis put it,

> Indeed, if we consider the unblushing promises of reward and the staggering nature of the rewards promised in the Gospels, it would seem that Our Lord finds our desires not too strong, but too weak. We are half-hearted creatures, fooling about with drink and sex and ambition when infinite joy is offered us, like an ignorant child who wants to go on making mud pies in a slum because he cannot imagine what is meant by the offer of a holiday at the sea. We are far too easily pleased.[8]

The best part of prayer is who you pray to. Answers to prayer are wonderful, but the Answerer is better. Spend enough time with Jesus, and you'll start to look and think and act like Jesus. Seeing is becoming. The church father Irenaeus said, "The glory of God is man fully alive, and the life of man is the vision of God." It's true: God is never more glorified than when we come alive to the vision of God. Prayer is anticipation and preparation for the great day promised in Scripture when we will see Christ fully and "will be like him, for we will see him as he really is."[9]

Augustine prayed,

> How shall I call upon my God, my God and my Lord, since in truth when I call upon him I call him into myself? Is there any place within me where God can dwell? How can God come into me, God who made heaven and earth? O Lord my God, is there any place in me that can contain you?[10]

Is there any place in us that can contain God? No, there is not. Something must expand us for that to happen. The Psalms are God's gracious gift to us to do that very thing. How sweet and kind of God to give us a book of prayers in his Word. This Word "is alive and powerful . . . sharper than the sharpest two-edged sword, cutting between soul and spirit, between joint and marrow. It exposes our innermost thoughts and desires."[11] This is the very Word he gives us to pray in the Psalms!

Paul coined a word to describe the character of Scripture: He said it is "inspired by God" (2 Timothy 3:16). The Greek is literally "God-breathed." The breath of God permeates the Bible. The breath of God is the Holy Spirit, the same Spirit who spoke light into darkness and turned dust into living beings made in the image of God. This is the Spirit who speaks to us in the Bible, making it "useful to teach us what is true and to make us realize what is wrong in our lives. It corrects us when we are wrong and teaches us to do what is right" (2 Timothy 3:16). With this thought no doubt in mind, the poet George Herbert described prayer as "God's breath in man returning to his birth."[12] The same Breath that gives us breath to pray comes to us through the God-breathed Scriptures. What we inhale in the Word of God, we exhale in prayer. Like language, what comes in comes out, changing us in the process.

Certainly, God invites us to pour out our hearts to him. The Psalms, which John Calvin called "an anatomy of all parts of the human soul," can help us do that.[13] All the joys, pleasures, hopes, fears, despairs, doubts, heartaches, terrors, and longings of which we are capable are mirrored, clarified, sanctified, and transformed in the Psalms, as are all the ways we may pray: supplication, intercession, praise, thanks, lament, and meditation. The Psalms, as many have said, are a mirror; they will reveal you. Yet they are much more. Read them and they will read you. Pray them and they will change you.

Prayer is better than a tool for mere self-expression, unless the self being expressed is the self being shaped by the Word of God into the image of Christ. And who is Christ, but the new Adam, the true human, the faithful Son who lived as we were all created by God to live? When we sin we are apt to excuse ourselves and say, "I'm only human." But Jesus knows better. He points to himself and says, in effect, "When you sin, you are less than human." We say, "Just be yourself when you pray." Jesus says, in effect, "You need to be a self, a true self, before you can be yourself."

To be in God's presence is to be transformed. At the end of *The Divine Comedy*, Dante writes of passing through the levels of hell and purgatory before ascending through heaven into God's very presence. He tries to describe what he saw when he looked into the face of God. Words fail him, for human language cannot express such a sight. But he does describe the effect gazing into the face of God has on his will and desire:

> But now my desire and will were revolved, like a wheel which is moved evenly, by the love that moves the sun and other stars.[14]

The same love that moves stars and constellations and nebulae moves you. The apostle Paul said that to be in the presence of God is to have a veil lifted so we ". . . can see and reflect the glory of the Lord. And the Lord—who is the Spirit—makes us more and more like him as we are changed into his glorious image."[15]

James Gilmour, the great Scottish missionary to Mongolia, went to the Psalms again and again when he was stuck in his prayer life, powerless to generate devotion on his own. "When I feel I cannot make headway in devotion, I open the Psalms and push in my canoe, and let myself be carried along in the stream of devotion which flows through the whole book. The current always sets toward God, and in most places is strong and deep."[16]

It's about *Us*

So learning to pray is learning to ask for the things that God wants to give. It is to be expanded in mind and spirit. There's a second thing I didn't understand about prayer that night in the janitor's closet: Prayer is not just about me; it's about us. This is especially the case with the Psalms—the "one size fits some" and the "one size fits all" types. The Psalms were first the prayers of Israel, the people of God. With the coming of Christ they continue to be the prayers of Israel, but now it is the new Israel, the church—all those Jesus "ransomed . . . for God from every tribe and language and people and nation . . . [and] caused . . . to become a Kingdom of priests for our God" (Revelation 5:9-10). For millennia the people of God have prayed the Psalms, corporately and individually, but with the accent always on corporate prayer.

My problem with the Psalms was my problem with prayer: There was too much "me and Jesus" in my praying, and there needed to be a lot more "we and Jesus." Eugene Peterson is right on the mark when he writes, "No Christian is an only child."[17] I never pray merely as an individual. Whether I am physically alone or in a group when I pray, I always pray as a member of the Body of Christ, a priest in a whole Kingdom of priests. To come into the presence of the living God is always to come with all those other people who, like me, have been given the same privilege. To ignore them is to reject the gift. "Prayer is an act, indeed *the* act of fellowship," writes Peter Taylor Forsyth. "We cannot truly pray for ourselves without passing beyond ourselves and our individual experience. . . . Even private prayer is common prayer."[18]

Now that is a liberating thought! When I pray, even if I am alone, I may imagine myself standing in the midst of a colossal assembly of God's people, "from every tribe and language and people and nation"[19] *praying with them*. That insight alone would have transformed that smelly janitor's closet into a place of wonder and awe. According to Hebrews 12, when we pray we enter into a scene that is something like the Rose Bowl on New Year's Day, times a billion: exuberant, majestic, noisy, the mother of all prayer meetings. For when we pray we come to:

> Mount Zion, to the city of the living God, the heavenly Jerusalem, and to countless thousands of angels in a joyful gathering . . . to the assembly of God's firstborn children, whose names are written in heaven . . . to God himself, who is the judge over all things . . . to the spirits of the righteous ones in heaven who have now been made perfect. (Hebrews 12:22-23)

We Don't Start the Praying, We Join the Praying

I am humbled and thrilled to know that the praying doesn't begin when I begin to pray. When I begin to pray, I join the praying! The implications are stunning. When we pray we participate in what the Apostles' Creed calls "the communion of saints." We stand before the throne of God with all who are his—past, present, and future. Peter Kreeft calls God the "eternal contemporary," meaning Abraham, Isaac, and Jacob are as alive to him as we are.[20] They are really there with us in God's presence, along with countless others, living and dead: Moses and Peter and Paul and J. S. Bach; Luther, Augustine, Aquinas, and my dad. And you. We're all there together.

Enter the Psalms: I may not personally be in the dark pit the man who prayed Psalm 88 was in, but there are many who were and are this very moment, my sisters and brothers in the persecuted church worldwide. We are part of the same Body; we're family in a family closer and more enduring than any earthly family. The psalm enables me to enter into real fellowship with them, whether or not I ever meet them on earth, whether or not I ever experience personally what they experience. Their experiences are ours. I can pray that psalm, and as I do, I pray with them and for them. I may not know their names, but I am, in a very concrete way, obeying Scripture's command to "rejoice with those who rejoice; mourn with those who mourn."[21] The first time I prayed Psalm 88 that way, tears flowed as I saw myself standing with those who grieve so deeply, and praying with them as I prayed for them,

O Lord, God of my salvation,
  I cry out to you by day.
  I come to you at night.
Now hear my prayer;
  listen to my cry.
For my life is full of troubles,
  and death draws near.
I am as good as dead,
  like a strong man with no strength left.
They have left me among the dead,
  and I lie like a corpse in a grave.
I am forgotten,
  cut off from your care.
You have thrown me into the lowest pit,
  into the darkest depths.[22]

Your Place in God's Story

It took a while for me to appreciate what Paul meant when he said we Gentiles, by the grace of God, have been grafted into the vine of Israel.[23] But when the lights came on, I was stunned and delighted to realize that their story is my story too. It's *our* story. What happened to Israel at the Red Sea and Sinai and Meribah is as much about me as it is about them. I began to see my name written into the whole biblical story. I started reading and praying the Psalms like a child learning how to read, learning a new "vocabulary, a grammar, and a plot line"[24]—discovering a family tree I didn't know I had. Huge parcels of the Psalms that had formerly seemed to belong to someone else started feeling like home, like Psalm 106:

The people made a calf at Mount Sinai;
  they bowed before an image made of gold.
They traded their glorious God
  for a statue of a grass-eating bull.

They forgot God, their savior,
who had done such great things in Egypt—
such wonderful things in the land of Ham,
such awesome deeds at the Red Sea.
So he declared he would destroy them.
But Moses, his chosen one, stepped between the LORD and the people.
He begged him to turn from his anger and not destroy them.[25]

I had known that story for a long time—how those foolish folks had sinned so stupidly but Moses had prayed for them and God had relented in his judgment. I had even made "life application" from that story as the Scriptures encouraged me to do: "These things happened to them as examples for us. They were written down to warn us who live at the end of the age."[26] Yes, of course, I do the same kinds of things they did. God forgive me.

But now! I was no longer learning *from them*; I was learning *about us*. This sin problem is not just my problem; it's our problem. The implications are critical to spiritual health. I tended to think I sinned mainly in isolation, as an individual. I thought I was taking responsibility for my own actions when I confessed my sins privately, but I was really separating myself from the protection of the community of God's people, the Body of Christ. Sin flourishes in isolation, for we belong to Christ's Body, not as members of a group, but as organs in a body. A member of a group can survive outside the group, but a member of a body dies outside the body. My individualistic approach to my sin increased the power that sin had over me. There is great comfort and strength in being able to pray, after a long litany of confession like Psalm 106, "Save *us*, O LORD our God! Gather *us* back from among the nations, so *we* can thank your holy name and rejoice and praise you."[27]

Merely knowing this much that night in the janitor's closet would have been a great encouragement to that little band of praying students. The walls with their shelves of detergent and disinfectants would have been pushed back and opened to include a lot more people—and some very fascinating people, at that. We would have been strengthened to see that our prayers were not about us as individuals in agreement; they were about us as living stones fitted together in the temple of the Holy Spirit, as royal priests, a holy nation.[28] We were a cast of millions, maybe trillions. Prayer is not about me, or you; it is about all of us who belong to God.

Not about Us, but about God

But the third, and biggest, thing I didn't appreciate that night in the janitor's closet is that prayer ultimately is not even about us but about God. It's not about the living stones that make up the temple but the Spirit in the temple. Overcoming this third misconception has been the most transforming of all to my prayer life.

Question: Who are the Psalms about? On the surface, they are about a lot of people: David, especially, but also Moses, Asaph, the sons of Korah, Jeduthun and Heman and Ethan and all Israel. Bigger question: Who is the Bible about? On the surface, the list is even longer. But Jesus made it radically short when he said to his opponents, "You search the Scriptures because you think they give you eternal life. But the Scriptures point to me!"[29] John 5:39

This wasn't a throwaway line for Jesus, an odd and obscure saying on the periphery of his teachings, something for future generations of scholars to puzzle over. It was right at the center, because he insisted that his whole mission was not to cancel what we know as the Old Testament Scriptures but to fulfill them.[30] To fulfill is to fill-full, to complete what was implicit and incomplete in what came before.

So in Luke's account of the Resurrection, establishing this fulfillment theme was very high on the Lord's priority list. The Gospel writer tells us that, shortly after stepping out of the tomb, Jesus sought out two disciples walking to the village of Emmaus and explained to them what he meant when he said the "Scriptures point to me." Luke says Jesus "took them through the writings of Moses and all the prophets, explaining from all the Scriptures the things concerning himself."[31] Later he appeared to the apostles and reiterated what he'd said earlier:

> "When I was with you before, I told you that everything written about me in the law of Moses and the prophets and in the Psalms

must be fulfilled." Then he opened their minds to understand the Scriptures.[32]

Every Psalm Whispers His Name

Jesus said he fulfilled all the Bible, including the Psalms of the Bible! The apostles grabbed hold of this and ran with it. On the Day of Pentecost, when Peter stood before the crowds in Jerusalem to preach the gospel, he went to one of David's psalms, Psalm 16, to explain Christ's resurrection. Peter said,

> King David said this about him:
>
> "I see that the LORD is always with me.
> I will not be shaken, for he is right beside me.
> No wonder my heart is glad,
> and my tongue shouts his praises!
> My body rests in hope.
> For you will not leave my soul among the dead
> or allow your Holy One to rot in the grave.
> You have shown me the way of life,
> and you will fill me with the joy of your presence."[33]

Then Peter did something with the psalm that took tremendous chutzpah and would have been absolutely outrageous if the Lord had not given him the authority to do it: He said that David wasn't really talking about himself; he was talking about Jesus!

> Dear brothers, think about this! You can be sure that the patriarch David wasn't referring to himself, for he died and was buried, and his tomb is still here among us. But he was a prophet, and he knew God had promised with an oath that one of David's own descendants would sit on his throne. David was looking into the future and speaking of the Messiah's resurrection. He was saying that God would not leave him among the dead or allow his body to rot in the grave.[34]

Peter could say this because Jesus had opened the door for him to say it. The church has been going through that door ever since. The writers of the New Testament write with the conviction that every story and psalm of the Old Testament "whispers his name."[35] The Bible is all about Jesus. As Peter explained it on the Day of Pentecost, when you pray the psalms of David as the psalms of Jesus, you pray exactly as David intended! You pray with David's greater Son. Your voice resonates with a voice deeper than yours or David's. You pray with Jesus. As Bonhoeffer put it, "If we want to read and pray the prayers of the Bible and especially the Psalms, therefore, we must not ask first what they have to do with us [and, I would add, or David or Israel!], but what they have to do with Jesus Christ."[36]

So use your imagination. It helps me to think of it this way: I bow my head and begin to pray a psalm. I sense Someone's presence, I hear Someone's voice in my head, speaking as I speak. I look up, and behold! There is Jesus praying beside me. He smiles, and I know without his saying a word that when I began to pray it was not I who got his attention; it was he who got my attention. He didn't join me in my concerns; I joined him in his. As I prayed his Word, my voice joined his voice. Precious mystery! Divine communion! Sweet intimacy!

There is more. I look at Jesus and see gathered around him his Body—countless multitudes there with me, also joined to him in prayer. Gathered from every tribe and language and nation, our voices are somehow subsumed, incorporated into Christ. Yet the intimacy with Jesus is not diluted! We are not a mass but members of a body. Just as every organ in a body is as directly connected to the head as any other organ—the nose no more connected to the head than the little toe—each of us in Christ's Body is as close to Jesus as we would be if we were the only one. But—and this is crucial—*there would be no intimacy outside the Body*.

My wife grew up in a wonderful, loving family—a mom and a dad with six kids, living on the meager salary of a professor at a Christian college. There may not have been enough money, but there was no shortage of love. When they became adults, the brothers and sisters laughed uproariously when they discovered that each thought he or she was the parents' favorite child! That's a little bit like the Body of Christ: love and intimacy not in spite of the family but because of the family.

All the members of the Body of Christ are empowered to pray with Jesus, but never alone with Jesus. His brothers and sisters join their voices with his and pray whatever he prays, as family: "So now Jesus and the ones he makes holy have the same Father. That is why Jesus is not ashamed to call them his brothers and sisters."[37] If you are in Jesus, you are now permitted to say whatever he says—not in yourself as an individual, but only as a member of Christ's Body, with everyone else in his Body.

Body and Spirit

This unique relationship of union to Christ in prayer, with others, touches on what is sometimes called the communion of the saints, or the fellowship of the Holy Spirit. Blaise Pascal saw with clarity how our love for God, for ourselves, and for each other—and therefore our prayers—are inextricably bound together in the Body (note: Pascal doesn't capitalize the word *Body* as I do).

> But in loving the body [each member] loves itself, because it has no being except in the body, through the body, and for the body. . . . We love ourselves because we are members of Christ. We love Christ because he is the body of which we are members. All are one. One is in the other like the three persons [of the Trinity].[38]

Here I must tread cautiously and reverently, for I touch on a mystery that goes far beyond my understanding. But for prayer it is a very practical mystery. The organic union of the Body of Christ is rooted in the loving union of the Trinity: Father, Son, and Holy Spirit. Together, the "community" of God helps us pray. In fact, we are drawn up into the communion of the Godhead when we pray. Jesus, the Son, teaches us to pray to the Father and intercedes for us as we do.[39] The Spirit also helps us to pray, as something of a translator. In our weakness we don't know what God wants us to pray for.

> The Holy Spirit prays for us with groanings that cannot be expressed in words. And the Father who knows all hearts knows what the Spirit is saying, for the Spirit pleads for us believers in harmony with God's own will.[40]

How to Pray through This Book

Given the mystery of prayer, you may wonder how this book can help you learn to pray through the Psalms. *God's Prayer Book* is a beginner's guide to learning to pray the Psalms, a "devotional commentary." My aim is not to *tell* you what to pray. I want to say just enough about each psalm to stir your heart and imagination to lead you into prayer. So it's far more devotional than commentary, more workbook than textbook. There are several wonderful commentaries any serious student of the Psalms should acquire. But the guides to prayer in this book say, "Here's a psalm, here are a few things you should know about it, now use it." Like a tool—a shovel, a hammer, or a saw—a psalm is best understood by using it, by praying it. Eugene Peterson likes the phrase "owner's manual"[41] for a book like this. I do too. The main idea is to give you enough information and reflection to get you started using the Psalms to teach you to pray.

Each devotional commentary has three parts:

A Psalm Text

This book contains the complete text of 62 psalms that I believe can transform your prayer life. Read through each psalm slowly and thoughtfully two or three times. The psalm will be better than anything I say about it. Take note of any word or phrase that "glimmers"—stands out or gives you pause. The Holy Spirit may use these "glimmerings" to prompt you to pay attention to some specific matter in your personal life.

A Devotional Window

I offer a short devotional perspective on each psalm only as an aid in understanding and an encouragement to pray. But I am no more than a servant of the Word of God, a kind of pastoral docent in an art museum. Its halls are lined with the works of masters, objects of profound wisdom and breathtaking beauty. My job is to point out a thing or two about these great works and then get out of the way so you can look *into them* more deeply and personally and be taught by the Holy Spirit to pray more like Jesus. Be careful what you look into—the Psalms are mirrors that will look *into you* and read you more searchingly than you will ever read them.

A Prayer Route

The prayer points listed after each devotional are suggested ways to pray the psalm, routes one may take to pray through it, like climbing a great rock.

My son Andy is an expert rock climber. In May 2007 he climbed El

Capitan in the Yosemite Valley, an imposing mass of granite that rises three thousand feet above the valley floor. It's the kind of climb that normally takes a few days and nights—which means climbers typically anchor themselves in portable "ledges" in which to sleep at night.

One of the fascinating things about any great "wall," as climbers term the rocks they climb, is that there is usually more than one way to the top. The wall is what it is, and it cannot be altered. It must be respected. There is one wall, and no amount of wishing it to be something other than what it is will make it so. Disaster awaits anyone who climbs wishfully. But within the parameters or boundaries the wall offers, there may be several routes for the climber, strategies one may take to move along the contours of the rock.

Like the God who gave them, the Psalms are like these great rocks. They are what they are, and no amount of wishing them to be otherwise will change that. Any attempt to make a psalm what it is not invites spiritual peril. But there are usually a variety of ways to pray through a psalm, while respecting its integrity. The prayer prompts after each devotional window are my suggested routes. They are based on my own prayers and analysis of the Psalms from dialogue with commentators and others I pray with—particularly my wife and the fine folks who have been praying with me these past four years in the school of prayer at Santa Barbara Community Church. But if you are moved to pray in different directions (see above, "A Psalm Text"), by all means do so.

You probably don't know that you know one of the main Hebrew words for belief. It's *amen*. It means to rest on something, to put your full weight down, to lash yourself to a truth as you would a tent to a stake or a rope to a rock face. Every time you pray a psalm, you anchor your soul to God's truth the way a climber rests his or her weight on a handhold on El Capitan—Spanish for something like "*the Lord*."

One more thing: During Andy's three-day climb, my wife, Lauretta, and I went on a Web site to follow the route he took to the top. The wall is named the Salathe, and the Web site was loaded with photos of the breathtaking vistas he was enjoying on his climb. The prayer routes are like those photos. They're vistas I got when I prayed the Psalms. It is my earnest prayer that they will encourage you to take your own photographs—or better, to paint your own pictures.

But this book is still just a beginner's guide—or perhaps a change of pace for those seasoned in prayer. As you read through each devotional, I invite you to try out some other ways to learn prayer from the Psalms that may serve you over your lifetime. I'll list five.

1. Say Them Out Loud

Just read the Psalms slowly and thoughtfully, assenting to what they say with as much understanding as you have, intellectually and emotionally. Don't just read them, pray them; *say them from the heart.*

Does it strike you as odd that the Word of God, the Bible, should have at its center a prayer book, the Psalms? It's better than odd; it's beautiful and mysterious, for the Psalms contain both the Word God has to say to us about prayer and the words he wants us to say to him in prayer. "This is pure grace," exclaimed Dietrich Bonhoeffer, "that God tells us how we can speak with him and have fellowship with him."[42]

2. Festoon Them

Think of a psalm as a Christmas tree. Read it and then festoon it with your own prayers, as you would decorate a tree. Your prayers are answers to what God says to you in the psalm. Or think of its words as a road map—let it show you where to go, and then go there. The psalm is your guideline, the Holy Spirit is your guide, and you are the traveler.[43]

A simple way to understand a psalm's intent is to read it through the lens of the "three Rs": Rejoice, Repent, and Request. Ask these three questions:

> **Rejoice:** What do I find here that gives me cause to rejoice, to give praise and thanks? Then do it.
>
> **Repent:** What do I read here that brings to light sin in my life? Then confess and repent.
>
> **Request:** What in this psalm can inform the way I pray for others and myself? Then make your requests of God accordingly.

3. Paraphrase Them

Meditate and study a psalm until you understand it well enough to put it into your own words. Then paraphrase the psalm as you have come to understand it, and pray your paraphrase.

The Living Bible, a paraphrase by Ken Taylor, opened a generation's eyes to the vitality of the Bible. You don't have to be as skilled as Ken Taylor to write a paraphrase that helps you pray from the heart what you hear God saying to you in his Word. No one need read or hear what you have written but you and the Lord, who delights in the prayers of his people.

4. Learn Them by Heart

Memorize the Psalms—but not by rote. Rather, learn them by heart; make their words your words. Come to understand them so well you can recite them—by inflection and tone—as though you had written them yourself. This is, by far, the best way I know to learn to pray the Psalms. I can think of no more powerful way to allow the Word of God to change who you are and how you think. Over the years I have been grateful for every line of Scripture I have committed to memory, but the prayers of the Psalms have offered incomparable comfort and clarity in desperate, murky, and confusing situations, when I didn't have a worthwhile word of my own to say—when I quite literally didn't have a prayer.

5. Marinate in Them

Some people use the Bible like they use spice to liven up the taste of food—a little Tabasco here, some salt and pepper and oregano there; a favorite verse, a "one size fits all" psalm like Psalm 23 or 103 to read when you are (check one) sad or glad or afraid or lonely or struggling with doubt. Nothing wrong with that, unless that's the only way you come to Scripture.

But it's better to use the Psalms as you would a marinade. A spice touches only the surface of the food; a marinade changes its character. Chicken soaked in lemon juice or a steak drenched in garlic and teriyaki sauce isn't the same thing it was before the treatment. The soul should marinate in Scripture by repeated, thoughtful, slow, comprehensive, and Spirit-enlightened reading. Make it your aim for Scripture to be for you what Charles Spurgeon said it was for John Bunyan: "Prick him anywhere, his blood is bibline."[44]

Soak in the Psalms, using any of the methods I've suggested above: saying, festooning, paraphrasing, and memorizing. Mature Christians have long known that the best way to learn to pray is to pray through the Psalms systematically, psalm by psalm, day in and day out, week by week and month by month for a lifetime. Liturgical traditions use prayer books with assigned daily readings arranged on a monthly cycle. Anyone can divide them up for monthly (thirty-day) or bimonthly (sixty-day) cycles; just divide 150 by the number of days. A thirty-day cycle would pray Psalms 1 to 5 on the first day of the month, Psalms 6 to 10 on the second day, and so on. It's not complicated.

Woody Allen once said that 80 percent of success is just showing up. So it is that 80 percent of learning to pray is just showing up—and doing it. Saint Benedict promised that this steady practice of prayer would eventually cause the mind to "echo in harmony with the voice."[45] Serious prayer is the work of a pilgrim, not the occasional dalliance of a tourist. It comes from what Nietzsche called "a long obedience in the same direction." Certainly this was what Jesus did. The man who prayed the Psalms so meaningfully on the cross had been drenched in the Psalms from boyhood. As a matter of fact, the first psalm in the Psalter is quite specifically about Jesus, the Messiah, the Son of David.

PSALM 1

1 Oh, the joys of those who do not
follow the advice of the wicked,
or stand around with sinners,
or join in with mockers.
2 But they delight in the law of the Lord,
meditating on it day and night.
3 They are like trees planted along the riverbank,
bearing fruit each season.
Their leaves never wither,
and they prosper in all they do.

4 But not the wicked!
They are like worthless chaff, scattered by the wind.
5 They will be condemned at the time of judgment.
Sinners will have no place among the godly.
6 For the Lord watches over the path of the godly,
but the path of the wicked leads to destruction.

> For the LORD watches over the path of the godly, but the path of the wicked leads to destruction. (6)

Get ready. Things are going to get violent, even bloody, very quickly. No choice about that. The question is not whether you'll be in the fight but on whose side you'll fight. The choices, just two, spoken of in brief outline in this psalm, will present themselves full blown in the psalms that follow. In Psalm 1 we know them as the path of the godly and the path of the wicked.

These paths are not merely two separate directions, one going east, the other going west, and never colliding. They are two different ways of life, implacably opposed to one another. Neither will tolerate the other.

So get ready. The first two psalms have been called the gateway to the book of Psalms. Strictly speaking, they aren't even prayers but preparation for prayer—meditations on the nature of things in the universe, the world we move in when we pray. So take note; be forewarned: The world of prayer is a world of intense conflict. The enemy is never far away when we pray. Prayer is not escape; it is engagement.

Erwin McManus tells the story of the night his little boy Aaron didn't want the lights off when he went to bed. He was afraid of the demons he had heard about the week before at summer camp. McManus groaned inside and fought back the temptation to say, "They're not real." He knew they are real. Before he could answer, Aaron asked him to pray for him:

> "Daddy, Daddy, would you pray for me that I would be safe?" I could feel it. I could feel warm-blanket Christianity beginning to wrap around him, a life of safety, safety, safety.

> I said, "Aaron, I will not pray for you to be safe. I will pray that God will make you dangerous, so dangerous that demons will flee when you enter the room."
>
> And he goes, "All right. But pray I would be really, really dangerous, Daddy."[46]

I don't know what McManus did next, but it wouldn't have been a bad idea to begin to teach Aaron to pray the Psalms. They are the prayers of a warrior, *the* Warrior.

+ + +

Oh, the joys of those who do not follow the advice of the wicked, or stand around with sinners, or join in with mockers. (1)
Examine your life: what you listen to and look at, whom you associate with and identify with. There seems to be a progression in this verse—a descent into hell—from listening to acting to the worst possible place one can ever be: mocking what is true and good.

Old Testament scholar Bruce Waltke compares listening to the advice and ways of sin to looking at the Greek mythological figure Medusa. One look at her and you freeze. To have a frozen heart is to be cold and hard, not only toward God, but also toward other people.

Stop now. Confess the ways you are frozen hearted.

But they delight in the law of the LORD, meditating on it day and night. (2)
Again, examine your life. Do you spend quality time in the Word of God? Is it your delight? Pray that it will be.

Sin is directional: It only looks around, horizontally, but not up. The advice of the wicked, the society of sinners, is all it knows. Righteousness is directional too: It looks up to God and meditates on his ways, his truth, his law. It sees things from heaven's point of view. Heaven's perspective is breathtaking and delightful!

James Packer describes this upward look of prayerful meditation as an activity of

> calling to mind, thinking over, dwelling on, and applying to oneself the various things one knows about the works and

> ways and purpose and promises of God . . . of holy thought, consciously performed in the presence of God, under the eye of God, by the help of God, as a means of communication with God. Its purpose is to clear one's mental and spiritual vision of God, and to let his truth make its full and proper impact on one's mind and heart. It is a matter of talking to oneself about God and oneself.
>
> It is, indeed, often a matter of arguing with oneself, reasoning oneself out of moods of doubt and unbelief into a clear apprehension of God's power and grace.[47]

To pray is to meditate, to hear God and answer God. To hear well is to pray well. We would never speak to God unless God had first spoken to us. Your prayer life will never go further than your grasp of God's Word.

Right now—ask the Lord to speak his Word with "its full and proper impact" into your life.

They are like trees planted along the riverbank, bearing fruit each season. Their leaves never wither, and they prosper in all they do. **(3)** Remember, since life is war, you must be sustained for the long haul. Pursue the life of meditation and prayer the way tree roots seek water.

Dietrich Bonhoeffer believed meditation on the Word of God to be as vital to the health of his soul as water to the vitality of a tree:

> Because I am a Christian, therefore, every day in which I do not penetrate more deeply into the knowledge of God's Word in Holy Scripture is a lost day for me. I can only move forward with certainty upon the firm ground of the Word of God. And, as a Christian, I learn to know the Holy Scriptures in no other way than by hearing the Word preached and by prayerful meditation.[48]

Your choice is either to flourish like a well-watered tree or to allow yourself to be blown about like chaff, to be a person of substance or to be shallow and hollow inside. Pray that God will help you choose well.

PSALM 2

1 Why are the nations so angry?
Why do they waste their time with futile plans?
2 The kings of the earth prepare for battle;
the rulers plot together
against the LORD
and against his anointed one.
3 "Let us break their chains," they cry,
"and free ourselves from slavery to God."

4 But the one who rules in heaven laughs.
The Lord scoffs at them.
5 Then in anger he rebukes them,
terrifying them with his fierce fury.
6 For the Lord declares, "I have placed my chosen king on the
throne
in Jerusalem, on my holy mountain."

7 The king proclaims the LORD's decree:
"The LORD said to me, 'You are my son.
Today I have become your Father.
8 Only ask, and I will give you the nations as your inheritance,
the whole earth as your possession.
9 You will break them with an iron rod
and smash them like clay pots.'"

10 Now then, you kings, act wisely!
Be warned, you rulers of the earth!
11 Serve the LORD with reverent fear,
and rejoice with trembling.
12 Submit to God's royal son, or he will become angry,
and you will be destroyed in the midst of all your
activities—
for his anger flares up in an instant.
But what joy for all who take refuge in him!

Why are the nations so angry? Why do they waste their time with futile plans? The kings of the earth prepare for battle; the rulers plot together against the LORD and against his anointed one. (1-2)

When my mentor retired, I asked him what advice he had for me in my work as a pastor. He had been a wise and courageous minister for decades and had taught me so much. Was there anything else he thought I needed to know? "Don't take it personally" was what he told me.

"Don't take what personally?" I asked.

"Don't take it personally when you get beat up, harassed, and depressed in the ministry. You're in a war. It goes with the territory."

I thought about that for a minute, and agreed. When a soldier gets shot at in a battle, he doesn't get his feelings hurt. It's not about him; it's about the war he's in. He doesn't look over the top of his foxhole and ask the enemy, "Was it something I said?"

What my mentor told me applies to all believers, not just pastors. Anyone who belongs to Jesus Christ will get Christ's enemies in the bargain.

That's what this psalm is about: the enemies of the Christ. *Christ* is Greek for the Hebrew "anointed one." The nations and kings of the earth hate him. They actually meditate on their hatred. For the word translated "plans" in verse 1 of this psalm is the same word translated *meditate* in Psalm 1.

Remarkable! Just as the Christ delights in and meditates on God's law,[49] his enemies meditate on how to overthrow him and his God. While he prays for God's Kingdom to come, they pray for God's Kingdom to be overthrown.

This primal conflict is never far from the Psalms, and those who pray the Psalms are usually engaged in spiritual warfare. The New Testament brings an added insight to this war:

> We are not fighting against flesh-and-blood enemies, but against evil rulers and authorities of the unseen world, against mighty powers in this dark world, and against evil spirits in the heavenly places.[50]

There are unseen powers behind the thrones of this world, darker and more malevolent than the darkest powers we know. The likes of Hitler, Stalin, and Osama bin Laden, along with the multibillion-dollar pornography and abortion industries, are merely slaves, houseboys, and lackeys for these powers.

Psalm 2 not only assures us of the outcome of the battle; it also shows us how to fight the battle—in prayer.

+++

"Let us break their chains," they cry, "and free ourselves from slavery to God." (3)
This is the battle cry of all God's enemies. The freedom that comes from obedience seems like slavery to them, so they rebel.

Think of rebellion in all its forms—in nations, peoples, families, individuals. How have you raised your fist to God and railed against his authority? Confess brazen rebellion in your own spirit. Confess the rebellious audacity of your community, your nation, even your church.

For the Lord declares, "I have placed my chosen king on the throne in Jerusalem, on my holy mountain." (6)
Declare the Lord Christ's sovereignty in your heart. Praise him that God has appointed him ruler over all creation, that every tongue will confess that he is Lord, and that every knee will bow to him in heaven and on earth and under the earth to the glory of God.[51]

Only ask, and I will give you the nations as your inheritance, the whole earth as your possession. (8)
The nations are the Father's to give to his Son—and to his church! Using the very language of this psalm, the risen Christ promises that the church will share in his victory and sovereignty:

To all who are victorious, who obey me to the very end,
    To them I will give authority over all the nations.
They will rule the nations with an iron rod
    and smash them like clay pots.
They will have the same authority I received from my Father,
    and I will also give them the morning star![52]

Christ's command that his people make disciples of all nations flows directly from the message of Psalm 2. The warfare of this psalm is no less than the battle to preach the gospel to the nations and to win the obedience of faith from all peoples. Both Christ's command and the words of this psalm are the fulfillment of God's promise to Abram to bless all the nations of the earth through him.[53]

This is a very big psalm—and so is the mission of the church to share in the victory it promises: Christ's victory! As Emil Brunner notes, "The church exists by mission as a fire exists by burning."

Stand before a map or globe and lay your hands on the nations represented there. Pray that Christ's victory will be complete and that you and your church will play your part in that victory. Pray for missionaries, and pray for the church in every nation to be faithful to the very end to preach the Good News of the risen Lord.

Submit to God's royal son, or he will become angry, and you will be destroyed in the midst of all your activities—for his anger flares up in an instant. But what joy for all who take refuge in him! (12)
Consider carefully what is at stake in this battle: either the joy of refuge in Christ or the horror of destruction outside of him. Let the weight and urgency of the gospel move you to prayer for the lost—and to be a bold witness for Christ.

PSALM 3

A psalm of David, regarding the time David fled from his son Absalom.

1 O LORD, I have so many enemies;
so many are against me.
2 So many are saying,
"God will never rescue him!" *Interlude*

3 But you, O LORD, are a shield around me;
you are my glory, the one who holds my head high.
4 I cried out to the LORD,
and he answered me from his holy mountain.
Interlude

5 I lay down and slept,
yet I woke up in safety,
for the LORD was watching over me.
6 I am not afraid of ten thousand enemies
who surround me on every side.

7 Arise, O LORD!
Rescue me, my God!
Slap all my enemies in the face!
Shatter the teeth of the wicked!
8 Victory comes from you, O LORD.
May you bless your people. *Interlude*

> Arise, O LORD! Rescue me, my God! Slap all my enemies in the face! Shatter the teeth of the wicked! (7)

Were this psalm a movie, the folks who rate films according to their suitability for children would probably give it an R rating for violence and strong language. A slap is one thing, but asking God to break your enemy's teeth is another. True, David was under extreme duress when he prayed this; his son Absalom had led a full-scale rebellion, and many were trying to kill him, grinning mockingly and crowing, "God will never rescue him!" But still, aren't words like that excessively violent for a Christian? Aren't we called to a higher and gentler standard?

Some modern Christians have even excluded psalms like this from use in lectionaries and prayer books. What are we to make of this? I'll let Patrick Henry Reardon answer for me:

> This is unmitigated nonsense. The enemies here are the real enemies, the adversaries of the soul, those hostile forces spoken of in the very first verse of the Book of Psalms. . . . To relinquish any of the psalms on the excuse that its sentiments are too violent for a Christian is a clear sign that a person has also given up the very battle that a Christian is summoned from his bed to fight. The psalms are prayers for those engaged in an ongoing spiritual conflict. No one else need bother even opening the book.[54]

The New Testament urges us to see the warfare as spiritual, but that changes nothing about the language and attitudes we should use to pray. Our adversaries may not be "flesh-and-blood enemies,"[55] but they are enemies nonetheless. These spiritual powers wage war against our very souls[56]—which Jesus says is a far greater evil than anything mere flesh-and-blood powers can do.

The whole world doesn't equal the value of just one soul:

> What do you benefit if you gain the whole world but lose your own soul? Is anything worth more than your soul?[57]

Nothing in all creation is worth more than your soul, absolutely nothing. Anything or anyone who would try to destroy a soul is an enemy deserving our fiercest anger and prejudice—and our most fervent and desperate prayers for protection.

Do you pray this way for yourself? For your family, for your friends, for the persecuted church?

+++

But you, O LORD, are a shield around me; you are my glory, the one who holds my head high. (3)

Paul said we should put on the whole armor of God to fight this spiritual battle—things like the belt of truth, the body armor of God's righteousness, the shoes of peace, the helmet of salvation, and the shield of faith.[58] But how, on earth, does one put on things like that? The answer is we put these on with prayer, by praying "in the Spirit at all times and on every occasion."[59] The point is, the spiritual armor we wear to fight the battle is not a collection of inanimate objects, of "things." *The armor is God.* That's why we pray to fight. As David puts it here, "But you, O LORD, are a shield around me." Merely to pray is to be surrounded and protected by God. So pray for protection—by praying!

Saint Patrick understood the life of spiritual warfare. A long prayer attributed to him, which has no doubt morphed and been added onto through the centuries, is called his "breastplate prayer." Pray it as a way of praying Psalm 3.

> I bind unto myself today
> The power of God to hold and lead,
> His eye to watch, his might to stay,
> His ear to hearken to my need;

The wisdom of my God to teach,
His hand to guide, his shield to ward;
The word of God to give me speech,
His heavenly host to be my guard.

Christ be with me, Christ within me,
Christ behind me, Christ before me,
Christ beside me, Christ to win me,
Christ to comfort and restore me,
Christ beneath me, Christ above me,
Christ in quiet, Christ in danger,
Christ in hearts of all that love me,
Christ in mouth of friend and stranger.

I lay down and slept, yet I woke up in safety, for the LORD was watching over me. (5)
For centuries the church has recommended praying this prayer in the morning, thanking God for what is easily overlooked by many of us—that when we let go and fell into sleep the night before, God took care of us, even as he ran the universe, watched over little birds, and kept track of the hairs on our heads.[60] We have no guarantees that we can fall asleep and wake again, apart from God's kindness.

With this in mind, pray these words when you awake from sleep each morning.

Victory comes from you, O LORD. May you bless your people. (8)
Declare God's ultimate victory over the things that appear formidable, even overwhelming. Say it out loud—it can make the exultation of final victory more vivid and real. You might list concerns such as:

war and famine across the globe
poverty and hopelessness
HIV/AIDS
estranged couples and wayward children
depression

Then say after each, "Victory comes from you, O LORD. May you bless your people."

PSALM 4

For the choir director: A psalm of David, to be accompanied by stringed instruments.

1 Answer me when I call to you,
O God who declares me innocent.
Free me from my troubles.
Have mercy on me and hear my prayer.

2 How long will you people ruin my reputation?
How long will you make groundless accusations?
How long will you continue your lies? *Interlude*

3 You can be sure of this:
The LORD set apart the godly for himself.
The LORD will answer when I call to him.

4 Don't sin by letting anger control you.
Think about it overnight and remain silent.
Interlude

5 Offer sacrifices in the right spirit,
and trust the LORD.

6 Many people say, "Who will show us better times?"
Let your face smile on us, LORD.
7 You have given me greater joy
than those who have abundant harvests of grain
and new wine.
8 In peace I will lie down and sleep,
for you alone, O LORD, will keep me safe.

Don't sin by letting anger control you. Think about it overnight and remain silent. . . . In peace I will lie down and sleep, for you alone, O LORD, will keep me safe. (4, 8)

I am named after a distant cousin my dad loved dearly. His name was Benny. Yes, that's my given name: not Ben, but Benny. But you can call me Ben. Please.

It's not totally clear why my dad liked him so much, but I have a pretty good idea. The only thing I know about Benny is a story my dad told over and over again with great amusement.

Benny had a younger brother who was constantly pestering and provoking him. Benny would lose his temper, then haul off and slug his little brother in the face, on the arm, in the stomach—whatever was closest—and his brother would run wailing to his mom. Benny would get a spanking, which was probably why his little brother did what he did, and Benny would hate his little brother even more. Thus the cycle of violence would repeat itself.

That's where my dad got involved. Benny needed to learn to control his anger, my dad thought. He needed to slow down his reaction time to his little brother's provocations. He needed to do something in the spirit of verse 4 of this psalm. "Don't sin by letting anger control you. Think about it overnight and remain silent."

So my dad advised Benny that the next time his little brother did something outrageous to him, he should count to ten before he acted. Ten is a pretty big number for a boy, my dad reasoned. Perhaps he'd slow down and think twice as he counted, and consider the dire consequences that would come if he acted on his impulse to double up his fist and wallop his brother.

I can still see my dad laughing until tears came as he told us what Benny did with his advice. Once again, the little brother goaded Benny to the point of violence. Benny raised his fist to strike his brother but saw my dad watching. His eyes locked onto my dad's eyes; he lowered his fist slightly, counted loudly to ten as fast as he could, and then hit his brother as hard as he could.

Obviously, he needed to do more than just wait before he acted. He needed to *think about it*. Other translations read "ponder" (ESV) or "search your hearts" (NIV). What Benny needed to think about is something that doesn't necessarily come any easier with age and maturity. It isn't simply a matter of "anger management," of learning to control one's impulses. It is a matter of faith, of what you believe to be the ultimate truth about God and your relationship to him. The last verse of the psalm says it: "In peace I will lie down and sleep, for you alone, O LORD, will keep me safe."

Since David knew who he belonged to, he didn't have to act as his own agent. He belonged to God, and it was God's business to take care of him. His enemies would have to answer to God, because when they attacked David they were really attacking the God who "set apart the godly for himself" (verse 3). God is better than anyone else at doing the right thing! No more sleepless nights brooding over slander and plots. God would take care of him—and them.

To believe this is to be free to lie down and sleep in peace. To live this way is to live—and sleep!—like Jesus, who "did not retaliate when he was insulted or threaten revenge when he suffered. He left his case in the hands of God, who always judges fairly."[61]

+ + +

How long will you people ruin my reputation? How long will you make groundless accusations? How long will you continue your lies? (2)

Thomas à Kempis's counsel on how to deal with slander is good. Remember that just because someone slanders you, the words don't make it so. Keep a sane perspective:

> Do not let your peace depend on the hearts of men; whatever they say about you, good or bad, you are not because of it another man, for as you are, you are.[62]

This advice is good, but it's not ultimately satisfying. Lies hurt. More than that, lies are usually impossible to correct. The more you protest your innocence, the more guilty you will probably look.

Prayer is better. Do what David did: Though his accusers were not actually there in his presence, he spoke to them in God's presence. They would not hear or heed what he said, but God would.

Speak your frustration and anger to the God who hears and cares.

Many people say, "Who will show us better times?" Let your face smile on us, LORD. (6)
Some kinds of friends can be as bad as enemies, maybe worse. The rhetorical question "Who will show us better times?" is really a statement—the kind of thing one says when he or she doesn't believe the Lord will come through, so we might as well do what Job's wife told him to do: Curse God and die.

You must pray about those who doubt God's faithfulness, just as you pray about your enemies. Think of them as professional joy busters. Tell God what they're saying and ask him to please "let your face smile on us, LORD."

You can be sure of this: The LORD set apart the godly for himself. The LORD will answer when I call to him. (3)
There is a reason we suffer the attacks of the enemy: We belong to the Lord. This is exactly as Jesus said it would be, and should be, given the fallen world we live in: "If the world hates you, remember that it hated me first."[63]

That's why we suffer in the world. And it's same reason we should remain joyful in the suffering and confident that God hears our prayers. We belong to him. We're in the best company.

Pray thankfully for any ways you are treated unfairly!

In peace I will lie down and sleep, for you alone, O LORD, will keep me safe. (8)
Just as the church has recommended praying Psalm 3 in the morning (see devotional on Psalm 3), so it has recommended praying this psalm in the evening, before going to sleep.

Sleep, sweet sleep, for those whom God loves![64] Poet George Herbert says this love is better than a cushy bed:

> My God, thou art all love.
> Not one poor minute scapes thy breast,
> But brings a favor from above;
> And in this love, more than in bed, I rest.[65]

The great saints also have seen sleep as a prefigurement of death—viewing letting go and falling asleep as preparation for a good death in the hope of the resurrection. Amazingly, on the night before his execution, Nicholas Ridley, bishop of London in the late sixteenth century, rejected the offer of a fellow priest to spend the last hours before his execution with him. He refused, reciting Psalm 4:8 and declaring his intent to go to bed and sleep as peacefully as he ever did in his life.

We don't know how well he slept that night. But you may know how well you can sleep when you pray, as you lay your head on your pillow, "In peace I will lie down and sleep, for you alone, O Lord, will keep me safe."

PSALM 5

For the choir director: A psalm of David, to be accompanied by the flute.

1 O LORD, hear me as I pray;
pay attention to my groaning.
2 Listen to my cry for help, my King and my God,
for I pray to no one but you.
3 Listen to my voice in the morning, LORD.
Each morning I bring my requests to you and wait expectantly.

4 O God, you take no pleasure in wickedness;
you cannot tolerate the sins of the wicked.
5 Therefore, the proud may not stand in your presence,
for you hate all who do evil.
6 You will destroy those who tell lies.
The LORD detests murderers and deceivers.

7 Because of your unfailing love, I can enter your house;
I will worship at your Temple with deepest awe.
8 Lead me in the right path, O LORD,
or my enemies will conquer me.
Make your way plain for me to follow.

9 My enemies cannot speak a truthful word.
Their deepest desire is to destroy others.
Their talk is foul, like the stench from an open grave.
Their tongues are filled with flattery.
10 O God, declare them guilty.
Let them be caught in their own traps.
Drive them away because of their many sins,
for they have rebelled against you.

11 But let all who take refuge in you rejoice;
let them sing joyful praises forever.
Spread your protection over them,
that all who love your name may be filled with joy.
12 For you bless the godly, O LORD;
you surround them with your shield of love.

Listen to my voice in the morning, LORD. Each morning I bring my requests to you and wait expectantly. (3)

+

Jack Sanford looks back fondly on childhood visits to the old family farmhouse in New Hampshire. In particular, he's never forgotten the old well that stood outside the front door. The water from the well was surprisingly pure and cold, and no matter how hot the summer or how severe the drought, the well was always dependable, a source of refreshment and joy. The faithful old well was a big part of his memories of summer vacations at the family farmhouse.

Time passed and eventually the farmhouse was modernized. Wiring brought electric lights, and indoor plumbing brought hot and cold running water. The old well was no longer needed, so it was sealed shut.

Years later while vacationing at the farmhouse, Sanford hankered for the cold, pure water of his youth. So he unsealed the well and lowered the bucket for a nostalgic taste of the delightful refreshment he once knew. But he was shocked to discover that the well that had once survived the worst droughts was bone dry. Perplexed, he began to ask questions of the locals who knew about these kinds of things. He learned that wells of that sort were fed by hundreds of tiny underground rivulets, which seep a steady flow of water. As long as water is drawn out of the well, new water will flow in through the rivulets, keeping them open for more to flow. But when the water stops flowing, the rivulets clog with mud and close up. The well dried up not because it was used too much but because it wasn't used enough.

Our souls are like that well. If we do not draw regularly and frequently on the living water that Jesus promised would well up in us like a spring,[66] our hearts will close and dry up. The consequence of not drinking deeply of God is to eventually lose the ability to drink at all. Prayerlessness is its own worst punishment, both its disease and cause.

David's description of his prayer life is a picture of a man who knew the importance of frequent, regular prayer—disciplined prayer, each morning. *Each morning I bring my requests to you and wait expectantly.* He knew how important it was to keep the water flowing—that from the human side of prayer, the most important thing to do is just to keep showing up. Steady, disciplined routine may be the most underrated necessity of the prayerful life.

Steady, disciplined prayer is also orderly prayer. The Hebrew for *bring*, in "Each morning I bring my requests to you and wait expectantly," is something like "prepare," as in preparing a meal; or "set forth," as in stating a case; or "lay out," as in a priest arranging the parts of an offering on an altar.[67]

We all love the exalted feelings prayer can bring, the sense of holy transcendence and passion that can bring tears to the eyes and a lump in the throat. But for every moment of exaltation, there are hours of regularity and discipline that, though not the cause of great feelings, are what can position us to receive them. Like the water in the well, the life of God flows from a heart and a will we cannot cause or create. But we can do much to create the conditions necessary to receive what flows. We can keep lowering the bucket.

+++

LORD, hear me as I pray; pay attention to my groaning. (1)
The Hebrew word for *groaning* is a word for deep, inaudible sighing. There is more to be done in prayer than mere sighing and moaning. Yet if that is where you are spiritually and emotionally, God will hear you. Besides, we have it on good authority that the Holy Spirit groans too—with us and for us: "The Holy Spirit prays for us with groanings that cannot be expressed in words."[68]

Go ahead and moan your prayers if you must. What we don't understand about ourselves, the Spirit understands, and he will pray with us and for us with great love, patience, and wisdom.

Listen to my cry for help, my King and my God, for I pray to no one but you. (2)
Always remember who you are praying to—and why. David speaks to his King and his God, which is to say that he prays, not only on his own behalf, but for the sake of his King. Before he is David, the son of Jesse, he is David, the servant of the King. He is under orders, and he prays as one who seeks God's Kingdom. Pray your prayers boldly and humbly in that great context: boldly because you serve the King, humbly for the same reason!

Each morning I bring my requests to you and wait expectantly. (3)
Morning is not the only time for prayer. For those who don't become fully functional before 10 or 11 a.m., that is a relief. For people who love to get an early start to their day, morning probably is the best time to set aside time to pray. For all of us, whether "morning people" or not, it is essential that the day begin with prayer in some degree and of some sort—a word of thanksgiving for safety through the night and the day ahead, a brief request that God's will be done in all you do, and that he be your Shepherd through the day. The reason is playfully demonstrated in a poem by an anonymous author:

> Dear God,
> So far today,
> I've done all right.
> I haven't gossiped.
> I haven't lost my temper.
> I haven't been greedy, grumpy, nasty, selfish, or overindulgent.
> I'm very thankful for that.
> But in a few minutes, God, I'm going to get out of bed;
> and from then on, I'm going to need a lot more help.
> Amen.

Plan prayer for each morning. Then work your plan. The amount of time you spend in prayer is not as important as that you regularly begin the day this way.

Because of your unfailing love, I can enter your house; I will worship at your Temple with deepest awe. (7)

The best part of prayer is God. To be in his presence—to find in him a refuge, to be under his protection—is our greatest joy, the purpose for living. Thank God for the mercy that gives this greatest gift and that enables you to pray with full confidence:

> You will show me the way of life, granting me the joy of your presence and the pleasures of living with you forever.[69]

Lead me in the right path, O LORD, or my enemies will conquer me. Make your way plain for me to follow. (8)

This world is no friend to those who want to walk the right path. Nor is the devil or your own sinful nature. The enemies of your soul will lie to you at every turn in the road, pointing to the wrong way (verses 9-10). This pattern is ingrained in their daily lives and can be summarized this way: "Inhale. Lie. Exhale. Lie."[70] Pray for protection and clarity from the untruths that might cause you to stray from God's will.

PSALM 6

For the choir director: A psalm of David, to be accompanied by an eight-stringed instrument.

1 O LORD, don't rebuke me in your anger
or discipline me in your rage.
2 Have compassion on me, LORD, for I am weak.
Heal me, LORD, for my bones are in agony.
3 I am sick at heart.
How long, O LORD, until you restore me?

4 Return, O LORD, and rescue me.
Save me because of your unfailing love.
5 For the dead do not remember you.
Who can praise you from the grave?

6 I am worn out from sobbing.
All night I flood my bed with weeping,
drenching it with my tears.
7 My vision is blurred by grief;
my eyes are worn out because of all my enemies.

8 Go away, all you who do evil,
for the LORD has heard my weeping.
9 The LORD has heard my plea;
the LORD will answer my prayer.
10 May all my enemies be disgraced and terrified.
May they suddenly turn back in shame.

+ I am sick at heart. How long, O LORD, until you restore me? (3)

*W*hen Hunter Thompson, the so-called gonzo journalist, committed suicide on February 20, 2005, he died as a man without the spiritual strength to pray. His health was gone; he was in constant pain—and football season was over.

His brief suicide message was scrawled in black marker and titled "Football Season Is Over." It read:

> No More Games. No More Bombs. No More Walking. No More Fun. No More Swimming. 67. That is 17 years past 50. 17 more than I needed or wanted. Boring. I am always [cranky]. No Fun—for anybody. 67. You are getting Greedy. Act your old age. Relax—This won't hurt.[71]

A man without a prayer: In the end, all he had to say to whoever might listen was regrets and the hope that he could end his life painlessly. Apparently the "this won't hurt" was a reference to the way he would kill himself. God did not create us to die that way.

Psalm 6 is the prayer of a man with hardly the strength to pray. But pray he does. He does what every one of us should do with sin and despair: He subjects his raw, chaotic emotions to theological and spiritual discipline. He voices his lament in the light of God's truth. He also does what few of us can do: He makes the prayer a poem. We don't know if David created this poem/prayer at the end of a long process of struggle, or if he prayed it at the beginning. In either case the Holy Spirit inspired him to produce a prayer that is a gift to those who feel they haven't a prayer to pray.

Prepare to pray by observation. Go through the psalm and make three brief lists: a list of the words he uses to describe his condition,[72] a list of the things David asks of the Lord,[73] and a list of the things he has to say about his enemies.[74] The psalm isn't long, and it won't take a lot of time to do this, but the exercise will reward you with a deeper sense of the profound emotions that go into not only David's prayer but your own as well. (If you don't have the time to do this, I have noted each list with a few of my own observations.)

Psalm 6 is the first of what the church has designated as the seven penitential psalms—the others being Psalms 32, 38, 51, 102, 130, 143. As prayers of confession and repentance, they offer superb opportunities to meditate on the nature of the sin that so disastrously separates us from God and the grace and mercy we desperately need, lest we die.

+ + +

Lord, don't rebuke me in your anger or discipline me in your rage. (1)
To say that God is angry is not to say that he is peeved or in a snit over some things he doesn't like. God's wrath is his rage at the evil that destroys his good creation. The evil is willful, deliberate rebellion against his holy character and will. Only God's mercy can save us from God's wrath.

Pray as David does: not that God will not discipline you for your sin, but that he will not do so in his wrath, but mercifully, as a father, in love.[75]

Have compassion on me, LORD, for I am weak. Heal me, LORD, for my bones are in agony. (2)
The power of sin seeps deep into our very selves, bodies included. Like bone marrow cancer, it eats away from the inside and takes the whole body down.

Pray that the effects of sin on your body will be healed.

I am sick at heart. How long, O LORD, until you restore me? (3)
The plea "How long, O LORD" appears several times in the Psalms. It's not impatience with God but an expression of an earnest desire to see

things restored and see what is wrong set right. Stoic resignation has no place in the prayers of a child of God.

Be eager as you pray your confession. You have no right to demand anything from God. But you may humbly plead for him to set your feet on solid ground again.[76]

Return, O LORD, and rescue me. Save me because of your unfailing love. (4)
Only God's love can avert God's wrath—not anything good you and I may try to do to cover up and rationalize sin. This is our one and only hope: *Save me because of your unfailing love.*

For the dead do not remember you. Who can praise you from the grave? (5)
The wages of sin is death—literal, physical death—and much, much more. As Patrick Henry Reardon puts it, "What we see death do to the body, sin does to the soul. Death is the externalizing of sin."[77] Our sins are not naughty little excursions into forbidden pleasures; they are things we do to put our desiccated bodies in the ground.

Acknowledge your sin for what it is—death. Thank God that though the wages of sin is death, the gift of God is eternal life through Christ.[78]

The LORD has heard my plea; the LORD will answer my prayer. (9)
Pray your confidence in God's promise that if we confess our sins, he will forgive them.[79]

PSALM 7

A psalm of David, which he sang to the LORD concerning Cush of the tribe of Benjamin.

1 I come to you for protection, O LORD my God.
Save me from my persecutors—rescue me!
2 If you don't, they will maul me like a lion,
tearing me to pieces with no one to rescue me.
3 O LORD my God, if I have done wrong
or am guilty of injustice,
4 if I have betrayed a friend
or plundered my enemy without cause,
5 then let my enemies capture me.
Let them trample me into the ground
and drag my honor in the dust. *Interlude*

6 Arise, O LORD, in anger!
Stand up against the fury of my enemies!
Wake up, my God, and bring justice!
7 Gather the nations before you.
Rule over them from on high.
8 The LORD judges the nations.
Declare me righteous, O LORD,
for I am innocent, O Most High!
9 End the evil of those who are wicked,
and defend the righteous.
For you look deep within the mind and heart,
O righteous God.

10 God is my shield,
saving those whose hearts are true and right.
11 God is an honest judge.
He is angry with the wicked every day.

12 If a person does not repent,
God will sharpen his sword;
he will bend and string his bow.

13 He will prepare his deadly weapons
and shoot his flaming arrows.

14 The wicked conceive evil;
they are pregnant with trouble
and give birth to lies.
15 They dig a deep pit to trap others,
then fall into it themselves.
16 The trouble they make for others backfires on them.
The violence they plan falls on their own heads.

17 I will thank the Lord because he is just;
I will sing praise to the name of the Lord Most High.

A psalm of David, which he sang to the LORD concerning Cush of the tribe of Benjamin.

There is far more to this superscription than meets the eye.

We don't know who Cush was, but knowing that he was from the tribe of Benjamin is probably all we need to know. Saul, the king David deposed, was of this tribe, and David was of the tribe of Judah. Many from the tribe of Benjamin saw David's ascension to the throne not as God's doing but as David's doing. David, in their view, was just a power-hungry schemer from Judah who became king by treachery, not by God's sovereign choice. Shimei, a Benjamite, heaped curses on David as the king fled from Jerusalem during Absalom's rebellion. Cush and Shimei present a vivid picture of the deep animosity that existed between David and this tribe.

> The LORD is paying you back for all the bloodshed in Saul's clan. You stole his throne, and now the LORD has given it to your son Absalom. At last you will taste some of your own medicine, for you are a murderer![80]

There was no love lost between David and the tribe of Benjamin. The murderous threats David so feared from Cush were common.

What is remarkable is what the superscription says David did in the face of these threats. He wrote this psalm as a prayer to be sung to God. If we are being attacked by a homicidal foe, the last thing most of us feel like doing is sitting down to compose a song about it. We scream and we groan, but we don't polish our language. But that is exactly what David did: He reflected on his desperate situation theologically, and he wrote lyrics to be prayed.

There is a wonderful lesson here to be learned about prayer. The things we fear can have terrible effects on us, not the least of which is what we become when we are afraid. Fear can stampede our emotions and actions, and we can start to look like the enemy, matching threat for threat and curse for curse. How much better to stop and remember what we know to be true about God and sin and guilt, and to turn that into a prayer. The very act of writing down our fears in the light of the truth, of wrestling with syntax and metaphor in order to pray them, can be a godly discipline in being, "quick to listen, slow to speak, and slow to get angry. [For] human anger does not produce the righteousness God desires."[81]

Perhaps you were taught that written prayers are inauthentic and contrived. If so, consider this: All the Psalms are written prayers! It may be that the most authentic prayers are the written ones, for they are the fruit of a heart that has struggled to think God's thoughts after him. The great prayers of Scripture come from people who so internalized God's words and thoughts that they came out of their mouths and through their pens as their own. They had wrestled to understand God and had come away changed and enlightened.

Use this psalm as a model of how to pray when you are threatened by the enemy.

+++

I come to you for protection, O LORD my God. Save me from my persecutors—rescue me! (1)
You don't have to set God up to hear your need or get him in the right mood by circling around your real concern with flowery language.
Go directly to what you need, and say it as directly and bluntly as you know how.

If you don't, they will maul me like a lion, tearing me to pieces with no one to rescue me. (2)
Pray the reality of evil. No matter what the identities of the people involved or the specifics of the situation, behind all evil and violence is

the devil, who "prowls around like a roaring lion, looking for someone to devour."[82] Cry out for God to close the mouths of the lions in the same way he did for Daniel in the lions' den.

LORD my God, if I have done wrong or am guilty of injustice, if I have betrayed a friend or plundered my enemy without cause, then let my enemies capture me. (3-5)
As you pray for protection from evil, also acknowledge the possibility that you may have been complicit with it in some way. David's "ifs" are more than merely rhetorical; they are the prayers of a man who loves justice and wants it done, even if he, too, feels its hard edge. When you ask God to set things straight around you, be willing to have yourself set straight too.

Gather the nations before you. Rule over them from on high. (7)
Put your personal prayer for protection and justice in the larger context of what God must do for the whole world. Pray for the Kingdom of God to come to all people, even as you pray for his hand to save you.

If a person does not repent, God will sharpen his sword; he will bend and string his bow. . . . The wicked conceive evil; they are pregnant with trouble and give birth to lies. They dig a deep pit to trap others, then fall into it themselves. (12, 14-15)
Declare before God that you believe what he has said about the ultimate destiny of all who do evil. Thank him that he has spoken and that what he says will be accomplished—though the wicked dig a pit for others, they will fall into it themselves.

I will sing praise to the name of the LORD Most High. (17)
The name David uses for God is an immense comfort to the beleaguered. He is the Lord Most High, the God above all gods and all threats, who rules from on high. Praise the name of the God who tells the weak that what he opens no one can shut and what he closes no one can open.[83]

PSALM 8

For the choir director: A psalm of David, to be accompanied by a stringed instrument.

1 O LORD, our Lord, your majestic name fills the earth!
Your glory is higher than the heavens.
2 You have taught children and infants
to tell of your strength,
silencing your enemies
and all who oppose you.

3 When I look at the night sky and see the work of your fingers—
the moon and the stars you set in place—
4 what are mere mortals that you should think about them,
human beings that you should care for them?
5 Yet you made them only a little lower than God
and crowned them with glory and honor.
6 You gave them charge of everything you made,
putting all things under their authority—
7 the flocks and the herds
and all the wild animals,
8 the birds in the sky, the fish in the sea,
and everything that swims the ocean currents.

9 O LORD, our Lord, your majestic name fills the earth!

Yet you made them only a little lower than God
and crowned them with glory and honor. (5)

*H*amlet's famous eulogy could easily have been written after reading this psalm:

> What a piece of work is a man! how noble in reason! how infinite in faculty! in action how like an angel! in apprehension how like a god! the beauty of the world! the paragon of animals![84]

What a piece of work, indeed. I remember seeing the title of a book written in the sixties that I think was aimed at urban youth: *God Don't Make No Junk*. That's not exactly Shakespeare, but in its own way it is just as biblical. Both are ways of saying what God had in mind when he created human beings in his own image:

> God said, "Let us make human beings in our image, to be like us. They will reign over the fish in the sea, the birds in the sky, the livestock, all the wild animals on the earth, and the small animals that scurry along the ground."[85]

Psalm 8 is a commentary on what it means to be created in God's image. It poses a rhetorical question of God—"What are mere mortals that you should think about them?"—and answers it resoundingly, echoing God's words in Genesis. We mere mortals aren't so mere to God; we are made in his image and given the godlike mandate to rule the creation in his name.

+++

You gave them charge of everything you made, putting all things under their authority—the flocks and the herds and all the wild animals, the birds in the sky, the fish in the sea, and everything that swims the ocean currents. (6-8)

Both Genesis 1 and Psalm 8 locate our human dignity in our likeness to God and in the call to work—to care for the earth he created as his representatives.

Psalm 8 is a commentary on Genesis 1, but it, too, has a commentary. According to Hebrews 2:5-10, the deeper meaning of this psalm is that it is about Jesus Christ. The writer of Hebrews quotes verse 6 of the psalm—"You gave them charge of everything you made, putting all things under their authority"—and explains:

> Now when it says "all things," it means nothing is left out. But we have not yet seen all things put under their authority. What we do see is Jesus, who was given a position "a little lower than the angels"; and because he suffered death for us, he is now "crowned with glory and honor."[86]

The upshot of all this is that if you want to know what it means to be a human being, you must look not at human beings but at Jesus Christ. We are broken and corrupted images, but he is the true image of God, the model, the prototype. As William Sloane Coffin put it, Jesus is the window to God and the mirror of humanity. "Christ is no afterthought; He is the original meaning of humanity. Christ is what God had in mind when He reached down and formed the first lump of mud into a man."[87]

Psalm 8 can teach us how to pray on at least three levels. It can be a marvelous instrument to worship the glory of Christ. It can help us celebrate and give thanks for God's gracious creation of our humanity in his image. And it can help us pray that our work on earth be good and godly labor.

LORD, our Lord, your majestic name fills the earth! Your glory is higher than the heavens. (1, 9)

The great astronomer Galileo believed God spoke in two books: Holy Scripture and the book of creation. Scripture affirms this and invites us to praise what we see of God's character—his name—in his creation. The seas and the fields and the air teem with signs of his name. Name the names of what you know of the creatures of earth, air, and sea, and thank God for the fecundity of his imagination and love.

You have taught children and infants to tell of your strength, silencing your enemies and all who oppose you. (2)
God is so big he doesn't need our money or cleverness or arms to defend him against his enemies. Praising him will do the job. In fact, even the praise of infants will silence his foes.[88] Praise God—it's the most powerful form of spiritual warfare there is.

You gave them charge of everything you made, putting all things under their authority. (6)
How do you begin your work each day? Enthusiastically, like the seven dwarfs in the Disney classic *Snow White*? "Hi ho, hi ho, it's off to work we go!" Or resignedly, like the bumper sticker, "I owe, I owe, it's off to work I go"? Try this: Go to work with this psalm on your lips, and with it a profound sense of wonder and gratitude for the place God has given you and your work in his creation.

No matter how small and insignificant your day's work may seem to you, if it is worth doing at all, it is a piece of God's world to be cared for in his majestic name. That amounts to nothing less than glory—God's and, in a derivative way, yours too.

So frame your day's work in worship. Begin with praise—the way a child praises God (verse 2), surrendering yourself simply and unquestioningly to his greatness. Affirm, with humble thankfulness, your place in this great God's world (verses 5-6). Then work as though you believe this is true, learning from Christ, who shows us how to work with gentleness and humility (Matthew 11:25-30).

Worship the Lord Christ who shows us how to work and who strengthens us by his Spirit to work to the glory of God.

> My Father is always working, and so am I. . . . I tell you the truth, the Son can do nothing by himself. He does only what he sees the Father doing. Whatever the Father does, the Son also does.[89]

PSALM 12

For the choir director: A psalm of David, to be accompanied by an eight-stringed instrument.

1 Help, O Lord, for the godly are fast disappearing!
The faithful have vanished from the earth!
2 Neighbors lie to each other,
speaking with flattering lips and deceitful hearts.
3 May the Lord cut off their flattering lips
and silence their boastful tongues.
4 They say, "We will lie to our hearts' content.
Our lips are our own—who can stop us?"

5 The Lord replies, "I have seen violence done to the helpless,
and I have heard the groans of the poor.
Now I will rise up to rescue them,
as they have longed for me to do."
6 The Lord's promises are pure,
like silver refined in a furnace,
purified seven times over.
7 Therefore, Lord, we know you will protect the oppressed,
preserving them forever from this lying generation,
8 even though the wicked strut about,
and evil is praised throughout the land.

Help, O LORD, for the godly are fast disappearing!
The faithful have vanished from the earth!
Neighbors lie to each other, speaking with
flattering lips and deceitful hearts. (1-2)

Blaise Pascal, the great seventeenth-century scientist and Christian apologist, summed up much of the meaning of Psalm 12 in one elegant epigram:

> Truth is so obscured nowadays and lies so well established that unless we love the truth we shall never recognize it.[90]

Pascal saw with the same clarity as David how truth will be obscured and lies firmly established whenever "evil is praised throughout the land" (verse 8). Cocky liars will strut brazenly about and say to themselves (for few liars ever say out loud what they believe in their hearts), "We will lie to our hearts' content. Our lips are our own—who can stop us?" (verse 4).

How can these liars get away with such nonsense? The psalm says it's because they speak with "flattering lips." They say the things we like to hear. They massage our vanity and scratch our itching egos. As Pascal put it, "Unless we love the truth we shall never recognize it." So there must be something in all of us that doesn't fully love the truth.

Case in point: In 2003, teenagers in the United States spent a whopping $112.5 billion on the consumption of goods and services. Divide that figure by the number of teenagers in the United States, roughly 20.5 million, and it translates to the average teenager spending more than one hundred dollars a week, mainly on clothes.[91] In the United States, consumerism, materialism, and individualism are the names of the evil "praised throughout the land." Each, in its own way, tells us the big lie that our worth and meaning come from the value of the things we possess. It's a whopper. It's outrageous. But we believe it to the extent that we believe a deeper and bigger lie: that we are the center of the universe and that therefore whatever we want and own and can consume is good.

And this falsehood oppresses and enslaves us in a subtle and puzzling way. Our evil renders us banal and trivial.

> The puzzle is why so many people live so badly. Not so wickedly but so inanely. Not so cruelly but so stupidly. There's little to admire and less to imitate in the people who are prominent in our culture. We have celebrities but not saints. Famous entertainers amuse a nation of bored insomniacs. Infamous criminals act out the aggressions of timid conformists. Petulant and spoiled athletes play games vicariously for lazy and apathetic spectators. Aimless and bored, people amuse themselves with trivia and trash. Neither the adventure of goodness nor the pursuit of righteousness gets headlines.[92]

Only the God of truth can free us from lies. We must learn to love the God of truth.

+++

The LORD's promises are pure, like silver refined in a furnace, purified seven times over. (6)

The Word of the Lord is everything the words of liars are not. It is pure, like highly refined silver. Silver is subjected to intense heat to burn out impurities. Silver put to the fire, purified, allowed to cool, then put to the fire again, seven times over, is the purest of silver. God's promises, and everything else he says, are like that.

Praise God that his words are not like the lies of the world. Then commit yourself to meditate deeply on his Word, to so soak yourself in the purity of truth that your innermost self will react with disgust and horror at the flattery of lying tongues. Pray that as God's eyes cannot bear to look on sin,[93] your heart would revolt against flattering lies.

Confess the ways you may have been sucked in by such untruths.

Help, O LORD, for the godly are fast disappearing! The faithful have vanished from the earth! (1)
A big part of David's lament is that he feels he is the only one who cares about truth. Eugene Peterson's rendering of his prayer in *The Message* captures David's loneliness and the panic that rises up in his heart:

> Quick, GOD, I need your helping hand! The last decent person just went down, all the friends I depended on gone.

This is not weakness on David's part. God made us to need each other to walk in the truth. The church should be a fellowship of people who love the truth and encourage each other to live truthfully.

Pray that your church fellowship would be a fellowship of truth lovers. Several verses in Ephesians may help: 4:15, 25, 29; 6:14.

May the LORD cut off their flattering lips and silence their boastful tongues. (3)
In the final analysis, we are too weak in ourselves to fight against lies. The Lord must fight for us. Pray that our warrior King will strike down the enemy.

The words of this prayer may sound excessively violent to our ears. If they do, it may be because we have grown accustomed to deceit. Have you ceased to be horrified by the soul-destroying malevolence of liars and their lies? Set your face like steel against their evil, and pray accordingly, for they serve the devil.

The LORD replies, "I have seen violence done to the helpless, and I have heard the groans of the poor. Now I will rise up to rescue them, as they have longed for me to do." (5)
The purpose of liars' lies is to control and exploit others for their own gain. The helpless may be those who are exploited economically, who don't have enough to live. Or they may be those who are helpless spiritually, like the average teenager who spends one hundred dollars a week on lies—who has more than enough to live but who doesn't know how to live.

Name the helpless on your heart today, and ask the Lord to rescue them.

PSALM 14

For the choir director: A psalm of David.

1 Only fools say in their hearts,
"There is no God."
They are corrupt, and their actions are evil;
not one of them does good!

2 The LORD looks down from heaven
on the entire human race;
he looks to see if anyone is truly wise,
if anyone seeks God.
3 But no, all have turned away;
all have become corrupt.
No one does good,
not a single one!

4 Will those who do evil never learn?
They eat up my people like bread
and wouldn't think of praying to the LORD.
5 Terror will grip them,
for God is with those who obey him.
6 The wicked frustrate the plans of the oppressed,
but the LORD will protect his people.

7 Who will come from Mount Zion to rescue Israel?
When the LORD restores his people,
Jacob will shout with joy, and Israel will rejoice.

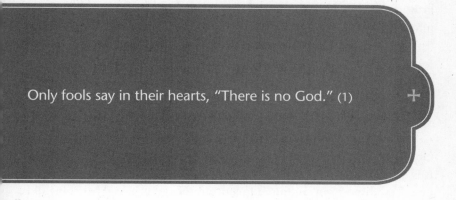

Only fools say in their hearts, "There is no God." (1)

Whatever fools say with their mouths, they say first in their hearts.

Comedian Julia Sweeney of *Saturday Night Live*, who is an atheist, was asked how she explained belief in God to her young daughter.

> I said God is this idea of a big man who lives up in the clouds and he created everything. And she goes, "Well I believe that!" And I go: "Well yeah, because it sounds like a cartoon character. But the truth isn't that, and I'll tell you the truth."
>
> And then I actually teach her about evolution, and she asks me about it all the time as a bedtime story. She'll say, "Tell me about how the dinosaurs weren't here when people were here." And then we'll go over it again. I don't know how much of it she really gets, but she likes the story. And then, she's kind of over it now, but she would go, "I believe in God at school, but when I come home I don't."[94]

Whatever fools say with their mouths, they say first in their hearts. The same applies to the wise. Jesus said, "Whatever is in your heart determines what you say. A good person produces good things from the treasury of a good heart, and an evil person produces evil things from the treasury of an evil heart" (Matthew 12:34-35).

The "heart" described in the Bible is that central core of ourselves, the wellspring of our feelings and attitudes and beliefs. So the wise father of

Proverbs advises his son, "Guard your heart above all else, for it determines the course of your life" (Proverbs 4:23).

Note that the heart is not the same as the intellect, the seat of reason. Contrary to the way we might like to think of ourselves as rational creatures, our ability to reason is often merely a tool in the hands of our hearts—a very sharp and effective tool, but still just a tool. The intellect serves the heart.

According to the Bible, Sweeney's—or any atheist's—conclusion about God's nonexistence is not the result of a rigorous sifting of the evidence. It is rather the result of a rigorous *selection* of the evidence, based on the heart's predisposition. Sigmund Freud, another atheist, said belief in God is based on wish fulfillment: We so want there to exist a benevolent and all-powerful being we call God, we come to believe there actually is. But the wish-fulfillment argument cuts both ways: Who is to say that it wasn't Freud's wish that there not be a God that led him to believe there wasn't? As the song from the Disney movie *Pinocchio* goes, "When you wish upon a star . . . dreams come true." All manner of dreams.

Blaise Pascal's laser-beam intellect saw through the pretensions of the intellect when he wrote, "The heart has reasons of which reason knows nothing."[95] He was echoing and applying what David and the Lord Jesus said about human nature—whatever fools say with their mouths, they say first in their hearts.

Confess your sins. Examine your actions and your words: What do they say about the condition of your heart? Ask the Holy Spirit to reveal the wellsprings of your attitudes and emotions.

Confess some more. There are two kinds of atheists: those who disbelieve the existence of God (theoretical atheists) and those who believe but act as though they don't (practical atheists). John Baillie describes the latter:

> According to the teaching of our Lord, what is wrong with the world is precisely that it does not believe in God. Yet it is clear that the unbelief which he so bitterly deplored was not an intellectual persuasion of God's non-existence. Those whom he rebuked for their lack of faith were not men who denied God with the top of their minds, but men who, while apparently incapable

of doubting him with the top of their minds, lived as though he did not exist.[96]

Pray for the alignment of your actions with your theology. Ask God to cleanse you of practical atheism.

+++

Who will come from Mount Zion to rescue Israel? When the LORD restores his people, Jacob will shout with joy, and Israel will rejoice. (7)

The contrast between the corrupt fools of verse 1—locked up in themselves, suffocating in corruption—and the worshipers of verse 7 is dramatic. Their arms are raised in praise, their eyes are open, and their hearts are tender. Exuberant worship is not an argument for God's existence, but it is an eye-opener, an organ of perception. Just as the eyes receive light and the ears receive sound, exuberant worship can be a receptor of God's presence. A stubborn heart can be coaxed and wooed into the truth by celebrating the truth.

Worship the Lord! As you do, pray also for the appearance of the One "who will come from Mount Zion to rescue Israel" (verse 7).

PSALM 16

A psalm of David.

1 Keep me safe, O God,
for I have come to you for refuge.

2 I said to the LORD, "You are my Master!
Every good thing I have comes from you."
3 The godly people in the land
are my true heroes!
I take pleasure in them!
4 Troubles multiply for those who chase after other gods.
I will not take part in their sacrifices of blood
or even speak the names of their gods.

5 LORD, you alone are my inheritance, my cup of blessing.
You guard all that is mine.
6 The land you have given me is a pleasant land.
What a wonderful inheritance!

7 I will bless the LORD who guides me;
even at night my heart instructs me.
8 I know the LORD is always with me.
I will not be shaken, for he is right beside me.

9 No wonder my heart is glad, and I rejoice.
My body rests in safety.
10 For you will not leave my soul among the dead
or allow your holy one to rot in the grave.
11 You will show me the way of life,
granting me the joy of your presence
and the pleasures of living with you forever.

You will show me the way of life, granting me the joy of your presence and the pleasures of living with you forever. (11)

Jonathan Edwards thought of God the way David thought of God in this psalm. It was for "sweet delight in God" that he gave himself to God. He wrote,

> The first instance I remember of that sort of inward, sweet delight in God and in divine things, that I have lived much in since, was on reading these words, 1 Timothy 1:17: "Now unto the King eternal, immortal, invisible, the only wise God, be honor and glory for ever and ever. Amen." As I read the words, there came into my soul, and was as it were, diffused through it, a sense of the glory of the Divine Being; a new sense, quite different from anything I ever experienced before. Never any words of Scripture seemed to me as these did. I thought with myself, *how excellent a Being that was, and how happy I should be, if I might enjoy that God,* and be rapt up to Him in Heaven, and be, as it were, swallowed up in Him forever.[97]

Edwards's words are a variation on the theme of verse 11: "You will show me the way of life, granting me the joy of your presence and the pleasures of living with you forever."

This psalm is the prayer of a single-minded man who declared, "I said to the LORD, 'You are my Master! Every good thing I have comes from you'" (verse 2). God alone is his inheritance and his cup of blessing. God is at his right hand, and he will not be shaken. The pleasure of God's company is the only path of freedom and life.

+++

Keep me safe, O God, for I have come to you for refuge. (1)
Pray for protection—you need it. Your enemies may be people or disease, but more likely they are the "evil rulers and authorities of the unseen world [and] . . . evil spirits in the heavenly places" (Ephesians 6:12)—what classic Christian theology has called the devil, the world, and your own sinfulness.

Every good thing I have comes from you. (2)
Think of all you love; open a photo album, walk around your home, or stroll in a park. Make a list and say of each, "Every good thing I have comes from you."

Then, to add to your joy, thank God for being the kind of God who gives such good gifts. He is better than the good things he gives. So pray,

> LORD, you alone are my inheritance, my cup of blessing. You guard all that is mine. The land you have given me is a pleasant land. What a wonderful inheritance! (verses 5-6)

The godly people in the land are my true heroes! I take pleasure in them! (3)
Can you pray this with a full heart? You can't love God truly unless you love those he loves. Thank God for the people of God. Ask him to increase your love and appreciation for the church. As you do, be sure to name the names of the people who have played an important role in your spiritual life.

Troubles multiply for those who chase after other gods. I will not take part in their sacrifices of blood or even speak the names of their gods. (4)
Renounce any of the other gods that compete for your loyalty. Do the things you own really own you? Do the things you desire, things that occupy your imagination, lead you away from or toward the Lord?

I will bless the LORD who guides me; even at night my heart instructs me. (7)
David is so confident of God's guidance that even at night his heart—his inner being—ponders what it means. David speaks to David about the Lord as he sleeps. He would awake sometimes with a deeper understanding of the truth than he had when he went to sleep. Pray that your heart will have such a deep resonance with God's voice that as you rest, your heart will speak about the Lord. It's a wonderful experience when God answers that kind of prayer.

My body rests in safety. For you will not leave my soul among the dead or allow your holy one to rot in the grave. You will show me the way of life, granting me the joy of your presence and the pleasures of living with you forever. (9-11)
Death, the last enemy and the thing we most fear, was conquered by Jesus. Use these words to pray your thanks to God, who raised Jesus from the dead. If you belong to Christ, his victory is your victory too.[98]

PSALM 19

For the choir director: A psalm of David.

1 The heavens proclaim the glory of God.
The skies display his craftsmanship.
2 Day after day they continue to speak;
night after night they make him known.
3 They speak without a sound or word;
their voice is never heard.
4 Yet their message has gone throughout the earth,
and their words to all the world.

God has made a home in the heavens for the sun.
5 It bursts forth like a radiant bridegroom after his wedding.
It rejoices like a great athlete eager to run the race.
6 The sun rises at one end of the heavens
and follows its course to the other end.
Nothing can hide from its heat.

7 The instructions of the LORD are perfect,
reviving the soul.
The decrees of the LORD are trustworthy,
making wise the simple.
8 The commandments of the LORD are right,
bringing joy to the heart.
The commands of the LORD are clear,
giving insight for living.
9 Reverence for the LORD is pure,
lasting forever.
The laws of the LORD are true;
each one is fair.
10 They are more desirable than gold,
even the finest gold.
They are sweeter than honey,
even honey dripping from the comb.

11 They are a warning to your servant,
a great reward for those who obey them.

12 How can I know all the sins lurking in my heart?
Cleanse me from these hidden faults.
13 Keep your servant from deliberate sins!
Don't let them control me.
Then I will be free of guilt
and innocent of great sin.

14 May the words of my mouth
and the meditation of my heart
be pleasing to you,
O Lord, my rock and my redeemer.

> The heavens proclaim the glory of God. The skies display his craftsmanship. . . . The instructions of the LORD are perfect, reviving the soul. The decrees of the LORD are trustworthy, making wise the simple. (1, 7)

One July 4, John Piper sat on a curb with his wife and son, watching the fireworks explode over the night sky of Minneapolis. After a while, he noticed a white light behind some trees. It was the moon, rising quietly and modestly among the fireworks, ancient and terrifying in its splendor, and *unnoticed*.

Piper reflected on the moon: It rises 240,000 miles above the earth, roughly 500,000 times higher than the highest fireworks. It moves in its orbit at a speed of 2,300 miles per hour, about five times that of the fireworks. Its thickness is the distance from San Francisco to Cleveland, 2,160 miles. Its weight is 81 quintillion tons. It has mountain ranges nearly the height of Everest, empty seas 750 miles across, and craters 146 miles wide and 20,000 feet deep. Each day this silent behemoth does something no man-made power can do: It effortlessly lifts the oceans of the earth, incalculable trillions of tons of water, into the air and lowers them back down again—some nineteen feet in Eastport, Maine, ten feet in Boston, and up to forty-three feet in the Bay of Fundy in Nova Scotia. Were we to stand in the light of the moon, our body fluids would boil. Were we to stand in its shadow, we would freeze instantly. Add to all this the fact that the moon reflects light from a medium-sized star we call the sun, from a distance of 93 million miles. Any closer and it, and we, would be incinerated. All of this, it seemed, went unnoticed that night and goes largely unnoticed most nights.[99]

"The world is charged with the grandeur of God," wrote the priest-poet Gerard Manley Hopkins. "It will flame out like shining from shook foil."[100] David would add, "It will flame out like light from the Scriptures too." The medieval church thought Galileo a heretic when he asserted that God had two books, the creation and the Bible. But David was a "heretic" thousands of years before, when he praised the God who speaks both in the skies (verses 1-6) and the Scriptures (verses 7-14).

There is no greater celebration of the Scriptures in the Bible than this psalm. One passage is longer (Psalm 119) and one is more succinct (2 Timothy 3:16-17), but none is greater. What does David think of when he looks at the sun and the other stars? He thinks of the Bible (verses 1-6)!

Is the Bible hard for you? dry? uninteresting? Don't worry, you're in good company. John Bunyan said, "Sometimes there has been more in a line of Scripture than I could bear to stand under. Other times, the Bible has been to me as dry as a stick." You shouldn't worry, but you shouldn't be blasé, either. Remember, the Bible is a critical part of the dialogue with God we call prayer, the chief part of his side of the conversation.

One thing you can do to reconnect with God through Scripture is to practice the lesser-known spiritual discipline of imaginative association: Connect in your imagination the wonder and beauty you see in the sky with the contents of this book. Look at glorious things, the splendid and majestic things, in God's world—like the sun, the moon, and the Milky Way, and say, "The Bible is like that." Our natural surroundings and Scripture are both amazing revelations of God that are available to us every day—but that we too often ignore.

+++

They are more desirable than gold, even the finest gold. They are sweeter than honey, even honey dripping from the comb. (10)
Ask yourself, *How would I act if I believed there is treasure hidden in the Bible?* If you had in your hands a map showing where you could find great material treasure, wouldn't you apply yourself diligently to crack any code or language and overcome any mountain, weather, or foe to find the treasure?

Now turn your face heavenward. Open your mouth to the Lord and say, "Lord, let me taste the sweetness of your Word."

How can I know all the sins lurking in my heart? Cleanse me from these hidden faults. Keep your servant from deliberate sins! Don't let them control me. Then I will be free of guilt and innocent of great sin. (12-13)

Ask yourself, *Do I really expect, or want, to meet God when I read the Bible?* "It's not what I don't understand in the Bible that worries me," wrote Mark Twain. "It's what I do understand." If you need to, confess your apathy toward the Bible. Perhaps it is a smoke screen to hide your fear of exposure.

Look at the words David uses for the power and deceit of sin: *lurking, hidden, deliberate*—all controlling your will and desires. Cry out to God, "Don't let them do this to me!"

May the words of my mouth and the meditation of my heart be pleasing to you, O LORD, my rock and my redeemer. (14)

Ask the Lord to so fill you with the purity and sweetness of his law (like fine gold and honey) that your interior life will be transformed, that your every thought will reflect his character.

What a pleasure it is for your heavenly Father to answer this prayer!

PSALM 22

For the choir director: A psalm of David, to be sung to the tune "Doe of the Dawn."

1 My God, my God, why have you abandoned me?
Why are you so far away when I groan for help?
2 Every day I call to you, my God, but you do not answer.
Every night you hear my voice, but I find no relief.

3 Yet you are holy,
enthroned on the praises of Israel.
4 Our ancestors trusted in you,
and you rescued them.
5 They cried out to you and were saved.
They trusted in you and were never disgraced.

6 But I am a worm and not a man.
I am scorned and despised by all!
7 Everyone who sees me mocks me.
They sneer and shake their heads, saying,
8 "Is this the one who relies on the LORD?
Then let the LORD save him!
If the LORD loves him so much,
let the LORD rescue him!"

9 Yet you brought me safely from my mother's womb
and led me to trust you at my mother's breast.
10 I was thrust into your arms at my birth.
You have been my God from the moment I was born.

11 Do not stay so far from me,
for trouble is near,
and no one else can help me.
12 My enemies surround me like a herd of bulls;
fierce bulls of Bashan have hemmed me in!
13 Like lions they open their jaws against me,
roaring and tearing into their prey.

14 My life is poured out like water,
and all my bones are out of joint.
My heart is like wax,
melting within me.
15 My strength has dried up like sunbaked clay.
My tongue sticks to the roof of my mouth.
You have laid me in the dust and left me for dead.
16 My enemies surround me like a pack of dogs;
an evil gang closes in on me.
They have pierced my hands and feet.
17 I can count all my bones.
My enemies stare at me and gloat.
18 They divide my garments among themselves
and throw dice for my clothing.

19 O LORD, do not stay far away!
You are my strength; come quickly to my aid!
20 Save me from the sword;
spare my precious life from these dogs.
21 Snatch me from the lion's jaws
and from the horns of these wild oxen.

22 I will proclaim your name to my brothers and sisters.
I will praise you among your assembled people.
23 Praise the LORD, all you who fear him!
Honor him, all you descendants of Jacob!
Show him reverence, all you descendants of Israel!
24 For he has not ignored or belittled the suffering of the needy.
He has not turned his back on them,
but has listened to their cries for help.

25 I will praise you in the great assembly.
I will fulfill my vows in the presence of those who worship
you.
26 The poor will eat and be satisfied.
All who seek the LORD will praise him.
Their hearts will rejoice with everlasting joy.

27 The whole earth will acknowledge the LORD and return to him.
All the families of the nations will bow down before him.
28 For royal power belongs to the LORD.
He rules all the nations.

29 Let the rich of the earth feast and worship.
Bow before him, all who are mortal,
all whose lives will end as dust.
30 Our children will also serve him.
Future generations will hear about the wonders of the Lord.
31 His righteous acts will be told to those not yet born.
They will hear about everything he has done.

My God, my God, why have you abandoned me? Why are you so far away when I groan for help? Every day I call to you, my God, but you do not answer. Every night you hear my voice, but I find no relief. (1-2)

What was Jesus thinking as he hung dying on the cross? We can't know much, but what we can know is stunning. This psalm, which he quoted on the cross, is a window into Jesus' soul.

What did he mean when he cried, "My God, my God, why have you abandoned me?" Certainly in some profound way, deeper than any human can fathom, he felt abandoned by God. But why did he choose Psalm 22 to say this? He could have gone to one of the following psalms, all of which have the same kind of anguish in them:

> O Lord, why do you stand so far away? Why do you hide when I am in trouble? (Psalm 10:1)
>
> "O God my rock," I cry, "Why have you forgotten me?" (Psalm 42:9)
>
> You are God, my only safe haven. Why have you tossed me aside? (Psalm 43:2)
>
> O God, why have you rejected us so long? Why is your anger so intense against the sheep of your own pasture? (Psalm 74:1)
>
> O Lord, why do you reject me? Why do you turn your face from me? (Psalm 88:14)

Surely Jesus picked this psalm because it was so very prophetic. No psalm has the startling and gruesome detail this psalm has:

> My enemies surround me like a pack of dogs; an evil gang closes in on me. They have pierced my hands and feet. I can count all my bones. My enemies stare at me and gloat. They divide my garments among themselves and throw dice for my clothing. (verses 16-18)

But I think there was another reason he chose this psalm. No passage provides the big picture of Christ's sufferings the way Psalm 22 does. It begins in dark anguish but ends in soaring hope. It goes from "Why have you abandoned me?" to "I will praise you in the great assembly. I will fulfill my vows in the presence of those who worship you" (verse 25). What starts with the rejection of God's Holy One ends with the joyous worship of the whole earth:

> The whole earth will acknowledge the Lord and return to him. All the families of the nations will bow down before him. (verse 27)

So what was Jesus thinking when he hung on the cross? *Thinking* is too mild a word. Better is, what was his *passion*? His passion was to do the will of his Father, no matter how much it hurt, for the greater glory that would come. He knew this psalm by heart, and it erupted out of his heart in hope as he died for the sins of the world.

✢ ✢ ✢

My life is poured out like water, and all my bones are out of joint. **(14)**

How are we to pray such a psalm? Pray Psalm 22 as a way to meditate on the sufferings of Christ. Read it slowly and thoughtfully. As you do, pause to sing a hymn of the Cross, such as Thomas Kelly's "Stricken, Smitten, and Afflicted":

> Stricken, smitten, and afflicted, see Him dying on the tree!
> 'Tis the Christ by man rejected; yes, my soul, 'tis He, 'tis He!
> 'Tis the long-expected Prophet, David's son, yet David's Lord;
> By His Son God now has spoken; 'tis the true and faithful Word.

> Ye who think of sin but lightly nor suppose the evil great
> Here may view its nature rightly, here its guilt may estimate.
> Mark the sacrifice appointed, see who bears the awful load;
> 'Tis the Word, the Lord's Anointed, Son of Man and Son of God.

My enemies surround me like a pack of dogs; an evil gang closes in on me. They have pierced my hands and feet. (16)
Remember that all prayer is soaked in the blood of Christ. Thank Jesus that the reason that you can pray anything is because of his sufferings detailed in Psalm 22:

> Dear brothers and sisters, we can boldly enter heaven's Most Holy Place because of the blood of Jesus. By his death, Jesus opened a new and life-giving way through the curtain into the Most Holy Place. And since we have a great High Priest who rules over God's house, let us go right into the presence of God with sincere hearts fully trusting him. For our guilty consciences have been sprinkled with Christ's blood to make us clean, and our bodies have been washed with pure water.[101]

Future generations will hear about the wonders of the Lord. His righteous acts will be told to those not yet born. (30-31)
Pray that the purpose for which Christ died will be fulfilled. Psalm 22 makes it clear that Jesus' death was the death of a missionary! He longed for the day when it could be said, "Let the rich of the earth feast and worship. Bow before him, all who are mortal, all whose lives will end as dust. Our children will also serve him" (verses 29-30).

PSALM 23

A psalm of David.

1 The LORD is my shepherd;
I have all that I need.
2 He lets me rest in green meadows;
he leads me beside peaceful streams.
3 He renews my strength.
He guides me along right paths,
bringing honor to his name.
4 Even when I walk
through the darkest valley,
I will not be afraid,
for you are close beside me.
Your rod and your staff
protect and comfort me.
5 You prepare a feast for me
in the presence of my enemies.
You honor me by anointing my head with oil.
My cup overflows with blessings.
6 Surely your goodness and unfailing love will pursue me
all the days of my life,
and I will live in the house of the LORD
forever.

The LORD is my shepherd; I have all that I need. (1)

Over the years I have been a pastor, I've heard a lot of stories, some glad, some sad. This is one of the sadder stories.

A woman in my church had come home from work the day after her divorce was final. Her husband had jettisoned her for a younger woman and left her with a ten-year-old son to raise. She expected her son to be home a little before her, so she was surprised to find the house so quiet and cold. It was winter, and if her son were there, she thought, he would have turned on the heat. She called his name, but there was no answer. She called his name again as she searched the house. Still no answer, but she thought she heard something. She stopped and listened, and heard it again. It was a sob, her son's sob. She found him sitting in his bedroom closet, crying softly, knees drawn up, arms tightly wrapped around them.

She asked, though she knew, what was the matter.

He said, "Who's going to show me how to be a man?"

That kind of question is everyone's question. It can be about anything that matters in life: being a man, being a woman, what to do, where to go, who to be. Who can I trust? What am I here for? Who can make me safe?

This wonderful psalm is used so often for the very sick or at memorial services for the dead, that it can be overlooked for the more pressing issues of just living. God says we are his sheep and he is our Shepherd. Jesus says he is the Good Shepherd, the ultimate Shepherd.[102] Most of life is very, very daily and ordinary. It's great to have a Shepherd for the big things and the little things.

The idea of God being a Shepherd to his people is not unique to this psalm. The picture appears many other places.[103] It was also used widely in the ancient Near East, and in the Bible, as a metaphor for a king. It worked well. Most people knew what shepherds did to protect and care for their flocks.

What makes this psalm so special is how personal it is. For God to be a Shepherd to his flock or his people, the nation of Israel, is one thing; but for God to be David's personal Shepherd is something else, something quite wonderful.

Read this psalm aloud, slowly, and take in the staggering message that God makes *you* rest in green meadows, leads *you* beside peaceful streams, and renews *your* strength (verses 2-3). Say these things to yourself and to God, over and over.

Praise God for his care for you and those you care for. He cares for them more than you do—and better than you do! If God is not really this way toward each of us personally, to pray this psalm is to engage in an act of almost criminal narcissism. But Jesus assured us that he does care for us[104] and that he has even numbered the hairs on our heads.[105] Let that truth sink in as you pray this psalm. There is great joy in the comfort it brings.

Praise the Good Shepherd for being both vast and near. An astronomer who was also a Christian lectured at a university on the immensity of the universe. During the question-and-answer session that followed, a student who was not a believer asked the astronomer a provocative question: "How can a God big enough to manage the cosmos you just described possibly be involved in the personal lives of his followers—as you believe he is?" The scientist answered quietly, "The God I believe in is bigger than you think." God's love and wisdom are immeasurable, both in the extent he goes into space and the depth he enters into our hearts. A truly big God can do both.

Praise God for the decisive defeat of your enemies. The hope that God would prepare a feast for me in the presence of my enemies didn't sound all that appealing to me at first. The food might be good, but my digestion wouldn't be, with all those unsavory people reclining at the table with me! But this line describes what kings in the ancient Middle East would do to their defeated enemies: They would make them sit in chains and watch from afar as the king had a party. Not bad!

This promise takes on even greater meaning when you note that this psalm follows Psalm 22, which describes in gruesome detail the sufferings of Christ at the hands of his enemies. God will be victorious; he will vindicate his chosen one.

+++

Surely your goodness and unfailing love will pursue me all the days of my life, and I will live in the house of the LORD forever. (6)
Be awed, and be joyful. Savor also this truth: The Shepherd wants your friendship. His goodness and mercy will pursue you all your life, so you may dwell in his house forever.

As you contemplate this astounding promise, pray this prayer of Fanny Crosby's:

All the way my Savior leads me;
Oh, the fullness of his love!
Perfect rest to me is promised
In my Father's house above:
When my spirit, clothed immortal,
Wings its flight to realms of day,
This my song through endless ages:
Jesus led me all the way.

PSALM 24

A psalm of David.

1 The earth is the LORD's, and everything in it.
The world and all its people belong to him.
2 For he laid the earth's foundation on the seas
and built it on the ocean depths.

3 Who may climb the mountain of the LORD?
Who may stand in his holy place?
4 Only those whose hands and hearts are pure,
who do not worship idols
and never tell lies.
5 They will receive the LORD's blessing
and have a right relationship with God their savior.
6 Such people may seek you
and worship in your presence, O God of Jacob.
Interlude

7 Open up, ancient gates!
Open up, ancient doors,
and let the King of glory enter.
8 Who is the King of glory?
The LORD, strong and mighty;
the LORD, invincible in battle.
9 Open up, ancient gates!
Open up, ancient doors,
and let the King of glory enter.
10 Who is the King of glory?
The LORD of Heaven's Armies—
he is the King of glory.

> Open up, ancient gates! Open up, ancient doors, and let the King of glory enter. Who is the King of glory? The LORD, strong and mighty; the LORD, invincible in battle. (7-8)

The original context of this psalm was probably the triumphant entry of King David and the Ark of the Covenant into Jerusalem. David, as God's anointed one, had subdued his enemies and was entering the city to rule. "Open up, ancient doors," the psalm commands. "Let the King of glory enter!" Read the scriptural account sometime; it's a great story.[106]

The church has long believed this psalm to have been fulfilled in the ascension of Christ into heaven. What do you believe?

Let me tell you what I used to believe. I used to think that when Christ ascended into heaven after his resurrection, he went off to a galaxy far, far away. I wasn't sure why he went away; maybe it was for a much-needed rest or to enjoy the rewards of his victory. But for the time being he'd pretty much left earthly matters in the hands of his disciples, with the help of his Holy Spirit, of course. We were to be his hands and feet until he came back—his only hands and feet.

One sermon illustration I heard on more than one occasion had the angels breathlessly questioning Jesus: "What's your plan for the continuation of your work on earth, now that you're up here in heaven?"

His answer was, "They're my plan."

The angels were shocked: "Them?! That ragtag bunch you call your church? What if they fail? Don't you have a backup plan?"

He said solemnly, "I have no other plan."

The preacher would then exhort us to live out our responsibility to be the hands and feet of Jesus on earth.

The trouble with this idea of the church being Christ's hands and feet is that it is partly true: The church is the Body of Christ. The error is in thinking that Jesus went off somewhere, as an absentee Lord, leaving matters in our hands. On the contrary, when Christ ascended, he rose to a place of the highest honor and power to rule, not to relax. The ascended Christ is more present in his church than he ever could have been when he lived on earth. The key to praying this psalm accurately is with its New Testament counterpart in mind—Paul's prayer for the Ephesians:

> I also pray that you will understand the incredible greatness of God's power for us who believe him. This is the same mighty power that raised Christ from the dead and seated him in the place of honor at God's right hand in the heavenly realms. Now he is far above any ruler or authority or power or leader or anything else—not only in this world but also in the world to come. God has put all things under the authority of Christ and has made him head over all things for the benefit of the church. And the church is his Body; it is made full and complete by Christ, who fills all things everywhere with himself.[107]

+++

The earth is the LORD's, and everything in it. The world and all its people belong to him. (1)

What keeps you up at night? Is it worry over teenagers? a financial shortfall? violence and chaos in the world? My wife calls this song by David a "middle of the night psalm." Pray this truth into your fear. Memorize and repeat it when you are anxious and afraid. Verse 1 reminds us that no circumstance can negate this one truth: Christ is Lord, the earth is his, and we are his. So say it out loud, "The earth is the LORD's. . . ." Say it often. Make it your first response to the things that trouble you.

Pray this truth into your presumption or aimlessness in work. We own nothing; everything belongs to God. What we possess we possess only as managers who must one day give it all back to the Owner and give an account for how we cared for his property.

Confess any tendency to treat your possessions as your own.

Bishop Edwin Hughes once preached a stirring sermon on "God's Ownership." A wealthy parishioner didn't like it, so he invited the bishop to lunch on his estate. After they ate, he walked him through his elaborate gardens, woodlands, and farm. When the tour was finished, he demanded, "Now are you going to tell me that all this land does not belong to me?" Bishop Hughes smiled and proposed, "Ask me that same question a hundred years from now."[108]

Commit yourself to working hard and managing your resources well to the glory of God.

Who may climb the mountain of the LORD? Who may stand in his holy place? Only those whose hands and hearts are pure, who do not worship idols and never tell lies. (3-4)
Thank the Lord Christ that because of his ascension he now stands in the holy place. The question "Who may stand in the holy place?" damns us all. No one but Christ meets the requirements and passes the test. But by his ascension, he has entered the holy place as our Priest, our Representative, and our Redeemer. Now we may go in too!

> Since we have a great High Priest who has entered heaven, Jesus the Son of God, let us hold firmly to what we believe. This High Priest of ours understands our weaknesses, for he faced all of the same testings we do, yet he did not sin. So let us come boldly to the throne of our gracious God. There we will receive his mercy, and we will find grace to help us when we need it most.[109]

Open up, ancient gates! Open up, ancient doors, and let the King of glory enter. Who is the King of glory? The LORD of Heaven's Armies—he is the King of glory. (9-10)
Pray again and again that what is true up in heaven may be true down here on earth and in your life. Invite the King of glory into your heart. Confess the ways you have attempted to dethrone him. Pray that Christ would fully be the Lord of your church.

Remember that the great commission is grounded in the authority of Christ's ascension: "I have been given all authority in heaven and on earth."[110] Pray therefore that the church, the servants of the King, would declare his kingship to the entire world and make disciples of all peoples.

PSALM 27

A psalm of David.

1 The LORD is my light and my salvation—
so why should I be afraid?
The LORD is my fortress, protecting me from danger,
so why should I tremble?
2 When evil people come to devour me,
when my enemies and foes attack me,
they will stumble and fall.
3 Though a mighty army surrounds me,
my heart will not be afraid.
Even if I am attacked,
I will remain confident.

4 The one thing I ask of the LORD—
the thing I seek most—
is to live in the house of the LORD all the days
of my life,
delighting in the LORD's perfections
and meditating in his Temple.
5 For he will conceal me there when troubles come;
he will hide me in his sanctuary.
He will place me out of reach on a high rock.
6 Then I will hold my head high
above my enemies who surround me.
At his sanctuary I will offer sacrifices with shouts of joy,
singing and praising the LORD with music.

7 Hear me as I pray, O LORD.
Be merciful and answer me!
8 My heart has heard you say, "Come and talk with me."
And my heart responds, "LORD, I am coming."
9 Do not turn your back on me.
Do not reject your servant in anger.
You have always been my helper.

Don't leave me now; don't abandon me,
O God of my salvation!
10 Even if my father and mother abandon me,
the LORD will hold me close.

11 Teach me how to live, O LORD.
Lead me along the right path,
for my enemies are waiting for me.
12 Do not let me fall into their hands.
For they accuse me of things I've never done;
with every breath they threaten me with violence.
13 Yet I am confident I will see the LORD's goodness
while I am here in the land of the living.

14 Wait patiently for the LORD.
Be brave and courageous.
Yes, wait patiently for the LORD.

The one thing I ask of the LORD—the thing I seek most—is to live in the house of the LORD all the days of my life, delighting in the LORD's perfections and meditating in his Temple. (4)

I'm the campus pastor at Westmont College. One of my responsibilities is planning the school's chapel services, which are held three times a week in the gymnasium. In the first chapel service of every semester, I begin by asking the students a rhetorical question: "Where are we? Let's get our bearings." Every returning student knows what I will say. Many of them laugh and say the answer along with me:

We are in
Murchison Gym,
955 La Paz Road,
Santa Barbara,
California,
United States,
North America,
western hemisphere,
planet Earth,
solar system,
Milky Way galaxy,
universe,
mind of God.

This is similar to how Emily, in Thornton Wilder's play *Our Town*, inscribed her schoolbooks. And it's very close to the words of the apostle Paul when he quoted the ancient Greek poet Epimenides to the Athenian philosophers on Mars Hill: "In him we live and move and have our being" (Acts 17:28, NIV).

The implications are profound. The God of the Bible obliterates the division between the sacred and the secular by doing away with the secular altogether. The whole creation is sacred because the whole creation is God's—in him and from him and through him and to him.[111] As Abraham Kuyper put it in his inaugural address at the Free University of Amsterdam, "There's not one inch of the universe that Christ does not lay his hand on and say, 'Mine!'" I want the students to think of their education, and everything else they do, as an act of worship, as service done in the presence of their Creator and Savior.

This is what David yearns for when he prays, "The one thing I ask of the LORD—the thing I seek most—is to live in the house of the LORD all the days of my life, delighting in the LORD's perfections and meditating in his Temple" (verse 4). It would be a serious misreading of his prayer to conclude that he wanted to exchange public life for the life of a priest or a monk. David knew that no one was allowed to live in the Temple; what he wanted was to enjoy daily and forever what the Temple stood for—the presence of God. God's house is the whole world;[112] what David wanted was the pleasure and protection of unbroken communion with God in his house.

It's not where you are but who you're with that makes all the difference. Threats, fear, and worry—which are David's lot in this psalm—cannot ultimately touch you in God's presence. Not even disaster and death can separate you from his love.[113] The endless distractions and demands of life are unified and ordered in God's presence. The one thing necessary[114] "is to live in the house of the LORD . . . delighting in the LORD's perfections and meditating in his Temple."

+++

The LORD is my light and my salvation—so why should I be afraid? The LORD is my fortress, protecting me from danger, so why should I tremble? (1)

What feels dark and dangerous to you today? Name the scary what-ifs and horrors. Then stand against them and say in their face, with pugnacity and boldness, "But the Lord is my light—why should I fear you?! He is my fortress, and you can't touch me!"

My heart has heard you say, "Come and talk with me." And my heart responds, "LORD, I am coming." (8)
It really couldn't be simpler. The Lord invites you to come in close and speak to him. He pats his knee as though to say, "Sit here with me. Let's talk." Visualize the intimacy—and wonder—of the invitation. Can you say, "Lord, I'm coming"?

Even if my father and mother abandon me, the LORD will hold me close. (10)
David assumed the last thing his father or mother would ever do would be to abandon him. It would be unthinkable. But even if the unthinkable happened, God would not be sucked into the unthinkable. He knew God was better than the best he knew.

But you may have known the unthinkable. Maybe your father or mother has abandoned you or been cruel and abusive. As a result, you have assumed that God's feelings toward you mirror those of your parents. If this describes you, you may alter the psalmist's words to say, "Lord, my father and mother have abandoned me, but you have held me close. You will never let me go."

Wait patiently for the LORD. Be brave and courageous. Yes, wait patiently for the LORD. (14)
No stamping of the feet like a petulant child, no fidgeting and whining; rather, a calm, secure waiting. If you are beset and besieged, and would love to see God bring his big fist down on the heads of the enemies of your soul, this is your psalm!

Ask the Lord to make you patient as you wait—eagerly and expectantly patient.

PSALM 30

A psalm of David. A song for the dedication of the Temple.

1 I will exalt you, Lord, for you rescued me.
You refused to let my enemies triumph over me.
2 O Lord my God, I cried to you for help,
and you restored my health.
3 You brought me up from the grave, O Lord.
You kept me from falling into the pit of death.

4 Sing to the Lord, all you godly ones!
Praise his holy name.
5 For his anger lasts only a moment,
but his favor lasts a lifetime!
Weeping may last through the night,
but joy comes with the morning.

6 When I was prosperous, I said,
"Nothing can stop me now!"
7 Your favor, O Lord, made me as secure as a mountain.
Then you turned away from me, and I was shattered.

8 I cried out to you, O Lord.
I begged the Lord for mercy, saying,
9 "What will you gain if I die,
if I sink into the grave?
Can my dust praise you?
Can it tell of your faithfulness?
10 Hear me, Lord, and have mercy on me.
Help me, O Lord."

11 You have turned my mourning into joyful dancing.
You have taken away my clothes of mourning and clothed me with joy,
12 that I might sing praises to you and not be silent.
O Lord my God, I will give you thanks forever!

For his anger lasts only a moment, but his favor lasts a lifetime! Weeping may last through the night, but joy comes with the morning. (5)

The Polish Jew had eluded the Nazis for months. His family hadn't been so lucky—all had been executed. As a friend leads him into a new hiding place, a small apartment, the friend says, "Keep as quiet as possible. You are now living in the lions' den." The head of the police lives next door; across the street is a hospital for wounded German soldiers.

The apartment has a piano. The fugitive, Wladyslaw Szpilman, is a virtuoso pianist, a man who would survive the horrors of World War II to become one of the leading concert pianists of the twentieth century. He can't take his eyes off the piano, and when his friend leaves he goes directly to the instrument, lifts the felt cover from the keys, and begins to play—to the accompaniment of a symphony orchestra!

The scene is from Roman Polanski's film *The Pianist*. As he plays, the camera pans to Szpilman's hands to show that his fingers are not actually touching the keys but are playing just inches above it. The music and the orchestra are all in his head, and his heart.

This scene is repeated day after day, sustaining him through a long and torturous exile. It is an act of hope and a prayer, for "hope is hearing the melody of the future. Faith is to dance to it."[115] It's like David's prayer, in which, no matter what, the soul can "practice [its] scales of rejoicing"[116] in the firm confidence that "weeping may last through the night, but joy comes with the morning."

+++

Sing to the LORD, all you godly ones! Praise his holy name. For his anger lasts only a moment, but his favor lasts a lifetime! Weeping may last through the night, but joy comes with the morning. . . . You have turned my mourning into joyful dancing. You have taken away my clothes of mourning and clothed me with joy. (4-5, 11)
Pray hopefully. We don't know what suffering David was going through as he wrote this psalm, but he knew it came directly from God as a chastening for his sin. He knew he was getting exactly what he deserved—fatherly discipline. He also knew that God's anger with his sons and daughters is always temporary. All suffering, whether deserved or not, is never the last word. Whatever your pain may be, pray David's very words with his confidence. And if you recognize that your own poor choices have led to the pain you're experiencing, say of your own suffering what David said of his: "His anger lasts only a moment, but his favor lasts a lifetime!"

When I was prosperous, I said, "Nothing can stop me now!" (6)
Confess your sins. David's sin was the worst kind of sin: arrogant pride. He had forgotten that his prosperity was not a result of something he had done but was due to God's kind favor. He was cocky when he should have been grateful: "When I was prosperous, I said, 'Nothing can stop me now!'" (verse 6). The moment the Lord turned away, he fell apart. "Your favor, O Lord, made me as secure as a mountain. Then you turned away from me, and I was shattered" (verse 7). Have you turned God's grace upside down? Has it become for you an entitlement instead of the heart-stopping miracle that it is? Confess your false security to God.

. . . that I might sing praises to you and not be silent. O LORD my God, I will give you thanks forever. (12)
Pray for God's glory. The goal of all prayer is the praise and glory of God. If David's prayer sounds insincere, it may be because we're not accustomed to his Hebrew *chutzpah*. He says, in effect, "What good will my destruction do for you? If I die you'll have one less worshiper." Like Moses before him, he appealed to God's praise and reputation in

the world.[117] "I cried out to you, O LORD. I begged the Lord for mercy, saying, 'What will you gain if I die, if I sink into the grave? Can my dust praise you? Can it tell of your faithfulness? Hear me, LORD, and have mercy on me'" (verses 8-10). Voice your prayer that way, in that tone. Don't be afraid—some of God's favorite people have been so bold. But note: David doesn't push too hard and ends up with a raw cry, "Help me, O LORD," and the promise, "that I might sing praises to you and not be silent. O LORD my God, I will give you thanks forever" (verses 10, 12).

PSALM 31

For the choir director: A psalm of David.

1 O LORD, I have come to you for protection;
don't let me be disgraced.
Save me, for you do what is right.
2 Turn your ear to listen to me;
rescue me quickly.
Be my rock of protection,
a fortress where I will be safe.
3 You are my rock and my fortress.
For the honor of your name, lead me out of
this danger.
4 Pull me from the trap my enemies set for me,
for I find protection in you alone.
5 I entrust my spirit into your hand.
Rescue me, LORD, for you are a faithful God.

6 I hate those who worship worthless idols.
I trust in the LORD.
7 I will be glad and rejoice in your unfailing love,
for you have seen my troubles,
and you care about the anguish of my soul.
8 You have not handed me over to my enemies
but have set me in a safe place.

9 Have mercy on me, LORD, for I am in distress.
Tears blur my eyes.
My body and soul are withering away.
10 I am dying from grief;
my years are shortened by sadness.
Sin has drained my strength;
I am wasting away from within.
11 I am scorned by all my enemies
and despised by my neighbors—
even my friends are afraid to come near me.

When they see me on the street,
they run the other way.
12 I am ignored as if I were dead,
as if I were a broken pot.
13 I have heard the many rumors about me,
and I am surrounded by terror.
My enemies conspire against me,
plotting to take my life.

14 But I am trusting you, O LORD,
saying, "You are my God!"
15 My future is in your hands.
Rescue me from those who hunt me down relentlessly.
16 Let your favor shine on your servant.
In your unfailing love, rescue me.
17 Don't let me be disgraced, O LORD,
for I call out to you for help.
Let the wicked be disgraced;
let them lie silent in the grave.
18 Silence their lying lips—
those proud and arrogant lips that accuse the godly.

19 How great is the goodness
you have stored up for those who fear you.
You lavish it on those who come to you for protection,
blessing them before the watching world.
20 You hide them in the shelter of your presence,
safe from those who conspire against them.
You shelter them in your presence,
far from accusing tongues.

21 Praise the LORD,
for he has shown me the wonders of his unfailing love.
He kept me safe when my city was under attack.
22 In panic I cried out,
"I am cut off from the LORD!"
But you heard my cry for mercy
and answered my call for help.

23 **Love the Lord, all you godly ones!**
For the Lord protects those who are loyal to him,
but he harshly punishes the arrogant.
24 **So be strong and courageous,**
all you who put your hope in the Lord!

I entrust my spirit into your hand. Rescue me, LORD, for you are a faithful God. (5)

What a way to go. What a way to pray as you go. In Luke's account of the Crucifixion, the words of Psalm 31:5 are the last Jesus prayed before he gave up his spirit and died.[118] Some biblical scholars believe these words were also the first prayer every Jewish mother taught her child to pray before going to sleep at night. When Jesus prayed this prayer on the cross, he added "Father" to it. Jesus died, it seems, the way a child falls to sleep in his father's arms.[119]

Falling to sleep has long been regarded as a prefigurement, a kind of rehearsal for dying. My mother taught me a prayer as a child that I prayed at night. For years it was a comfort, a sweet, innocuous palliative, until I thought about the words I was praying: "Now I lay me down to sleep, I pray the Lord my soul to keep. If I should die before I wake, I pray the Lord my soul to take."

That bit about dying before I wake kept me awake, but not indefinitely. As anxious as I got about the possibility of dying while I slept, I still succumbed to sleep. I eventually had to give up and let go. The choice was not whether to fall into sleep but how: in trust and hope or in fear and despair. The same is true when it comes to dying.

Here's another picture: The Christian's relationship to God is like the special relationship that must exist between a flier and a catcher on the high trapeze. The flyer is the one who lets go of the bar in midair; the catcher is the one who catches him. Absolutely critical in this exchange is that the flyer never try to catch the catcher, but remain still as he arcs out into space, with no visible support, and wait in trust for the catcher to . . . *catch*. For the flier to try to catch the catcher is to court disaster.[120]

Whether in life or in death it is the same: It's let go and let God; let the Catcher catch. It's "I entrust my spirit into your hand."

+++

I entrust my spirit into your hand. (5)

Jesus suffered not so we wouldn't have to. He suffered to show us how to suffer. He invites us to come to him to learn how to carry our burdens the way he carried his: "Take my yoke upon you. Let me teach you, because I am humble and gentle at heart, and you will find rest for your souls" (Matthew 11:29).

Identify the burdens that weigh you down. Think of those you know who suffer. Pray for yourself and for them to learn to pray the way Jesus prayed in verse 5: "I entrust my spirit into your hand."

Read these passages from the New Testament to help you pray this way: Acts 7:59; 1 Peter 2:20-25; 4:19.

My future is in your hands. (15)

Verse 15 focuses on what it meant for Jesus to entrust himself into his Father's hands. The word translated "future" in the New Living Translation is *times* in the Hebrew and speaks not only of the future but of all seasons of life.

What seasons have you lived? Thank God that your past—all of it, the good and the bad—was in his hands.

What is the nature of the time, the season, that you are in now? Name it, and affirm your faith that the present is in his hands.

What do you look forward to? Is there fear as you think ahead? Name your fears and again declare the hope of verse 15. You don't know what the future holds, but you know who holds the future.

Love the LORD, all you godly ones! For the LORD protects those who are loyal to him, but he harshly punishes the arrogant. So be strong and courageous, all you who put your hope in the LORD! (23-24)

Close your prayer time by praying these verses with force and vigor. Say to yourself or to those you may be praying with, "Love the Lord, ________!" and so on.

PSALM 32

A psalm of David.

1 Oh, what joy for those
whose disobedience is forgiven,
whose sin is put out of sight!
2 Yes, what joy for those
whose record the LORD has cleared of guilt,
whose lives are lived in complete honesty!
3 When I refused to confess my sin,
my body wasted away,
and I groaned all day long.
4 Day and night your hand of discipline was heavy on me.
My strength evaporated like water in the summer heat.
Interlude

5 Finally, I confessed all my sins to you
and stopped trying to hide my guilt.
I said to myself, "I will confess my rebellion to the LORD."
And you forgave me! All my guilt is gone. *Interlude*

6 Therefore, let all the godly pray to you while there is still time,
that they may not drown in the floodwaters of judgment.
7 For you are my hiding place;
you protect me from trouble.
You surround me with songs of victory. *Interlude*

8 The LORD says, "I will guide you along the best pathway for
your life.
I will advise you and watch over you.
9 Do not be like a senseless horse or mule
that needs a bit and bridle to keep it under control."

10 Many sorrows come to the wicked,
but unfailing love surrounds those who trust the LORD.
11 So rejoice in the LORD and be glad, all you who obey him!
Shout for joy, all you whose hearts are pure!

Oh, what joy for those whose disobedience is forgiven, whose sin is put out of sight! (1)

Very near the end of her life, Marghanita Laski surprised a television audience with her candor and vulnerability. One of the best-known British novelists and secular humanists of her time, she admitted, "What I envy most about you Christians is your forgiveness; I have nobody to forgive me."[121]

She had half a diagnosis, but no belief in a cure. What was it she had been feeling all those years? Many today would call it lack of self-confidence or low self-esteem. But she knew that was silly, that there was more to this vague sense of having somehow failed and fallen short—the aching fear of missing something exquisite and precious, of loneliness, lostness, and futility. But that's all she knew.

How good it is to know that this malaise and emptiness and sadness has a name: sin. How infinitely greater it is to know the name of the One who forgives sin. "Yes, what joy for those whose record the LORD has cleared of guilt, whose lives are lived in complete honesty!" (verse 2). That's what makes the Good News good, and grace so amazing. The apostle Paul says it's the heart of the Christian message and quotes this psalm to prove his point in Romans 4:7-8.

+++

Oh, what joy for those whose disobedience is forgiven, whose sin is put out of sight! (1)

Have you forgotten this? Think back on your sins, not as a way to open old wounds, but to remember how much God has forgiven you. Kierkegaard prayed this way:

> Father in Heaven! Hold not our sins up against us but hold us up against our sins, so that the thought of Thee when it wakens in our soul, and each time it wakens, should not remind us of what we have committed but of what Thou didst forgive, not of how we went astray but of how Thou didst save us![122]

When I refused to confess my sin, my body wasted away, and I groaned all day long. (3)

No one knows what David's unspecified ailment was. But a lot of things can go wrong with the rest of us when something as toxic as sin is left untended. The whole person compensates pathologically, like my friend who injured his knee playing college football. After the reparative surgery, he began to run again, but gingerly for fear of reinjuring his knee. As he ran, he compensated for the knee, favoring that side of his body. Over time his spine compensated too and got seriously out of alignment. Shooting pains down his sciatic nerve led to his next surgery—done to repair the lumbar disc damaged by the way he had compensated for his knee.

Has any unconfessed sin led you to try to compensate in other areas of your life? Sometimes we can try too hard to be "good" in an effort to offset the bad we've done. Guilt can make us frantic and driven to do good works—doing the right things for the wrong reasons.

Therefore, let all the godly pray to you while there is still time, that they may not drown in the floodwaters of judgment. For you are my hiding place. (6-7)

When we sin, moral and emotional chaos and turbulence rush in like a flood. Personal relationships and whole communities fall apart. Sin has consequences, always, but they need not destroy you. God promises final safety if you confess and repent.

Name your fears about what you may face because of your sin. Declare your trust in God's promise that it will not destroy you, and declare with David, "You are my hiding place."

I will guide you along the best pathway for your life. I will advise you and watch over you. Do not be like a senseless horse or mule that needs a bit and bridle to keep it under control. **(8-9)**

Regrets are not the same as genuine repentance. Anyone can feel bad for what he or she has done. The repentant resolves to learn from it. Better, the repentant sinner hears God's call to become a disciple and be taught by God. God's offer is really an invitation to fellowship with the One we've wronged. This is forgiveness squared! You may go from being an enemy of God to a friend of God, who offers to "guide you along the best pathway for your life," who will "advise you and watch over you."

What evidence can you see of how God is leading you along the best pathway for your life? Thank him for his faithfulness.

PSALM 36

For the choir director: A psalm of David, the servant of the LORD.

1 Sin whispers to the wicked, deep within their hearts.
They have no fear of God at all.
2 In their blind conceit,
they cannot see how wicked they really are.
3 Everything they say is crooked and deceitful.
They refuse to act wisely or do good.
4 They lie awake at night, hatching sinful plots.
Their actions are never good.
They make no attempt to turn from evil.

5 Your unfailing love, O LORD, is as vast as the heavens;
your faithfulness reaches beyond the clouds.
6 Your righteousness is like the mighty mountains,
your justice like the ocean depths.
You care for people and animals alike, O LORD.
7 How precious is your unfailing love, O God!
All humanity finds shelter
in the shadow of your wings.
8 You feed them from the abundance of your own house,
letting them drink from your river of delights.
9 For you are the fountain of life,
the light by which we see.

10 Pour out your unfailing love on those who love you;
give justice to those with honest hearts.
11 Don't let the proud trample me
or the wicked push me around.
12 Look! Those who do evil have fallen!
They are thrown down, never to rise again.

Your unfailing love, O LORD, is as vast as the heavens; your faithfulness reaches beyond the clouds. (5)

In C. S. Lewis's insightful fantasy *The Great Divorce*, the residents of hell are given the option of taking a bus trip to heaven to look around a bit and decide whether they'd like to stay on. They may if they wish, but practically no one wants to. Heaven is so real and hell so false and insubstantial that, compared to hell, even the grass of heaven hurts their feet.

There is a surprise at the end of the tale. Hell, at the beginning of the story, was so vast, some of its residents lived light-years away from one another. But after the narrator leaves hell, he is shocked to discover that it was actually no bigger than a tiny crack in the soil of earth, so small it had to be pointed out with a blade of grass. Dumbfounded, he asks his guide for an explanation:

> "Do you mean then that Hell—all that infinite empty town—is down in some little crack like this?"
>
> "Yes. All Hell is smaller than one pebble of your earthly world: but it is smaller than one atom of *this* world, the Real World. Look at yon butterfly. If it swallowed all Hell, Hell would not be big enough to do it any harm or to have any taste."
>
> "It seems big enough when you're in it, Sir."
>
> "And yet all loneliness, angers, hatreds, envies and itchings that it contains, if rolled into one single experience and put into the scale against the least moment of the joy that is felt by the least in Heaven, would have no weight that could be registered at all. Bad cannot succeed even in being bad as truly as good is good. . . .

> For a damned soul is nearly nothing: it is shrunk, shut up in itself. Good beats upon the damned incessantly as sound waves beat upon the ears of the deaf, but they cannot receive it. Their fists are clenched, their teeth are clenched, their eyes fast shut. First they will not, in the end they cannot, open their hands for gifts, or their mouths for food, or their eyes to see."[123]

This psalm's description of the wicked in verses 1-4 is another way of saying that a lost soul is "nearly nothing: it is shrunk, shut up in itself." Such people's blind conceit and deceit, their preoccupation with doing wrong, are evidence that each of their souls has imploded on itself.

Then the mercy and beauty of God explode into the psalm in verses 5-9! No eye has seen his greatness, no ear has heard it, no mind can conceive it. Set next to him, all the evil of the world has no weight at all. One atom of God's world dwarfs all the universes of sin. This psalm invites us to meditate on the two—the withered wickedness of the wicked and the expansive greatness of God—and to be instructed in wisdom and prayer.

+++

They have no fear of God at all. (1)

The root of all this evil is no fear, the absence of reverence for God. List the ways this shows itself in such things as blind conceit and falsehood, as well as a continual inertia toward darkness: "They lie awake at night, hatching sinful plots." The apostle Paul said these are the very sins all humankind is guilty of (Romans 3:18, 23). Where, in our contemporary world, do you think such evil is most obvious and troubling?

Confess your own sins to God, remembering that sin's greatest power comes when it conceals itself. "The most common lie," observed Friedrich Nietzsche, "is the lie one tells to oneself."

Ask the Holy Spirit to show you any ways your soul has been shrunk by sin.

Your unfailing love, O LORD, is as vast as the heavens. (5)

Celebrate the vastness of God's love and generosity. Bask in their light. Let them show sin for the wasted little fraud that it is. Say out loud, over and over, these words of praise.

Paraphrase verses 5-6 along the lines used by Eugene Peterson in *The Message*:

> God's love is meteoric, his loyalty astronomic, his purpose titanic, his verdicts oceanic. Yet in his largeness nothing gets lost; not a man, not a mouse, slips through the cracks.

Sing something!

Pour out your unfailing love on those who love you; give justice to those with honest hearts. **(10)**
Pray for others, appealing to God's unfailing love and generosity. Name names and situations of need, and say after each, litany-like, words based on verse 10 (e.g., "Father, remember my sister's sickness," "Pour out your unfailing love on ________, who loves you . . .").

Don't let the proud trample me or the wicked push me around. **(11)**
Using these very words, pray against the liars, impostors, and oppressors of the world. Included in God's goodness is his hatred of every pretense and force that sets itself against him.

PSALM 37

A psalm of David.

1 Don't worry about the wicked
   or envy those who do wrong.
2 For like grass, they soon fade away.
   Like spring flowers, they soon wither.

3 Trust in the LORD and do good.
   Then you will live safely in the land and prosper.
4 Take delight in the LORD,
   and he will give you your heart's desires.

5 Commit everything you do to the LORD.
   Trust him, and he will help you.
6 He will make your innocence radiate like the dawn,
   and the justice of your cause will shine like the
      noonday sun.

7 Be still in the presence of the LORD,
   and wait patiently for him to act.
Don't worry about evil people who prosper
   or fret about their wicked schemes.

8 Stop being angry!
   Turn from your rage!
Do not lose your temper—
   it only leads to harm.
9 For the wicked will be destroyed,
   but those who trust in the LORD will possess the land.

10 Soon the wicked will disappear.
   Though you look for them, they will be gone.
11 The lowly will possess the land
   and will live in peace and prosperity.

12 The wicked plot against the godly;
   they snarl at them in defiance.

13 But the Lord just laughs,
for he sees their day of judgment coming.

14 The wicked draw their swords
and string their bows
to kill the poor and the oppressed,
to slaughter those who do right.
15 But their swords will stab their own hearts,
and their bows will be broken.

16 It is better to be godly and have little
than to be evil and rich.
17 For the strength of the wicked will be shattered,
but the LORD takes care of the godly.

18 Day by day the LORD takes care of the innocent,
and they will receive an inheritance that lasts forever.
19 They will not be disgraced in hard times;
even in famine they will have more than enough.

20 But the wicked will die.
The LORD's enemies are like flowers in a field—
they will disappear like smoke.

21 The wicked borrow and never repay,
but the godly are generous givers.
22 Those the LORD blesses will possess the land,
but those he curses will die.

23 The LORD directs the steps of the godly.
He delights in every detail of their lives.
24 Though they stumble, they will never fall,
for the LORD holds them by the hand.

25 Once I was young, and now I am old.
Yet I have never seen the godly abandoned
or their children begging for bread.
26 The godly always give generous loans to others,
and their children are a blessing.

27 Turn from evil and do good,
and you will live in the land forever.
28 For the Lord loves justice,
and he will never abandon the godly.

He will keep them safe forever,
but the children of the wicked will die.
29 The godly will possess the land
and will live there forever.

30 The godly offer good counsel;
they teach right from wrong.
31 They have made God's law their own,
so they will never slip from his path.

32 The wicked wait in ambush for the godly,
looking for an excuse to kill them.
33 But the Lord will not let the wicked succeed
or let the godly be condemned when they are put on trial.

34 Put your hope in the Lord.
Travel steadily along his path.
He will honor you by giving you the land.
You will see the wicked destroyed.

35 I have seen wicked and ruthless people
flourishing like a tree in its native soil.
36 But when I looked again, they were gone!
Though I searched for them, I could not find them!

37 Look at those who are honest and good,
for a wonderful future awaits those who love peace.
38 But the rebellious will be destroyed;
they have no future.

39 The Lord rescues the godly;
he is their fortress in times of trouble.
40 The Lord helps them,
rescuing them from the wicked.
He saves them,
and they find shelter in him.

The lowly will possess the land and will live in peace and prosperity. (11)

*T*his psalm could be really irritating.

The last thing you want to hear when you're upset and angry is "Don't be upset and angry." It's irritating to be told not to be irritated, especially if you're troubled over the evil in the world—things you think you have a right to be angry over. But Psalm 37 says three times in the first eight verses: "Don't worry about the wicked" (verse 1), "Don't worry about evil people" (verse 7), "Do not lose your temper"—the same Hebrew verb for *worry* used in verses 1 and 7, which means something like "Don't get heated"(verse 8).

However, this psalm is a powerful tool against worry and rage in the face of evil. It empowers you in three ways.

First, it tells you *why*: God will bring about justice for his people in his own way, and very important, in his own *time*. His mills may grind slowly, but they grind exceedingly small. The wicked will end up with the thorough thrashing they deserve,[124] and the lowly will be blessed: "The lowly will possess the land and will live in peace and prosperity" (verse 11).

By the way, this is a very important psalm, because Jesus drew from it in one of his Beatitudes. It explains what he meant when he said, "God blesses those who are humble, for they will inherit the whole earth" (Matthew 5:5; see also Matthew 11:29). Just knowing this is reason enough to calm you down when you're worked up.

Second is the *way* it tells you why. The psalm is written in an alphabetic acrostic pattern in the Hebrew; that is, every other line begins with the next letter of the alphabet. It takes a clever poet to do this kind of thing, and it helps in memorization, but it can be a little arbitrary too—it doesn't always lend itself to the logical development of ideas. And, in fact, the psalm is repetitive as it insists on the same few basic ideas over and over again: God will bring about justice for his people in his own way, and very important, in his own *time*.

But the medium fits the message. When you are distraught and in a fury, you aren't able to be rational. You don't need an argument; you need the quiet and repeated reminder that things are going to be all right. You're like a child; you need to be held and reassured. God repeats his assurances over and over again in this psalm. Say them to yourself.

Third, this psalm tells you *how* to trust God despite the trouble and evil you encounter each day.

+ + +

Trust in the LORD. (3)

One of the advantages, or spiritual opportunities, that comes with evil running rampant is the reminder that God is God and we are not. Philosopher Peter Kreeft calls this the "grammar of existence." That it is. True, we can be led to doubt that God is God in times like this, but we can also be confronted with our absolute need for the Lord. You can choose to pray, "If you don't act, Lord, we're sunk; you're our only hope." Good choice, good prayer.

Take delight in the LORD. (4)

Most of life's frustrations come when circumstances or people thwart our desires. Then, of course, the circumstances and the people take the blame—we think, *How can I fly like an eagle when I'm surrounded by turkeys?* The problem may be more in our desires than in our circumstances (James 4:1-3). To delight in God is to desire what God desires—and never to wallow in disappointment, knowing we can trust his wise sovereignty and providence in any situation. We can do anything through the God who strengthens us (Philippians 4:13).

Are you delighting in God? If not, take your disappointments to him; then pray that he will give you the desires of *his* heart. Be frank about what you feel. Don't try to edit your emotions until you've gotten them out. God knows how you feel anyway, but when kept inside, your feelings can be a barrier. Expressed in prayer, they can be a bridge.

Commit everything you do to the Lord. (5)
Wait for God's choices for you. Go ahead and make your plans, but hold them lightly. Pray with Jesus, "Yet I want your will to be done, not mine" (Mark 14:36). Alexander MacLaren, the great nineteenth-century English preacher, counseled, "Hold the will in equilibrium that [God's] finger may incline the balance."[125]

Be still in the presence of the Lord, and wait patiently for him to act. (7)
After committing your way to the Lord, take a nap, go to bed early and get a good night's sleep, keep the Sabbath; in general, act as though you really believe that God heard your prayers. Maybe you should talk a little less too. Sometimes the chatter of the angry and worried only makes things worse. Be more leisurely in making decisions, especially big ones. Talk to God more than you talk about him and the things you think he should do.

PSALM 40

For the choir director: A psalm of David.

1 I waited patiently for the LORD to help me,
and he turned to me and heard my cry.
2 He lifted me out of the pit of despair,
out of the mud and the mire.
He set my feet on solid ground
and steadied me as I walked along.
3 He has given me a new song to sing,
a hymn of praise to our God.
Many will see what he has done and be amazed.
They will put their trust in the LORD.

4 Oh, the joys of those who trust the LORD,
who have no confidence in the proud
or in those who worship idols.
5 O LORD my God, you have performed many wonders
for us.
Your plans for us are too numerous to list.
You have no equal.
If I tried to recite all your wonderful deeds,
I would never come to the end of them.

6 You take no delight in sacrifices or offerings.
Now that you have made me listen, I finally
understand—
you don't require burnt offerings or sin offerings.
7 Then I said, "Look, I have come.
As is written about me in the Scriptures:
8 I take joy in doing your will, my God,
for your instructions are written on my heart."

9 I have told all your people about your justice.
I have not been afraid to speak out,
as you, O LORD, well know.

10 I have not kept the good news of your justice hidden in my heart;
I have talked about your faithfulness and saving power.
I have told everyone in the great assembly
of your unfailing love and faithfulness.

11 Lord, don't hold back your tender mercies from me.
Let your unfailing love and faithfulness always protect me.
12 For troubles surround me—
too many to count!
My sins pile up so high
I can't see my way out.
They outnumber the hairs on my head.
I have lost all courage.

13 Please, Lord, rescue me!
Come quickly, Lord, and help me.
14 May those who try to destroy me
be humiliated and put to shame.
May those who take delight in my trouble
be turned back in disgrace.
15 Let them be horrified by their shame,
for they said, "Aha! We've got him now!"

16 But may all who search for you
be filled with joy and gladness in you.
May those who love your salvation
repeatedly shout, "The Lord is great!"
17 As for me, since I am poor and needy,
let the Lord keep me in his thoughts.
You are my helper and my savior.
O my God, do not delay.

Then I said, "Look, I have come. As is written about me in the Scriptures: I take joy in doing your will, my God, for your instructions are written on my heart." (7-8)

*K*antega is a 22,300-foot peak in the Himalayas of Nepal, and a favorite of mountain climbers. The physical demands it makes on a climber are tremendous, especially in lung and heart strength. Therefore it was more than remarkable when, in the 1980s, a man with a heart transplant successfully climbed it. Born with a congenitally defective heart, the man had struggled for most of his life even to walk up the steps of the porch of his house. But now! With a new heart he could climb Kantega.

Spiritually speaking, this is what David says has happened to him. Because of God's mercy, he has a new heart with God's law written on it. It's not on the outside trying to get in but on the inside working its way out. What he always knew he should do but couldn't, he now really wants to do, and can. It is not merely his duty but his great joy to do God's will. His glowing testimony anticipates the promise God gave through the prophet Ezekiel to one day give his people new hearts able to do things they had never before been able to do.

> I will give you a new heart, and I will put a new spirit in you. I will take out your stony, stubborn heart and give you a tender, responsive heart. And I will put my Spirit in you so that you will follow my decrees and be careful to obey my regulations.[126]

David exults in doing God's will, but the deeper voice is David's greater son, Jesus. The writer of Hebrews quotes these lines to refer to

Jesus, whose whole life is the embodiment and fulfillment of what David expresses.[127] Christ's willing and perfect obedience to his Father is a matter of great significance in the New Testament. In fact, the only time Jesus speaks to his Father intimately as "Abba," or "Papa," is when in Gethsemane he lays down his will to do Abba's will.[128] What Jesus is by nature, he expressed in action by obedience.

To pray in the name of Christ is to pray with the heart of Christ, ready and willing to do his will. Patrick Henry Reardon is absolutely right to say, "'Your will be done,' is the spiritual center of prayer . . . [and] likewise the summation of the entire book of Psalms, and ultimately what makes Christian sense of the Psalter."[129]

Stop to praise and thank Jesus for his perfect obedience to Abba's will. Pray that by the power of his Spirit, the purpose of his sufferings would be perfected in your heart, by working in you willing and joyful obedience. A nineteenth-century hymn by Dora Greenwell can be a great way to pray this:

> And O, that He fulfilled may see
> The travail of His soul in me,
> And with His work contented be,
> As I with my dear Savior![130]

+++

I waited patiently for the LORD to help me, and he turned to me and heard my cry. He lifted me out of the pit of despair, out of the mud and the mire. He set my feet on solid ground and steadied me as I walked along. (1-2)

Remember what Christ saved you from. Remember his mercy in the past and give thanks. What initially prompted David to pray as he did was his deep gratitude for what God did to save him.

As John Newton's memory began to fail him in his old age, he said, "My memory is nearly gone; but I remember two things: that I am a great sinner, and that Christ is a great Saviour." Pray to be like John Newton.

He has given me a new song to sing, a hymn of praise to our God. Many will see what he has done and be amazed. They will put their trust in the LORD. (3)

Isaac Watts's hymn "When I Survey the Wondrous Cross" parallels the flow of the first eight verses of this psalm. A great love calls for a greatly thankful life—and an offering of love: "Love so amazing, so divine, demands my soul, my life, my all." Pray these words for yourself.

LORD, don't hold back your tender mercies from me. Let your unfailing love and faithfulness always protect me. For troubles surround me—too many to count! My sins pile up so high I can't see my way out. They outnumber the hairs on my head. I have lost all courage. (11-12)

Jesus never had to pray this part of the psalm, but we do—often. We were saved by Christ's perfect obedience on the cross. We are being saved continually by his mercy and forgiveness—and will be saved in the end. Confess your sins, thankful that he never tires of forgiving you.

PSALM 42

For the choir director: A psalm of the descendants of Korah.

1 As the deer longs for streams of water,
so I long for you, O God.
2 I thirst for God, the living God.
When can I go and stand before him?
3 Day and night I have only tears for food,
while my enemies continually taunt me, saying,
"Where is this God of yours?"

4 My heart is breaking
as I remember how it used to be:
I walked among the crowds of worshipers,
leading a great procession to the house of God,
singing for joy and giving thanks
amid the sound of a great celebration!

5 Why am I discouraged?
Why is my heart so sad?
I will put my hope in God!
I will praise him again—
my Savior and 6 my God!

Now I am deeply discouraged,
but I will remember you—
even from distant Mount Hermon, the source of the Jordan,
from the land of Mount Mizar.
7 I hear the tumult of the raging seas
as your waves and surging tides sweep over me.
8 But each day the LORD pours his unfailing love upon me,
and through each night I sing his songs,
praying to God who gives me life.

9 "O God my rock," I cry,
"Why have you forgotten me?

Why must I wander around in grief,
oppressed by my enemies?"
10 Their taunts break my bones.
They scoff, "Where is this God of yours?"

11 Why am I discouraged?
Why is my heart so sad?
I will put my hope in God!
I will praise him again—
my Savior and my God!

Why am I discouraged? Why is my heart so sad? I will put my hope in God! I will praise him again—my Savior and my God! (5, 11)

The great Christian poet and hymn writer William Cowper (1731–1800) suffered from what appears to have been bipolar disorder, or manic depression. By the time he was thirty-two, he had tried to commit suicide several times—with an almost comic lack of success. He tried to poison himself, but that didn't work. Then he decided to throw himself into the Thames River, but the night he tried was so foggy, the horse-drawn cabbie he hired to drive him to the river got lost. So Cowper, disgusted, decided to walk to the river. But after a lot of wandering he found himself back at his own doorstep—he had been walking in circles! The next morning he tried falling on his knife, but the knife broke. Then he hung himself, but he was found and cut down, unconscious but alive.

Days later, while reading his Bible, he came to faith in Christ. But his struggle with depression never ceased. He was immobile with depression the last seven years of his life. The last hymn he wrote we know by the title "God Moves in a Mysterious Way." He titled it "Light Shining Out of Darkness." It was his own version of saying what the psalmist said about his own deep sadness. Even though his experience in the moment was dreadful, Cowper hung on to the belief that there was a great and bright hope beyond his depression, and that where he was in the moment was not where he would always be. He reiterated his faith that all God does he does well and with wise and tender love.

God moves in a mysterious way
His wonders to perform;
He plants his footsteps in the sea,
And rides upon the storm.

Deep in unfathomable mines
Of never-ending skill,
He treasures up his bright designs,
And works his sovereign will.

Ye fearful saints, fresh courage take,
The clouds ye so much dread,
Are big with mercy, and shall break
In blessings on your head.

Judge not the Lord by feeble sense,
But trust him for his grace:
Behind a frowning providence
He hides a smiling face.

His purposes will ripen fast
Unfolding every hour;
The bud may have a bitter taste
But sweet will be the flower.

Blind unbelief is sure to err,
And scan his work in vain;
God is his own interpreter
And he will make it plain.[131]

His dear friend John Newton, with amazing intuition, somehow understood what we do now—that much depression can be a physical disorder. He preached at Cowper's funeral: "He was one of those who came out of great tribulations. He suffered much here. . . . But eternity is long enough to make amends for all. For what is all he endured in this life, when compared with the rest which remaineth for the children of God."[132]

+++

"O God my rock," I cry, "Why have you forgotten me? Why must I wander around in grief, oppressed by my enemies?" Their taunts break my bones. They scoff, "Where is this God of yours?" (9-10) Not all depressions are the same. Some are circumstantial, the result of loss or disappointment or fatigue; some are clinical and more complex. But whatever their nature or source, their symptoms are very similar: the numbing dread that the darkness and grief are impenetrable and immovable, and the lie that what is passing is really eternal. This psalm and the next give some helpful clues as to how to deal with depression.

The first is to talk to God about your depression. Pray the depression. That is what this psalm is: an address to God about how the psalmist feels. You can be brutally honest, just as the psalmist is.

Remember that it's always better to talk to God about how you feel about God than to others about how you feel about God. The most destructive aspect of any depression is the sense of abandonment by God. So talk to him about that! Prayer can turn the chasm into a bridge.

Why am I discouraged? Why is my heart so sad? I will put my hope in God! I will praise him again—my Savior and my God! (5, 11) Twice the psalmist reminds himself that he can banish his discouragement by placing his hope in God. Talk to yourself about your depression.

Feelings can be like unruly children, and like unruly children, they must not be allowed to have the last word. Let them sound off, but then tell yourself what is true. It may seem a little disingenuous to talk to yourself this way, but the power of depression is in its deception; it splits you off from what is true. It takes a piece of the picture and makes it the whole picture. Talk back to yourself and affirm the truth that "I will praise him again—my Savior and my God!"

In other words, allow yourself to express your negative feelings even as you affirm God's goodness. Be as mad or as fearful or as sad as you actually are, and at the same time, say with the writer of Lamentations,

> The thought of my suffering and homelessness is bitter beyond words. I will never forget this awful time, as I grieve over my loss. Yet I still dare to hope when I remember this: The faithful love of the LORD never ends! His mercies never cease. (Lamentations 3:19-22)

As the deer longs for streams of water, so I long for you, O God. I thirst for God, the living God. When can I go and stand before him? **(1-2)**

Remind yourself what your deepest need is, whether you are downhearted or not: God. Unpleasant as it is, depression can be a reminder that we are not whole without God, no matter how well we may feel. You may even be so bold as to thank him for that reminder!

PSALM 46

For the choir director: A song of the descendants of Korah, to be sung by soprano voices.

1 God is our refuge and strength,
always ready to help in times of trouble.
2 So we will not fear when earthquakes come
and the mountains crumble into the sea.
3 Let the oceans roar and foam.
Let the mountains tremble as the waters surge!
Interlude

4 A river brings joy to the city of our God,
the sacred home of the Most High.
5 God dwells in that city; it cannot be destroyed.
From the very break of day, God will protect it.
6 The nations are in chaos,
and their kingdoms crumble!
God's voice thunders,
and the earth melts!
7 The LORD of Heaven's Armies is here among us;
the God of Israel is our fortress. *Interlude*

8 Come, see the glorious works of the LORD:
See how he brings destruction upon the world.
9 He causes wars to end throughout the earth.
He breaks the bow and snaps the spear;
he burns the shields with fire.

10 "Be still, and know that I am God!
I will be honored by every nation.
I will be honored throughout the world."

11 The LORD of Heaven's Armies is here among us;
the God of Israel is our fortress. *Interlude*

God is our refuge and strength, always ready to help in times of trouble. (1)

A father watched his son struggle to move a big rock. The rock was just too big, and the boy was just too little, so he sat down dejectedly with his head in his hands.

The father went outside and asked, "What's wrong, Son? Can't you lift that rock out?"

"No, sir," the boy said, "I can't do it."

"Have you used all the strength that's available to you?" the father asked.

"Yes, sir," the boy replied.

"No, you haven't," the father said. "You haven't asked me to help you."[133]

"God is our refuge and strength, always ready to help in times of trouble." So let the worst come, the psalmist says. Bring it on—we can handle whatever comes, because our God is a God who answers prayer.

After affirming God's power and faithfulness, the psalmist conjures up the worst disasters, what we might today describe in terms of nuclear holocaust:

+++

So we will not fear when earthquakes come and the mountains crumble into the sea. Let the oceans roar and foam. Let the mountains tremble as the waters surge! (2-3)

Other bad things can and do happen: Enemies may attack us and nations continually fight among themselves (verses 5-6). But God is God and they are not, so we will not fear—we will pray.

Alexander MacLaren wrote, "Only he who can say, 'The Lord is the strength of my life' can say, 'Of whom shall I be afraid?'"

Declare your trust in the Lord. Say out loud, "The Lord is the strength of my life." If you're not sure you totally believe that, say it anyway, and ask that the Spirit would plant that truth deep in your heart.

A river brings joy to the city of our God, the sacred home of the Most High. (4)

Jerusalem is the city of God spoken of here, but Jerusalem had no river, as her powerful enemies did. Egypt had the Nile, Babylon had the Tigris and Euphrates, but Jerusalem had only a little creek, at most. The river that brought joy was the presence of God. God's people can drink to their deepest satisfaction from this "river of delights"![134]

Believe this, pray this, and let God rebuke your enemies and calm your fears.

The Lord of Heaven's Armies is here among us; the God of Israel is our fortress. (7, 11)

Martin Luther was inspired by this psalm when he wrote his famous hymn, "A Mighty Fortress Is Our God." Luther's use of the archaic *Lord Sabaoth* comes from verse 7 and simply means "Lord of Heaven's Armies." Sing or say it as another way of thanking God for his fortress-like presence with you. He *must* win the battle against the enemies of our souls!

> Did we in our own strength confide,
> our striving would be losing,
> were not the right man on our side,
> the man of God's own choosing.
> Dost ask who that may be?
> Christ Jesus, it is he;
> Lord Sabaoth, his name,
> from age to age the same,
> and he must win the battle.

Be still, and know that I am God! I will be honored by every nation. I will be honored throughout the world. (10)

One of the most famous verses in the Bible is verse 10: "Be still, and know that I am God!" It is often read in a tone of calm assurance and comfort or as a call to be still and peaceful in one's soul. While that is always good advice, it is probably not the tone the psalmist intended. The Hebrew is more like, "Hush!" or "Enough!" Since it is spoken to warring and violent peoples, we should read it as a stern rebuke; God gets in the face of arrogant and angry nations and says, "Stop! Right now!" The closest New Testament parallel are the words Jesus shouted to the storm, "Silence! Be still"![135] That's how God speaks to our enemies.

Pray *at* your enemies the way the psalm does. Say to them, "Hush, be still, for God is God and he will be honored here!" Intercede for those who suffer oppression. Say to their oppressors, "Hush, be still, for God is God and he will be honored here!" Confess your busyness. Repent of the ways you run here and there, reacting to circumstances and fears. Say to yourself, "Hush, be still, for God is God and he will be honored here!" Ponder these words of C. S. Lewis:

> The real problem of the Christian life comes where people do not usually look for it. It comes the very moment you wake up each morning. All your wishes and hopes for the day rush at you like wild animals. And the first job each morning consists in simply shoving them all back; in listening to that other voice, taking the other point of view, letting that other, larger, stronger, quieter life come flowing in. And so on, all day. Standing back from your natural fussings and frettings; coming in out of the wind.[136]

Vow to the Lord that with his help you will create more quiet spaces in your life.

> There is hardly ever a complete silence in our soul. God is whispering to us well-nigh incessantly. Whenever the sounds of the world die out in the soul, or sink low, then we hear these whisperings of God. He is always whispering to us, only we do not always hear, because of the noise, hurry, and distraction which life causes as it rushes on.[137]

PSALM 51

For the choir director: A psalm of David, regarding the time Nathan the prophet came to him after David had committed adultery with Bathsheba.

1 Have mercy on me, O God,
because of your unfailing love.
Because of your great compassion,
blot out the stain of my sins.
2 Wash me clean from my guilt.
Purify me from my sin.
3 For I recognize my rebellion;
it haunts me day and night.
4 Against you, and you alone, have I sinned;
I have done what is evil in your sight.
You will be proved right in what you say,
and your judgment against me is just.
5 For I was born a sinner—
yes, from the moment my mother conceived me.
6 But you desire honesty from the womb,
teaching me wisdom even there.

7 Purify me from my sins, and I will be clean;
wash me, and I will be whiter than snow.
8 Oh, give me back my joy again;
you have broken me—
now let me rejoice.
9 Don't keep looking at my sins.
Remove the stain of my guilt.
10 Create in me a clean heart, O God.
Renew a loyal spirit within me.
11 Do not banish me from your presence,
and don't take your Holy Spirit from me.

12 Restore to me the joy of your salvation,
and make me willing to obey you.

13 Then I will teach your ways to rebels,
and they will return to you.
14 Forgive me for shedding blood, O God who saves;
then I will joyfully sing of your forgiveness.
15 Unseal my lips, O Lord,
that my mouth may praise you.

16 You do not desire a sacrifice, or I would offer one.
You do not want a burnt offering.
17 The sacrifice you desire is a broken spirit.
You will not reject a broken and repentant heart, O God.
18 Look with favor on Zion and help her;
rebuild the walls of Jerusalem.
19 Then you will be pleased with sacrifices offered in the right spirit—
with burnt offerings and whole burnt offerings.
Then bulls will again be sacrificed on your altar.

Have mercy on me, O God, because of your unfailing love. (1)

*O*ne summer, the children's director of our church asked me to act out a Bible character for our third graders in vacation Bible school. I would come to class, dressed as that character might have dressed, and tell the children my story, with just enough artistic license to make it accessible—and entertaining—for them. She assigned me the role of Samson. It sounded like a lot of fun.

But when I went to the material on Samson in the book of Judges and read it through the eyes of a child, I was perplexed. How many episodes in his life could I leave out and still tell his story? Should I include his multiple sexual partners? I didn't think so. Or his night at a brothel in Gaza? His ripping the gates off the city the next morning to escape his enemies? His setting the cute little foxes on fire? Samson's story, were it made into a movie today, would get at least an R rating.

I've since thought it would be fun if, outside our church entrance, we posted a neon sign, shaped like an arrow and pointing inside, that flashed "Adult Books." When curious so-called "adults" peered in the door, they would find a stack of Bibles. In the truest sense of the word, the Bible is an adult book. We have to water it down to teach it to children.

The story behind this psalm is as lurid as anything Hollywood has ever filmed. It includes murder and adultery, lies and deception, and the untimely death of an infant. It unleashes a series of events that would break David's heart and nearly bring his kingdom down: rape and more murder within the family, and the treason of his beloved son Absalom

(2 Samuel 11–18). But out of it comes a great prayer, one of the most often prayed psalms in Christian history. David's confession of sin shows what sin and forgiveness are really about. It may be one man's story, but it is everybody's predicament.

+++

Against you, and you alone, have I sinned. (4)
To cover up the unwanted pregnancy that resulted from his affair with Bathsheba, David arranged for the murder of Uriah, her husband. Uriah, were he able, might argue with David's confession that it was against God and God alone that he had sinned. But this psalm of confession is a radical prayer. The word *radical* comes from the Latin *radix*, which means "root." David has thought long and hard about the roots of this sin against Uriah, and he sees that it began with his disregard of God. In this, he predates Paul's searching analysis in Romans 1:21:

> Yes, they knew God, but they wouldn't worship him as God or even give him thanks. And they began to think up foolish ideas of what God was like. As a result, that their minds became dark and confused.

From this fundamental futility and darkness comes every other transgression and iniquity against others. Uriah would never have been murdered if David had attended to his relationship with God.

But you desire honesty from the womb, teaching me wisdom even there. (6)
David's radical approach extends deep into his own heart, as he acknowledges that God isn't interested in outward, superficial obedience but in inward purity. Do you live by that same understanding? If not, pray for the same kind of wisdom.

Create in me a clean heart, O God. Renew a loyal spirit within me. Do not banish me from your presence, and don't take your Holy Spirit from me. (10-11)
Recognizing the depth of his depravity, David asks for a radical cure for radical sin.

Confess your sins as David did, using his language (or a paraphrase) and analysis. Your sin may not be as grievous as his was, but it is no less radical in its origin, and it requires no less radical a cure.

Have mercy on me, O God, because of your unfailing love. Because of your great compassion, blot out the stain of my sins. Wash me clean from my guilt. Purify me from my sin. (1-2)
What does David ask God for in his confession? Everything!

Mercy: Justice is what he deserves; mercy is what he doesn't deserve. If he gets justice he is dead. Mercy is his only hope.

Unfailing love: The Hebrew word is the word for God's covenant love, *chesedh*. Like mercy, it is the love God promises when he sovereignly chooses to make us his own. It isn't given because we were good, and it is not withdrawn when we are bad. David is asking God to keep his promises.

Compassion: A prayer for God to show David his tender warmth. He longs for God's smile as much as he fears his judgment. He desires a hug as much as an acquittal.

A thorough laundering: The words in the text are simply, "Wash me clean." The language is stronger in verse 7: "Purify me from my sins." The Hebrew is literally, "Purify me with the hyssop branch." Hyssop was used in the washing of lepers. It was more than the removal of dirt; it was deep cleansing of all corruption.

Let these words expand and deepen your grasp of what you need from God and may ask of him. Then ask him to cleanse and purify you from your own sin.

With deep gratitude and wonder, remember Jesus, who, though he never sinned, "God made . . . to be the offering for our sin, so that we could be made right with God through Christ" (2 Corinthians 5:21).

PSALM 52

For the choir director: A psalm of David, regarding the time Doeg the Edomite said to Saul, "David has gone to see Ahimelech."

1 Why do you boast about your crimes, great warrior?
Don't you realize God's justice continues forever?
2 All day long you plot destruction.
Your tongue cuts like a sharp razor;
you're an expert at telling lies.
3 You love evil more than good
and lies more than truth. *Interlude*

4 You love to destroy others with your words,
you liar!
5 But God will strike you down once and for all.
He will pull you from your home
and uproot you from the land of the living.
Interlude

6 The righteous will see it and be amazed.
They will laugh and say,
7 "Look what happens to mighty warriors
who do not trust in God.
They trust their wealth instead
and grow more and more bold in their wickedness."

8 But I am like an olive tree, thriving in the house of God.
I will always trust in God's unfailing love.
9 I will praise you forever, O God,
for what you have done.
I will trust in your good name
in the presence of your faithful people.

> But I am like an olive tree, thriving in the house of God. (8)

So just how bad was Doeg the Edomite? "Doeg, who?" you say? Which is the point the psalm makes: Doeg, who had such a high opinion of himself, ended up as a mere cipher, a question in a Bible trivia game. He has been pulled up and uprooted like a weed. But in his brief career as a villain, he was a very bad man, arguably worse than Judas, the betrayer of Jesus.[138] But as with all evil men, he ended up a boring and dull man, almost comical; just a foil for the justice of God.

Briefly, his story is as follows:[139] David is hiding out from King Saul and his murderous paranoia. The priest Ahimelech gives David refuge, Doeg tattles on Ahimelech, and Saul orders Ahimelech's death, but his soldiers won't kill a priest of the Lord. Doeg eagerly offers his services, Saul accepts, and not only Ahimelech but his entire clan are slaughtered—eighty-five people in all. When it's all over, Doeg is feeling pretty macho, a warrior to be reckoned with, which prompts David's sarcastic, "Why do you boast about your crimes, great warrior?" (verse 1). In *The Message*, Eugene Peterson paraphrases it this way: "Why do you brag of evil, 'Big Man'?"

Psalm 52 comes as close to a political cartoon as any psalm in the Psalter. It would not be far off the mark to substitute Doeg's name with Nero and Nebuchadnezzar, Hitler and Stalin, Idi Amin and Pol Pot. They all had their day and loomed large and terrifying in their time, but now they are gone and disgraced. David is sure of this, so he exults in God's justice, for God will not be mocked. God will pull Doeg up like a weed. "God will strike you down once and for all. He will pull you from your home and uproot you from the land of the living" (verse 5). But as for David and all who trust in the Lord, they can be confident and say, "But I am like an olive tree, thriving in the house of God" (verse 8). What God plants will never be uprooted.

This psalm is a great model for how to pray in the times the Doegs of this world are having their moment. Among other things, it gives you permission to pray with an "attitude," like David.

+++

Why do you boast about your crimes, great warrior? Don't you realize God's justice continues forever? (1)
In the presence of God, as you pray, substitute the names of the Doegs of this world: the traffickers in the sex trade, the drug dealers, and the dictators.

Proceed through the entire psalm with evil institutions and governments in mind. Let the words of the psalm give you a voice to fight against the spiritual forces of evil.

You love to destroy others with your words, you liar! But God will strike you down once and for all. (4-5)
Think of the lies told by the media and the advertising industry as you pray the words above. In particular, pray for the young people you know who may be affected by these deceptions.

But I am like an olive tree, thriving in the house of God. I will always trust in God's unfailing love. I will praise you forever, O God, for what you have done. I will trust in your good name in the presence of your faithful people. (8-9)
Declare your faith. For you pray with and in Jesus, who faced the most savage and vicious Doegs and saw the faithfulness of the Lord. Thank God for Christ's victory.

During a TV interview, Barbara Walters asked Katharine Hepburn, "If you were a tree, what kind would you be?" If that question were posed to David, this psalm gives us his answer. And it's a good prayer for each of us, too: Ask to be like an olive tree, thriving in the house of the Lord. This tree is a cultivated plant. It grows strong and vital over time, unlike evil that pops up like a weed anywhere. Sin comes easily; righteousness takes time and patience.

PSALM 53

For the choir director: A meditation; a psalm of David.

1 Only fools say in their hearts,
"There is no God."
They are corrupt, and their actions are evil;
not one of them does good!

2 God looks down from heaven
on the entire human race;
he looks to see if anyone is truly wise,
if anyone seeks God.
3 But no, all have turned away;
all have become corrupt.
No one does good,
not a single one!

4 Will those who do evil never learn?
They eat up my people like bread
and wouldn't think of praying to God.
5 Terror will grip them,
terror like they have never known before.
God will scatter the bones of your enemies.
You will put them to shame, for God has rejected them.

6 Who will come from Mount Zion to rescue Israel?
When God restores his people,
Jacob will shout with joy, and Israel will rejoice.

God looks down from heaven on the entire human race; he looks to see if anyone is truly wise, if anyone seeks God. (2)

"We have met the enemy and he is us."

That was the heading of an antipollution poster for Earth Day 1970. It came from *Pogo*, a comic strip created by Walt Kelly that was set in the Okefenokee Swamp of Georgia. From 1948 to 1975, Kelly used a wide variety of funny swamp creatures, but mainly Pogo the Possum and Albert the Alligator, to deliver trenchant political and social satire. It made me laugh even as it made me squirm. "We have met the enemy and he is us" is his most famous quotation, and a key to the meaning of this psalm.

Psalm 53 is virtually a word-for-word repeat of Psalm 14, with just a few variations. Why the same psalm twice? No one knows for sure, but my guess is that it has something to do with Walt Kelly's famous quote. Follow the flow of the psalm: There's the fool, the enemy everybody hates (verse 1). Then there's God, who looks down from heaven to see if there is anyone who isn't a fool, and guess what—he can't find anybody. "All have turned away; all have become corrupt. No one does good, not a single one!" (verse 3). The apostle Paul quotes this verse as he makes the same point in his indictment of the human race.[140] "We have met the enemy and he is us." This truth is hard to hear; maybe that's why we need to hear it twice.

What a sobering image of God—he looks down and all around the earth and can't find even one person who isn't the enemy. God doesn't miss anything. No one is overlooked in the search. But there's another picture in the Bible of God looking down and searching that's very comforting. It's 2 Chronicles 16:9: "The eyes of the LORD search the whole earth in order to strengthen those whose hearts are fully committed to him." The worst kinds of fools are those who don't know they're fools. They can't be helped. But God delights in those who know they have been fools. He strengthens them. That's the significance of verse 4. The worst fools are those who "wouldn't think of praying to God." The only fools God won't help are those who won't ask for help.

This takes us to the heart of the gospel. Christianity is not a self-help religion. It was Benjamin Franklin who said, "God helps those who help themselves," not Jesus. Jesus said he "came not to be served but to serve others and to give his life as a ransom for many" (Mark 10:45). To pray is to ask for help. The only fools Jesus can't and won't save are those who won't pray. There are fools, and there are *fools*.

+++

All have turned away; all have become corrupt. No one does good, not a single one! (3)

Confess your prayerlessness. P. T. Forsyth believed prayer is so central to the health of the Christian life that "the worst sin is prayerlessness. Overt sin . . . [is] the effect of this, or its punishment. We are left by God for lack of seeking him."[141] This psalm agrees and adds that prayerlessness is foolishness.

Ask the Lord to give you a greater hunger for prayer. Pledge yourself to spend more time talking with him. Resolve to lay your whole life out before God—all you do and desire—and make it the material of your prayers.

Imagine the face of Jesus as he "looks down from heaven on the entire human race . . . to see if anyone is truly wise, if anyone seeks God" (verse 2). Raise your arms to him and lift your eyes to heaven. Say, "I seek you, Lord."

Pray for the North American church and its prayerlessness. We are the richest and most educated church in history, and yet we are shrinking. The church in the southern hemisphere lacks money and education but has no lack of a sense of its need of God. And it is growing, not only in numbers but also in vitality.

When God restores his people, Jacob will shout with joy, and Israel will rejoice. (6)

Pray into the future in the spirit of verse 6. Thank and praise God for his ultimate victory, even as you ask him to restore and save his beleaguered church around the world in places like India, China, North Korea, Europe, and the inner cities.

PSALM 55

For the choir director: A psalm of David, to be accompanied by stringed instruments.

1 Listen to my prayer, O God.
Do not ignore my cry for help!
2 Please listen and answer me,
for I am overwhelmed by my troubles.
3 My enemies shout at me,
making loud and wicked threats.
They bring trouble on me
and angrily hunt me down.

4 My heart pounds in my chest.
The terror of death assaults me.
5 Fear and trembling overwhelm me,
and I can't stop shaking.
6 Oh, that I had wings like a dove;
then I would fly away and rest!
7 I would fly far away
to the quiet of the wilderness. *Interlude*

8 How quickly I would escape—
far from this wild storm of hatred.

9 Confuse them, Lord, and frustrate their plans,
for I see violence and conflict in the city.
10 Its walls are patrolled day and night against invaders,
but the real danger is wickedness within
the city.
11 Everything is falling apart;
threats and cheating are rampant in the streets.

12 It is not an enemy who taunts me—
I could bear that.
It is not my foes who so arrogantly insult me—
I could have hidden from them.

13 Instead, it is you—my equal,
my companion and close friend.
14 What good fellowship we once enjoyed
as we walked together to the house of God.

15 Let death stalk my enemies;
let the grave swallow them alive,
for evil makes its home within them.

16 But I will call on God,
and the LORD will rescue me.
17 Morning, noon, and night
I cry out in my distress,
and the LORD hears my voice.
18 He ransoms me and keeps me safe
from the battle waged against me,
though many still oppose me.
19 God, who has ruled forever,
will hear me and humble them. *Interlude*

For my enemies refuse to change their ways;
they do not fear God.

20 As for my companion, he betrayed his friends;
he broke his promises.
21 His words are as smooth as butter,
but in his heart is war.
His words are as soothing as lotion,
but underneath are daggers!

22 Give your burdens to the LORD,
and he will take care of you.
He will not permit the godly to slip and fall.

23 But you, O God, will send the wicked
down to the pit of destruction.
Murderers and liars will die young,
but I am trusting you to save me.

> Oh, that I had wings like a dove; then I would fly away and rest! I would fly far away to the quiet of the wilderness. . . . How quickly I would escape—far from this wild storm of hatred. (6-8)

*N*ot long ago, I officiated at the funeral of a woman I did not know. When she died of the ravages of cancer at the young age of forty, a lot more than her body had been ruined. There had been three husbands and five children from the three men, with all the lingering ravages of anger, sadness, and deep confusion the failed marriages had brought. Then there was the devastation of her alcoholism and various forms of substance abuse. She died a mess and left a mess behind, but she still was loved.

A friend of a friend of a friend contacted me to perform the memorial service. I nervously agreed, not knowing her and not knowing what to say about her, and knowing the tightrope I'd have to walk to speak the gospel truthfully and graciously into the emotional and spiritual morass of her family and friends. The service was planned by the family and included several bits of remembrance of the things she loved and the things they loved about her—sweet recollections of a family vacation, some laughter over her love of spaghetti and meatballs, and a recording of her favorite song—one she played over and over again every day in the weeks before she died. When she heard it, she would smile even through the fog of morphine. It was a song I like a lot, a song by Christopher Cross called "Sailing." They played it just before I preached. The refrain reflects the writer's longing to sail away—"just a dream and the wind to carry me, and soon I will be free."

As the song played, I looked out over the gathering at the faces of those who had known her. Many were smiling wistfully and tearfully. All

I could think of was how the song described the way she had lived: trying to escape, to sail away on a dream and the wind from all the hard things. How sad, how ironic, that all her efforts to sail away had kept her tied to the bleak shore she wanted to leave behind.

The temptation is understandable though. David feels it intensely. His good friend has turned against him, and others have joined the betrayer in a murderous conspiracy. The easiest thing, if it were possible, would be to get out of town and live the rest of his days in a quiet, peaceful place. But that would only guarantee his destruction.

So he doesn't cave in to the temptation; instead he prays—always a good idea.

+++

But I will call on God, and the LORD will rescue me. (16)
Turn your cares into prayers. Repent of the urge to run away from your problems. Resist what David resisted in verses 6-8; follow his lead in verse 16, or as the apostle Paul urges us in Philippians 4:6-7:

> Don't worry about anything; instead, pray about everything. Tell God what you need, and thank him for all he has done. Then you will experience God's peace, which exceeds anything we can understand. His peace will guard your hearts and minds as you live in Christ Jesus.

Morning, noon, and night I cry out in my distress, and the LORD hears my voice. (17)
Bring greater structure and regularity to your prayer life. In the chaos and disjointedness of the circumstances and emotions swirling around him, David spoke of praying three times a day. This kind of "saying your prayers" at appointed times can counterbalance the drift into greater confusion that hard times and fear—"wild storm[s] of hatred" (verse 8)—usually bring.

Instead, it is you—my equal, my companion and close friend. What good fellowship we once enjoyed as we walked together to the house of God. (13-14)
Pray this psalm with Jesus. Its description of betrayal by a close friend is exactly what Jesus experienced in the treachery of Judas Iscariot. Pray

this psalm as a way of sharing in the fellowship of Christ's sufferings (Philippians 3:10). If you are a Christian, you are in Christ, in his Body, the church. This kind of "praying with" is not only permitted by our Lord, it is a duty and a joy. Because we are in Christ, we may pray as he prays, in him and with him. This introduces us to a fellowship unlike any other in life.

Also use this psalm to pray for others. It may not describe what you are experiencing at the moment, but it does express what many others are experiencing. Stand with the betrayed and abandoned, and pray these verses for them, on their behalf: "Remember those in prison, as if you were there yourself. Remember also those being mistreated, as if you felt their pain in your own bodies" (Hebrews 13:3).

PSALM 56

For the choir director: A psalm of David, regarding the time the Philistines seized him in Gath. To be sung to the tune "Dove on Distant Oaks."

1 O God, have mercy on me,
for people are hounding me.
My foes attack me all day long.
2 I am constantly hounded by those who slander me,
and many are boldly attacking me.
3 But when I am afraid,
I will put my trust in you.
4 I praise God for what he has promised.
I trust in God, so why should I be afraid?
What can mere mortals do to me?

5 They are always twisting what I say;
they spend their days plotting to harm me.
6 They come together to spy on me—
watching my every step, eager to kill me.
7 Don't let them get away with their wickedness;
in your anger, O God, bring them down.

8 You keep track of all my sorrows.
You have collected all my tears in your bottle.
You have recorded each one in your book.

9 My enemies will retreat when I call to you for help.
This I know: God is on my side!
10 I praise God for what he has promised;
Yes, I praise the Lord for what he has promised.
11 I trust in God, so why should I be afraid?
What can mere mortals do to me?

12 I will fulfill my vows to you, O God,
and will offer a sacrifice of thanks for your help.
13 For you have rescued me from death;
you have kept my feet from slipping.
So now I can walk in your presence, O God,
in your life-giving light.

O God, have mercy on me, for people are hounding me. (1)

*B*ack in the days of the American frontier, deer hunters who were low on ammunition and wanted to make sure their shots found their targets came up with an interesting technique. A hunter would take his dogs, his hounds, with him and look for a deer watering by a lake or river. When the hunter found his quarry, he would sic the hounds on the deer. The dogs would chase the poor creature until it was exhausted, all the while herding it into deep water. Sometimes the deer would get so tired that it drowned, saving the hunter even one bullet.

That's where our expression "hounding a man to death" comes from. It's a good description of our text, for the persistent harassment of David's enemies goes on "all day long" and "constantly." There really aren't any knockout punches being thrown, just a lot of stinging jabs: "twisting what I say . . . plotting to harm me . . . watching my every step" (verses 5-6). But these things add up. They're not like the clean shot of a rifle; they're more like the yapping and bullying of the hounds as they drive their prey toward the water.

David's great comfort is in the God whose love is intimate and who doesn't miss one jab—not when a sparrow falls or when an enemy slanders one of his own. His tender love is accountant-like in its detailed specificity: Not only has God kept track of all of David's sorrows, but he has recorded each and every one of his tears.

When my son Joel was four years old, he had a big fall and scuffed his knees pretty badly. I held him as he cried, and when he stopped, I wiped away each and every tear that was left on his face, counting them as I did. I think there were thirteen or fourteen teardrops. This fascinated Joel, and he grew thoughtful as I went about my task. When I finished, he grinned impishly as he pointed to a spot near his ear and said, "You missed that one, Daddy." He knew what I was trying to do, and he was only too willing to let me do it. I was trying to love him the way God loves his children.

Let God love you that way. Begin by praying this psalm. There are two kinds of persons "keeping track" of David's life: One keeps track to harm; the other, God, keeps track to help and heal. David prays this way about those who keep track to harm:

+++

My foes attack me all day long. . . . They are always twisting what I say; they spend their days plotting to harm me. They come together to spy on me—watching my every step, eager to kill me. (1, 5-6)
David's words can do at least two things to help you pray: first, they can give you a voice if you are experiencing the kind of hounding David experienced. Second, if they don't describe you, they can help give you an ear to those they do describe. There are many in the world for whom these words poignantly apply. Pray for them the way David prayed. And of course, these words describe something of the sufferings of Jesus. Pray them thankfully for his great passion.

You keep track of all my sorrows. You have collected all my tears in your bottle. You have recorded each one in your book. (8)
God is keeping track too! He responds to your tears in a loving and intimate way. The thief may come to kill and destroy, but the Good Shepherd comes to give life abundantly. He knows each one of his sheep intimately (John 10:10-30). Read Psalm 23 to remember the gracious generosity of the Good Shepherd, who feeds and refreshes us, protects us from danger, saves us from death, and pursues us with his love. What could be better?

Tell the Lord you know that he has missed not one moment of your or anyone else's suffering. Name each of your sorrows, and thank him that he has written each one down in his book.

I trust in God, so why should I be afraid? What can mere mortals do to me? (4)
This kind of prayer—talking to yourself or to whomever you're with—appears often in the Psalms, and it's a great way to pray (e.g., Psalms 42, 43, and 103). Say to yourself, and to anyone around you as you pray, what you know to be true about God. True prayer isn't just speaking to God, but listening to God and speaking *of* God in his presence and the presence of his people.

I will fulfill my vows to you, O God, and will offer a sacrifice of thanks for your help. (12)
This is another common way of praying in the Psalms: to vow to give thanks—often publicly—when God answers the psalmists' petitions. Where and with whom will you vow to give thanks when God answers your prayer?

PSALM 57

For the choir director: A psalm of David, regarding the time he fled from Saul and went into the cave. To be sung to the tune "Do Not Destroy!"

1 Have mercy on me, O God, have mercy!
I look to you for protection.
I will hide beneath the shadow of your wings
until the danger passes by.
2 I cry out to God Most High,
to God who will fulfill his purpose for me.
3 He will send help from heaven to rescue me,
disgracing those who hound me. *Interlude*

My God will send forth his unfailing love and faithfulness.

4 I am surrounded by fierce lions
who greedily devour human prey—
whose teeth pierce like spears and arrows,
and whose tongues cut like swords.

5 Be exalted, O God, above the highest heavens!
May your glory shine over all the earth.

6 My enemies have set a trap for me.
I am weary from distress.
They have dug a deep pit in my path,
but they themselves have fallen into it. *Interlude*

7 My heart is confident in you, O God;
my heart is confident.
No wonder I can sing your praises!
8 Wake up, my heart!
Wake up, O lyre and harp!
I will wake the dawn with my song.
9 I will thank you, Lord, among all the people.
I will sing your praises among the nations.

10 **For your unfailing love is as high as the heavens.**
Your faithfulness reaches to the clouds.

11 **Be exalted, O God, above the highest heavens.**
May your glory shine over all the earth.

My enemies have set a trap for me. I am weary from distress. They have dug a deep pit in my path, but they themselves have fallen into it. (6)

*H*ow can I say this delicately? Euphemisms abound. Suffice it to say, a man relieving himself is in a very vulnerable posture, especially if what he is doing takes long enough for an enemy to sneak up and cut off a piece of his robe. That is exactly what happens to King Saul in the cave in the wilderness of En-gedi. As he squats to do what all men, high and low, rich and poor, must do, David crawls up behind him in the darkness and slices off a piece of his robe.

This is no practical joke, for Saul has come after him with murderous intent and three thousand special troops. David could easily harm Saul but doesn't, choosing rather to honor God and Saul by not taking matters into his own hands. After Saul leaves the cave, David waves the piece of his garment at him from across the way and shouts his loyalty to the king (1 Samuel 24).

Ironies abound too. Completely outmanned, David and his men had hidden in the back of a cave. They could hear the sounds of the enemy army outside the cave, and they trembled at the thought of being discovered there, backed up against the wall, fodder for slaughter. Their hiding place had become a cage. Then into the cave walks the leader of the enemy. They crouch in the shadows, their hands gripping their weapons, ready for the worst. Then they watch in astonished amusement as the predator becomes the prey and falls into the trap he set for David. Miraculously, the cage has become a snare. David remembers that moment in his prayer:

+++

My heart is confident in you, O God; my heart is confident. No wonder I can sing your praises! (7)
The memory of that marvelous reversal teaches David a lot about God and helps him to pray with confidence in the current crisis.

David's experience has also deepened his theological vocabulary, which in turn strengthens his courage to pray. Pray to David's God. Name this God as your confidence in prayer—for everything depends on the character of the God you speak to when you pray.

- Say, "I believe in . . . 'God Most High'" (verse 2).

  There is no one above him, absolutely no one! This is the title used for God in Genesis 14:18-22, when he comes to the side of Abraham, another homeless man. How like the Most High to look upon the lowly (see also Psalm 113:5-6; 138:6)!

- Say, "I believe in . . . 'God who will fulfill his purpose for me'" (verse 2).

  God has a purpose for you, and as someone has said, you are immortal until it is fulfilled. You need not fear premature death, for there can be no premature death with this God.

- Say, "I believe . . . 'he will send help from heaven to rescue me'" (verse 3).

  God's height is not the height of distance but of mastery. He is above all and unencumbered by the things that hinder humans. Because God is in heaven, he can do anything he pleases on earth (Psalm 115:3). Help from on high is better than any help from below.

Be exalted, O God, above the highest heavens. May your glory shine over all the earth. (5, 11)
This God being who he is, David knows he is all-important. So he prays the first thing Jesus said we should pray—that God's name be hallowed. In fact, he prays it twice.

To pray this way is a victory in itself. Fear and anxiety can shrink and crush your soul; wonderfully, the prayer that God's glory be over all the earth raises you with it. You become what you worship.[142] (see 2 Corinthians 3:18 and 1 John 3:2). Pray this prayer over and over again. Sing it.

I will thank you, Lord, among all the people. I will sing your praises among the nations. (9)
Because David's prayer goes so very high, it also spreads very wide. As he thinks of the grandeur of God, he vows to do his part in telling the world how great God is. It is the kind of prayer Jesus said should be the second thing we ask for: Your Kingdom come.

Pray this way with David.

PSALM 63

A psalm of David, regarding a time when David was in the wilderness of Judah.

1 O God, you are my God;
    I earnestly search for you.
My soul thirsts for you;
    my whole body longs for you
in this parched and weary land
    where there is no water.
2 I have seen you in your sanctuary
    and gazed upon your power and glory.
3 Your unfailing love is better than life itself;
    how I praise you!
4 I will praise you as long as I live,
    lifting up my hands to you in prayer.
5 You satisfy me more than the richest feast.
    I will praise you with songs of joy.

6 I lie awake thinking of you,
    meditating on you through the night.
7 Because you are my helper,
    I sing for joy in the shadow of your wings.
8 I cling to you;
    your strong right hand holds me securely.

9 But those plotting to destroy me will come to ruin.
    They will go down into the depths of the earth.
10 They will die by the sword
    and become the food of jackals.
11 But the king will rejoice in God.
    All who trust in him will praise him,
    while liars will be silenced.

O God, you are my God; I earnestly search for you. My soul thirsts for you; my whole body longs for you in this parched and weary land where there is no water. (1)

Read the superscription: "A psalm of David, regarding a time when David was in the wilderness of Judah." David must have been literally hungry and thirsty when he wrote this psalm in the desolate wilderness of Judea. But he saw in his body's longings a deeper meaning—his hunger and thirst were signposts to his need for God. That brought a dignity to his cravings—he was more than his belly; he was made for God. Hungry and thirsty in the same wilderness, Jesus did the same thing with his bodily yearnings when he rebuked Satan: "It is written, 'Man does not live on bread alone, but on every word that comes from the mouth of God'" (Matthew 4:4; Deuteronomy 8:3, NIV).

Here is a great way to pray: Turn your longings and hungers toward God. You may pray that they be removed. But pray also that they become reminders and parables of your need for God. Pain and suffering, frustration and anxiety can become sacramental experiences if you let them lead you to their deeper meaning in God.

That's what the great twentieth-century British preacher W. E. Sangster did when he learned that he had an incurable disease that would lead to progressive, radical muscular atrophy. It started with an uneasiness in his throat and a dragging in his leg but would eventually take away his voice, his ability to swallow, and finally his breath.

Sangster took his disease as a summons to go deeper spiritually, his radical loss a reminder of his more profound need for God. He begged God, "Let me stay in the struggle, Lord. I don't mind if I can no longer be a general, but give me a regiment to lead." He now had more time for prayer, so he prayed and organized prayer cells all over England. He wrote articles and books. To those who pitied him, he said, "I'm only in the kindergarten of suffering." *Kindergarten*: the great loss was a time to learn of greater needs.

On Easter morning, just a few weeks before he died, Sangster wrote his daughter: "It is terrible to wake up on Easter morning and have no voice to shout, 'He is risen!'—but it would be still more terrible to have a voice and not want to shout."[143]

Worse things can happen to you than great hunger and thirst or the loss of speech. The worst is to have no hunger or thirst and no sense of your need for God, to be able to speak but have no desire to praise him.

+++

Your unfailing love is better than life itself. (3)
Think of your hungers and longings. Name each of them and, as you do, say, "I have seen you in your sanctuary and gazed upon your power and glory. Your unfailing love is better than life itself; how I praise you!" (verses 2-3).

Confess the things you have feasted on that don't—and can't—satisfy your soul. Read Jeremiah 2:13 as a companion to this psalm:

> My people have done two evil things: They have abandoned me—the fountain of living water. And they have dug for themselves cracked cisterns that can hold no water at all!

All who trust in him will praise him, while liars will be silenced. (11)
Pray that God would indeed silence liars—all those voices in our culture that denigrate the "fountain of living water" and peddle pathetic little cracked cisterns.

Ask God to deepen and focus your hungers and longings on him as your true food and water. Pray to be like Jesus, who said, "My nourishment comes from doing the will of God, who sent me, and from finishing his work" (John 4:34).

PSALM 67

For the choir director: A song. A psalm, to be accompanied by stringed instruments.

1 May God be merciful and bless us.
May his face smile with favor on us. *Interlude*

2 May your ways be known throughout the earth,
your saving power among people everywhere.
3 May the nations praise you, O God.
Yes, may all the nations praise you.
4 Let the whole world sing for joy,
because you govern the nations with justice
and guide the people of the whole world. *Interlude*

5 May the nations praise you, O God.
Yes, may all the nations praise you.
6 Then the earth will yield its harvests,
and God, our God, will richly bless us.
7 Yes, God will bless us,
and people all over the world will fear him.

May your ways be known throughout the earth,
your saving power among people everywhere. (2)

I remember well the first sunrise I ever saw—I was seven or eight years old when it happened. My dad was a bus driver for the Los Angeles Rapid Transit District, which meant he often got up very early. One evening he asked me if I'd like to get up the next morning and go to work with him. His route that day was going to take him all over Los Angeles County; I'd see a lot, he said, and he would buy me a chili burger at Tommy's—an LA landmark. I was delighted.

But when he gently shook me awake at 5:30 a.m. the next day, I couldn't remember why I'd agreed to ride with him the night before. It was dark and cold, and my mind was mush. I dressed silently, ate a bowl of cereal, and got in the car with my dad. As we pulled out of our driveway I saw that first pristine glow on the horizon that has thrilled me so many times since. I was dazzled to see the light grow and move across the landscape with warmth and clarity. I've loved the early morning hours ever since (and Tommy's chili burgers).

For centuries the church has prayed this psalm each morning at the break of day. Benedict of Nursia prescribed it for his monks in the sixth century. Its vision of the glory and blessing of God moving across the darkness of the world to warm and embrace and give light to the nations was thought to be perfectly imaged in the rising of the sun—a grand earthly picture of something grander spiritually. I can't argue with that.

+++

May God be merciful and bless us. May his face smile with favor on us. . . . May the nations praise you, O God. Yes, may all the nations praise you. (1, 3)
Great praying and great theology go together. The prayers of the masters are saturated in Scripture. To read the prayers of David and Paul, Thomas à Kempis and John Calvin, John Bunyan and Martin Luther is to encounter hearts that have long soaked in the Word of God. To borrow a phrase of Spurgeon's, you may prick them anywhere and their blood will be "bibline."

Rooted in two magisterial passages—authoritative texts that inform many other texts with meaning—this psalm is a beautiful example of that very thing. The Aaronic blessing (Numbers 6:24-26), a plea for God to bless and make his face shine on his people, echoes in the words of verse 1, and throughout. In the same way, the call of Abraham (Genesis 12:1-2), with God's promise to bless all the nations of all the earth through his people, Israel, can be heard in the prayer of verse 3, and throughout.

Pray for God's people and for the world as this psalm prays for both; for the two are inextricably bound up with each other in Scripture. It's a splendid thing to lift your voice to God and join in with voices of the ages. Make this psalm, so rooted and saturated in Scripture, a model for the way you pray. To ask for the blessings God wants to give is to become a little more like the God you pray to!

Let the whole world sing for joy, because you govern the nations with justice and guide the people of the whole world. (4)
Pray for the Kingdom of God to break through every barrier and language and culture so that God's justice will indeed govern and guide all the people of all the world. Stand before a world map as you pray this prayer. Name names, substituting "the whole world" with countries like Rwanda, Belize, Indonesia, Venezuela, Japan, Tajikistan, and Saudi Arabia.

Yes, God will bless us, and people all over the world will fear him. (7)
Don't forget to ask God to bless his church everywhere—to the end that he might bless all people everywhere. A revived church is a missionary church, a city set on a hill, a lamp on a lamp stand.

PSALM 69

For the choir director: A psalm of David, to be sung to the tune "Lilies."

1 Save me, O God,
for the floodwaters are up to my neck.
2 Deeper and deeper I sink into the mire;
I can't find a foothold.
I am in deep water,
and the floods overwhelm me.
3 I am exhausted from crying for help;
my throat is parched.
My eyes are swollen with weeping,
waiting for my God to help me.
4 Those who hate me without cause
outnumber the hairs on my head.
Many enemies try to destroy me with lies,
demanding that I give back what I didn't steal.

5 O God, you know how foolish I am;
my sins cannot be hidden from you.
6 Don't let those who trust in you be ashamed because of me,
O Sovereign LORD of Heaven's Armies.
Don't let me cause them to be humiliated,
O God of Israel.
7 For I endure insults for your sake;
humiliation is written all over my face.
8 Even my own brothers pretend they don't know me;
they treat me like a stranger.

9 Passion for your house has consumed me,
and the insults of those who insult you have
fallen on me.
10 When I weep and fast,
they scoff at me.
11 When I dress in burlap to show sorrow,
they make fun of me.

12 I am the favorite topic of town gossip,
and all the drunks sing about me.

13 But I keep praying to you, LORD,
hoping this time you will show me favor.
In your unfailing love, O God,
answer my prayer with your sure salvation.
14 Rescue me from the mud;
don't let me sink any deeper!
Save me from those who hate me,
and pull me from these deep waters.
15 Don't let the floods overwhelm me,
or the deep waters swallow me,
or the pit of death devour me.

16 Answer my prayers, O LORD,
for your unfailing love is wonderful.
Take care of me,
for your mercy is so plentiful.
17 Don't hide from your servant;
answer me quickly, for I am in deep trouble!
18 Come and redeem me;
free me from my enemies.

19 You know of my shame, scorn, and disgrace.
You see all that my enemies are doing.
20 Their insults have broken my heart,
and I am in despair.
If only one person would show some pity;
if only one would turn and comfort me.
21 But instead, they give me poison for food;
they offer me sour wine for my thirst.

22 Let the bountiful table set before them become
a snare
and their prosperity become a trap.
23 Let their eyes go blind so they cannot see,
and make their bodies shake continually.

24 Pour out your fury on them;
consume them with your burning anger.
25 Let their homes become desolate
and their tents be deserted.
26 To the one you have punished, they add insult to injury;
they add to the pain of those you have hurt.
27 Pile their sins up high,
and don't let them go free.
28 Erase their names from the Book of Life;
don't let them be counted among the righteous.

29 I am suffering and in pain.
Rescue me, O God, by your saving power.

30 Then I will praise God's name with singing,
and I will honor him with thanksgiving.
31 For this will please the LORD more than sacrificing cattle,
more than presenting a bull with its horns and hooves.
32 The humble will see their God at work and be glad.
Let all who seek God's help be encouraged.
33 For the LORD hears the cries of the needy;
he does not despise his imprisoned people.

34 Praise him, O heaven and earth,
the seas and all that move in them.
35 For God will save Jerusalem
and rebuild the towns of Judah.
His people will live there
and settle in their own land.
36 The descendants of those who obey him will inherit the land,
and those who love him will live there in safety.

Come and redeem me; free me from my enemies. You know of my shame, scorn, and disgrace. You see all that my enemies are doing. (18-19)

When young Helen Roseveare went as a medical missionary to what was the Belgian Congo in the 1950s and 1960s, she had no idea of what she was getting into. Fresh out of medical school, she had skipped the final steps in her medical training, which were internships and a residency, because as she explained it, she couldn't stand the sight of blood. She had taken classes but hadn't actually practiced what she had learned in the classes. She naively thought her work as a missionary doctor would mainly involve dispensing pills and applying bandages. Her first patient was a woman in labor who required a C-section delivery—definitely not something she had planned on! But Helen got out her medical books, read the directions, and performed a successful C-section. She was beginning to get an idea of what she had gotten into.

Yet she had no inkling of what was to come in the years that followed. During the wars for independence that took place in Africa in the 1960s, she was held captive by the Simba rebels and repeatedly beaten and raped. On one occasion, when she was sure she would be executed, she feared God had abandoned her.

She cried out to God, and in that moment heard the Holy Spirit say to her, "Twenty years ago you asked me for the privilege of being identified with me. This is it. Don't you want it? This is what it means. These are not your sufferings; they are my sufferings. All I ask of you is the loan of your body."

Roseveare was overwhelmed with wonder at this privilege. She wrote about it later:

> He didn't stop the sufferings. He didn't stop the wickedness, the cruelties, the humiliation or anything. It was all there. The pain was just as bad. The fear was just as bad. But it was altogether different. It was in Jesus, for him, with him.[144]

It was exactly as the psalm says: "Passion for your house has consumed me, and the insults of those who insult you have fallen on me" (verse 9). There is no greater privilege than to be so identified with Jesus that you feel what he feels and people react to you as they did to him.

"All I ask of you is the loan of your body." That's all God asks of any of us. It's that simple, and that huge. We cannot know where that request will take us. All we can be sure of is who will go with us on the journey. It will be with Jesus. And those who, like Helen, have traveled with him into impossibly dark and difficult places always say the same thing: Jesus is worth it all.

Roseveare was asked years later if what she had accomplished in Africa as a missionary had made all her sufferings worth it. Did the success of her work offset the pain? Her answer was no, it did not; the pain was too great. But she added that the Lord had told her that was the wrong question. He said, "The question is not, was *it* worth it, but am *I* worthy?" Her answer was, "Of course you are, Lord."

A great way to pray this psalm is to pray it as much of the church has for centuries: as a meditation on the sufferings of Christ. Indeed, this psalm is one of only a handful, along with Psalm 22, that can give us insight into the prayer life of Jesus spoken of by the writer of the book of Hebrews:

> While Jesus was here on earth, he offered prayers and pleadings, with a loud cry and tears, to the one who could rescue him from death. And God heard his prayers because of his deep reverence for God.[145]

Ponder some of the psalm's lines in the light of what the New Testament tells us about Christ's passion, and give thanks to Jesus—who though he had no sin, was made "to be the offering for our sin, so that we could be made right with God through Christ."[146]

+++

Passion for your house has consumed me. (9)
After Jesus had violently purged the Temple, the disciples remembered this line as a prophecy of that act. Jesus further explained that his very body was the greater Temple that would be consumed for the sake of that passion—even more violently.[147]

Thanks be to you, Lord Jesus, Lamb of God.

The insults of those who insult you have fallen on me. (9)
In his letter to the Romans, Paul thought of this line as a description of the servant Jesus' determination to live, not to please himself, but to please his Father.[148] This is reflected in the way Jesus prayed in Gethsemane:

> He went on a little farther and bowed with his face to the ground, praying, "My Father! If it is possible, let this cup of suffering be taken away from me. Yet I want your will to be done, not mine."[149]

The fact that Paul simply makes the reference, with no attempt to develop it, shows this was already the common understanding in the early church.

Amazing love! Who can fathom the attitude that says to God, "It is my pleasure not to please myself but to please you, Father. Let their hatred of you fall on me."

Thanks be to you Lord Jesus, Lamb of God.

Save me, O God, for the floodwaters are up to my neck. Deeper and deeper I sink into the mire; I can't find a foothold. I am in deep water, and the floods overwhelm me. (1-2)
Jesus spoke of his coming suffering and death as a kind of baptism—a drenching in death, a wrenching, gasping drowning in the sin of the world.[150] Again, can anybody take this in? Amazing love!

Thanks be to you, Lord Jesus, Lamb of God.

Their insults have broken my heart, and I am in despair. If only one person would show some pity; if only one would turn and comfort me. But instead, they give me poison for food; they offer me sour wine for my thirst. (20-21)

These lines point to the bitter loneliness Jesus would know in the garden as his friends (!) slept, oblivious to his sorrow. Wouldn't anyone show some pity and give him some comfort? Must he be abandoned by the very men closest to him? "Couldn't you watch with me even one hour?"[151]

Then, on the cross, his misery would be compounded when he was offered sour wine to drink—a fact mentioned in all four of the Gospels.

Let their homes become desolate and their tents be deserted. (25)
Soon after Christ's resurrection and ascension, Peter and the early church saw in this line a direct reference to the dark and appalling figure of Judas—and moved to replace his empty position in the apostolic band.[152]

There is, however, another way to pray this psalm: as Helen Roseveare experienced the sufferings of Christ. If you have time, or perhaps on another day, pray through each line mentioned above, remembering what Jesus said to his disciples:

> If the world hates you, remember that it hated me first. The world would love you as one of its own if you belonged to it, but you are no longer part of the world. I chose you to come out of the world, so it hates you. Do you remember what I told you? "A slave is not greater than the master." Since they persecuted me, naturally they will persecute you.[153]

Passion for your house has consumed me, and the insults of those who insult you have fallen on me. (9)
May this be said of you, too?

PSALM 70

For the choir director: A psalm of David, asking God to remember him.

1 Please, God, rescue me!
Come quickly, LORD, and help me.
2 May those who try to kill me
be humiliated and put to shame.
May those who take delight in my trouble
be turned back in disgrace.
3 Let them be horrified by their shame,
for they said, "Aha! We've got him now!"
4 But may all who search for you
be filled with joy and gladness in you.
May those who love your salvation
repeatedly shout, "God is great!"
5 But as for me, I am poor and needy;
please hurry to my aid, O God.
You are my helper and my savior;
O LORD, do not delay.

Please, God, rescue me! Come quickly, LORD, and help me. (1)

*T*he two best prayers writer Anne Lamott claims she knows are: "Help me, help me, help me" and "Thank you, thank you, thank you." In sharp contrast are the words her friend prays each morning, "Whatever," and each evening, "Oh, well."[154] As grand simplifications go, Lamott's prayers are two of the best. Much of the Psalter can be divided into "Help me" prayers and "Thank you" prayers. Her friend's prayer of resignation is completely absent from the Bible. If the prayers of the Psalms are nothing else, they are urgent and passionate. How could they be anything less? Our need is great; the God we pray to, our only hope, is responsive; and his promises are extravagant.

From the earliest days of the church, the first verse of this psalm has been regarded as one of the best and most succinct of the "Help me" prayers. It's one of those "one size fits all" psalms I mentioned on page 3—a prayer that fits like my baseball cap that can be adjusted to fit all head sizes. No matter what situation you're in, it's always appropriate to pray, "Please, God, rescue me! Come quickly, LORD, and help me." If you're afraid, you know you need this prayer. If you're at peace, you may forget you need it, but you still do. It will keep you humble and alert. Happy or sad, in danger or secure, we always need God's help. One prayer fits all. Say it when you get up in the morning and when you go to bed at night. The Benedictine monks have made it the first prayer they pray at each one of the seven daily "hours" of prayer. It can be a great way to pray constantly—something to repeat throughout the day, a variation of the famous "Jesus Prayer" ("Lord Jesus Christ, Son of the living God, have mercy on me, a sinner").

Try praying this prayer constantly for a week, in every situation:

> Please, God, rescue me! Come quickly, LORD, and help me.

+++

May those who love your salvation repeatedly shout, "God is great!" (4)
Don't forget to add the other half of the prayer: "Thank you, thank you, thank you." Seize every opportunity, expecting there will be many occasions to say these words from your heart.

But as for me, I am poor and needy; please hurry to my aid, O God. You are my helper and my savior; O LORD, do not delay. (5)
This verse is a good prayer for the weary and discouraged. On the one hand there are the enemies who never relent (verse 2). They wear you down. On the other hand there are those who seem so diligent in their search for God (verse 4). They wear you down too, for they seem only to remind you of how weak you are. You pray them good success, but by comparison you are a spiritual slacker. The opening phrase of verse 5—"But as for me"—is a comfort and an invitation to pray with King David.

Help me! Thank you! Again, one size fits all.

PSALM 71

1 O LORD, I have come to you for protection;
don't let me be disgraced.
2 Save me and rescue me,
for you do what is right.
Turn your ear to listen to me,
and set me free.
3 Be my rock of safety
where I can always hide.
Give the order to save me,
for you are my rock and my fortress.
4 My God, rescue me from the power of the wicked,
from the clutches of cruel oppressors.
5 O Lord, you alone are my hope.
I've trusted you, O LORD, from childhood.
6 Yes, you have been with me from birth;
from my mother's womb you have cared for me.
No wonder I am always praising you!

7 My life is an example to many,
because you have been my strength and protection.
8 That is why I can never stop praising you;
I declare your glory all day long.
9 And now, in my old age, don't set me aside.
Don't abandon me when my strength is failing.
10 For my enemies are whispering against me.
They are plotting together to kill me.
11 They say, "God has abandoned him.
Let's go and get him,
for no one will help him now."

12 O God, don't stay away.
My God, please hurry to help me.
13 Bring disgrace and destruction on my accusers.
Humiliate and shame those who want to harm me.

14 But I will keep on hoping for your help;
I will praise you more and more.
15 I will tell everyone about your righteousness.
All day long I will proclaim your saving power,
though I am not skilled with words.
16 I will praise your mighty deeds, O Sovereign LORD.
I will tell everyone that you alone are just.

17 O God, you have taught me from my earliest childhood,
and I constantly tell others about the wonderful things
you do.
18 Now that I am old and gray,
do not abandon me, O God.
Let me proclaim your power to this new generation,
your mighty miracles to all who come after me.

19 Your righteousness, O God, reaches to the highest heavens.
You have done such wonderful things.
Who can compare with you, O God?
20 You have allowed me to suffer much hardship,
but you will restore me to life again
and lift me up from the depths of the earth.
21 You will restore me to even greater honor
and comfort me once again.

22 Then I will praise you with music on the harp,
because you are faithful to your promises, O my God.
I will sing praises to you with a lyre,
O Holy One of Israel.
23 I will shout for joy and sing your praises,
for you have ransomed me.
24 I will tell about your righteous deeds
all day long,
for everyone who tried to hurt me
has been shamed and humiliated.

Now that I am old and gray, do not abandon me, O God. Let me proclaim your power to this new generation, your mighty miracles to all who come after me. (18)

I have a friend who has covered the walls in his office with pictures of those who, as he puts it, "have finished strong." Included are the likes of Mother Teresa, C. S. Lewis, Dietrich Bonhoeffer, and Francis Schaeffer—an impressive gallery of people I'd like to join at the end of my life. I'd like to finish strong.

But it's not easy. Billy Graham, speaking to his daughter Anne Graham Lotz, admitted how challenging aging can be: "All my life, I've been taught how to die, but no one ever taught me how to grow old." The psalmist's prayer is a primer on the subject and a model of what to say to God about aging.

+++

Lord, you alone are my hope. I've trusted you, O LORD, from childhood. Yes, you have been with me from birth; from my mother's womb you have cared for me. No wonder I am always praising you! (5-6)

Grow old gratefully. The standard complaint about getting old is that the memory is the first to go. Don't wait until you're old to remember God's faithfulness through the seasons of your life. A well-cultivated memory can be like a well-nurtured tree—it will bear fruit in the late summer. Pray your gratitude frequently.

And now, in my old age, don't set me aside. Don't abandon me when my strength is failing. For my enemies are whispering against me. They are plotting together to kill me. They say, "God has abandoned him. Let's go and get him, for no one will help him now." (9-11)
There have long been enemies of the aged. Though we're not sure who wrote this psalm, it may have been a king who knew there was always someone wanting to usurp his throne. All of us are tempted to despair and grow bitter because of our fear of dying or because of our culture's foolish obsession with prolonging youth, a $56-billion industry in 2006. Pray for deliverance from these enemies of the soul.

Now that I am old and gray, do not abandon me, O God. Let me proclaim your power to this new generation, your mighty miracles to all who come after me. (18)
Embrace more fully and with greater abandon the special vocation of the aged: to pass on the faith to the next generation. Karl Barth shuddered at the thought of the elderly freezing in their sense of calling and living out their days in comfort and safety "as if it were permissible to freeze or solidify at the point where the river of responsibility should flow more torrentially than ever in view of the approaching falls, of the proximity of the coming Judge!"[155] Pray for God to give you the strength to do good work like this until the end of your days.

If you're not yet elderly, you will be one day—or else dead! Pray for a good death and a good dying.

You will restore me to even greater honor and comfort me once again. (21)
Pray for the grace to finish well and with honor. Pray the kind of prayer Robertson McQuilkin prayed for himself:

> It's sundown, Lord. The shadows of my life stretch back into the dimness of the years long spent. I fear not death, for that grim foe betrays himself at last, thrusting me forever into life: life with you, unsoiled and free. But I do fear. I fear the dark specter may come too soon—or do I mean too late? That I should end before I finish or finish, but not well. That I should stain your honor, shame your name, grieve your loving heart. Few, they tell me, finish well. . . . Lord, let me get home before dark.[156]

PSALM 73

A psalm of Asaph.

1 Truly God is good to Israel,
to those whose hearts are pure.
2 But as for me, I almost lost my footing.
My feet were slipping, and I was almost gone.
3 For I envied the proud
when I saw them prosper despite their wickedness.
4 They seem to live such painless lives;
their bodies are so healthy and strong.
5 They don't have troubles like other people;
they're not plagued with problems like everyone else.
6 They wear pride like a jeweled necklace
and clothe themselves with cruelty.
7 These fat cats have everything
their hearts could ever wish for!
8 They scoff and speak only evil;
in their pride they seek to crush others.
9 They boast against the very heavens,
and their words strut throughout the earth.
10 And so the people are dismayed and confused,
drinking in all their words.
11 "What does God know?" they ask.
"Does the Most High even know what's
happening?"
12 Look at these wicked people—
enjoying a life of ease while their riches multiply.

13 Did I keep my heart pure for nothing?
Did I keep myself innocent for no reason?
14 I get nothing but trouble all day long;
every morning brings me pain.

15 If I had really spoken this way to others,
I would have been a traitor to your people.

16 So I tried to understand why the wicked prosper.
But what a difficult task it is!
17 Then I went into your sanctuary, O God,
and I finally understood the destiny of the wicked.
18 Truly, you put them on a slippery path
and send them sliding over the cliff to destruction.
19 In an instant they are destroyed,
completely swept away by terrors.
20 When you arise, O Lord,
you will laugh at their silly ideas
as a person laughs at dreams in the morning.

21 Then I realized that my heart was bitter,
and I was all torn up inside.
22 I was so foolish and ignorant—
I must have seemed like a senseless animal to you.
23 Yet I still belong to you;
you hold my right hand.
24 You guide me with your counsel,
leading me to a glorious destiny.
25 Whom have I in heaven but you?
I desire you more than anything on earth.
26 My health may fail, and my spirit may grow weak,
but God remains the strength of my heart;
he is mine forever.

27 Those who desert him will perish,
for you destroy those who abandon you.
28 But as for me, how good it is to be near God!
I have made the Sovereign LORD my shelter,
and I will tell everyone about the wonderful things
you do.

Whom have I in heaven but you? I desire you more than anything on earth. (25)

*O*f the seven deadly sins, anger is possibly the most fun," writes Frederick Buechner. "To lick your wounds, to smack your lips over grievances long past, to roll over your tongue the prospect of bitter confrontations still to come, to savor to the last toothsome morsel both the pain you are given and the pain you are giving back—in many ways it is a feast fit for a king. The chief drawback is that what you are wolfing down is yourself. The skeleton at the feast is you."[157]

Asaph, the writer of this psalm, looks back on how things were for him at one time and admits that he was being consumed by bitterness and anger. He was full of envy for what seemed to be the unchecked arrogance and rapaciousness of the wicked. "These fat cats have everything their hearts could ever wish for!" (verse 7). Not only were they getting away with murder and theft, they were prospering. God seemed worse than an absentee landlord; he appeared unfazed and uninterested. The psalmist almost shot his mouth off about God and the uselessness of living a good life. He's glad he didn't (verse 15). In retrospect, he says to God, "I realized that my heart was bitter, and I was all torn up inside. I was so foolish and ignorant—I must have seemed like a senseless animal to you" (verses 21-22).

What changed things for him was entering the sanctuary one day and gaining a fresh vision of God's love and justice. In worship he remembered that a holy God will not let sin go unpunished (verses 16-20). Even better, in worship he remembered the sweetness of God's love. He prayed some of the sweetest words of friendship with God in all of Scripture:

> You hold my right hand. You guide me with your counsel, leading me to a glorious destiny. Whom have I in heaven but you? I desire you more than anything on earth. My health may fail, and my spirit may grow weak, but God remains the strength of my heart; he is mine forever. (verses 23-26)

Let the wicked enjoy their temporary successes! Asaph now knew that "the man that had everything minus God is a pauper; and the other who has God minus everything is 'rich to all the intents of bliss.'"[158] The cure for anger, envy, and bitterness is gratitude for the goodness of God's friendship.

How can you pray for this same renewal of faith?

+++

For I envied the proud when I saw them prosper despite their wickedness. . . . Did I keep my heart pure for nothing? Did I keep myself innocent for no reason? (3, 13)
Confess the things that come between you and God. Envy and hopelessness feed the beast of anger and kill gratitude. They are among the most corrosive of the attitudes that eat away at your pleasure in God.

If I had really spoken this way to others, I would have been a traitor to your people. (15)
Pray for a tender heart toward the people around you. It is significant that the first move Asaph makes away from his anger comes because of his love for those around him. He considers the disastrous effect on them if he were to indulge his crisis of faith with careless words. There is a direct connection between how we treat others and how we see the Lord.

Whom have I in heaven but you? I desire you more than anything on earth. My health may fail, and my spirit may grow weak, but God remains the strength of my heart; he is mine forever. (25-26)
Practice praying these words (verses 23-24 are full of hope too) in all circumstances, especially the very frustrating and sad. It is another

way of practicing what the apostle Paul commanded in 1 Thessalonians 5:16-18—"Always be joyful. Never stop praying. Be thankful in all circumstances, for this is God's will for you who belong to Christ Jesus." Say the psalmist's words whether or not you feel them—and until you do!

PSALM 75

For the choir director: A psalm of Asaph. A song to be sung to the tune "Do Not Destroy!"

1 We thank you, O God!
We give thanks because you are near.
People everywhere tell of your wonderful deeds.

2 God says, "At the time I have planned,
I will bring justice against the wicked.
3 When the earth quakes and its people live in turmoil,
I am the one who keeps its foundations firm.
Interlude

4 "I warned the proud, 'Stop your boasting!'
I told the wicked, 'Don't raise your fists!
5 Don't raise your fists in defiance at the heavens
or speak with such arrogance.'"
6 For no one on earth—from east or west,
or even from the wilderness—
should raise a defiant fist.
7 It is God alone who judges;
he decides who will rise and who will fall.
8 For the LORD holds a cup in his hand
that is full of foaming wine mixed with spices.
He pours out the wine in judgment,
and all the wicked must drink it,
draining it to the dregs.

9 But as for me, I will always proclaim what God has done;
I will sing praises to the God of Jacob.
10 For God says, "I will break the strength of the wicked,
but I will increase the power of the godly."

God says, "At the time I have planned, I will bring justice against the wicked." (2)

*M*any of the students in the makeshift little Ugandan Bible school lived with horrendous reminders of what they had endured during the murderous reign of Idi Amin. Some were missing an eye or an arm. Several had bulging red scars from what had been deep machete wounds. In the eyes of all was the shadow of the horror they had seen. But there was also the light of the hope of Christ. They were pastors studying to be better pastors in their village churches.

The professor was lecturing from Paul's first letter to the Thessalonians, in which the apostle is teaching about Christ's return, when he will come again to reign forever in glory, wiping away every tear and setting straight every injustice. A student's hand went up when he came to chapter 4, verse 16: "The Lord himself will come down from heaven with a commanding shout, with the voice of the archangel, and with the trumpet call of God."

"Yes?" said the professor. "What is your question?"

The man who had raised his hand hesitated for a moment and then asked softly, "What will the Lord shout?"

The professor didn't know what to say. Who would? Yet the accumulated suffering of the students in that classroom seemed to demand some kind of answer. What will the Lord say when he finally humbles all his enemies under his feet and puts death to death, when God is finally and forever utterly supreme over all things? What will the Lord shout when that happens?[159]

"I don't know," the professor admitted. Then he looked around the room, pausing to look at each student, and asked, "What do you think he will shout?"

A student's voice came from the back: "I think he will shout, 'Enough!'"

That's a good answer, and very much in the spirit of this psalm. God says, "At the time I have planned, I will bring justice against the wicked." Even in heaven, his answer to the cries of the martyred saints—"O Sovereign Lord, holy and true, how long before you judge the people who belong to this world and avenge our blood for what they have done to us?"—is very much the same. He tells them to wait patiently "until the full number of their brothers and sisters—their fellow servants of Jesus who were to be martyred—had joined them."[160] Justice will come when God's inexplicable wisdom and love have determined that there has been enough suffering for the sake of his name.

This psalm helps us pray into that great truth.

+++

We thank you, O God! . . . God says . . . But as for me . . . (1- 2, 9)
The structure of the psalm has three parts: the people praise God (verse 1), then God answers the people (verses 2-5), and finally the people respond to what God has said (verses 6-10).

Pray this way using the psalm as a guide. Declare your praise to God, then quote God to yourself, then respond to what he has said. This pattern can be repeated extemporaneously: You praise, you quote the Lord, then you respond to the Lord.

It is God alone who judges; he decides who will rise and who will fall. (7)
Even the wicked rulers of the world must move within the boundaries God sets. He keeps them all on a tight tether, so that even their rebellion must unwittingly serve his larger purposes. Praise God for this, as in Romans 8:28: "We know that God causes everything to work together for the good of those who love God and are called according to his purpose for them."

He pours out the wine in judgment, and all the wicked must drink it, draining it to the dregs. (8)

As the saying goes, the mill of God's judgment grinds slowly but exceedingly fine. The wicked will drink to the dregs God's judgment; it will be precise and complete. Thank God that, in what seems to us to be his delays, he is working his higher and more thorough wisdom.

But as for me, I will always proclaim what God has done; I will sing praises to the God of Jacob. (9)
"But as for me" is a great way to pray in the face of all that might seem to contradict your faith, especially when everyone around you is doubting God. It's akin to Joshua's "*As for me* and my family, we will serve the LORD" (Joshua 24:15, emphasis added). It is a declaration of courage and determination that is good for the soul.

PSALM 76

For the choir director: A psalm of Asaph. A song to be accompanied by stringed instruments.

1 God is honored in Judah;
his name is great in Israel.
2 Jerusalem is where he lives;
Mount Zion is his home.
3 There he has broken the fiery arrows of the enemy,
the shields and swords and weapons of war.
Interlude

4 You are glorious and more majestic
than the everlasting mountains.
5 Our boldest enemies have been plundered.
They lie before us in the sleep of death.
No warrior could lift a hand against us.
6 At the blast of your breath, O God of Jacob,
their horses and chariots lay still.

7 No wonder you are greatly feared!
Who can stand before you when your anger explodes?
8 From heaven you sentenced your enemies;
the earth trembled and stood silent before you.
9 You stand up to judge those who do evil, O God,
and to rescue the oppressed of the earth. *Interlude*

10 Human defiance only enhances your glory,
for you use it as a weapon.

11 Make vows to the LORD your God, and keep them.
Let everyone bring tribute to the Awesome One.
12 For he breaks the pride of princes,
and the kings of the earth fear him.

Jerusalem is where he lives; Mount Zion is his home. (2)

"How odd of God to choose the Jews."[161]

It's odd indeed, even preposterous, to claim that God's address is Jerusalem, that he keeps "his own suite of rooms in Zion."[162] But it is God's claim, not the Jews',[163] and though it seems odd by human standards, it is no more odd than his choosing you or me or any of us to be his people. Paul, who dubbed himself the quintessential Jew,[164] saw the same oddness of God at work in those he chose to be his church:

> Remember, dear brothers and sisters, that few of you were wise in the world's eyes or powerful or wealthy when God called you. Instead, God chose things the world considers foolish in order to shame those who think they are wise. And he chose things that are powerless to shame those who are powerful. God chose things despised by the world, things counted as nothing at all, and used them to bring to nothing what the world considers important. As a result, no one can ever boast in the presence of God. (1 Corinthians 1:26-29)

So there's a method in God's oddness. He chooses the weak and foolish to shame what the world in its pride deems strong and wise, and to underline in big, bold letters the most elemental fact of human existence: that "no one can ever boast in the presence of God."

From the new Jerusalem, the church, God means to break "the fiery arrows of the enemy, the shields and swords and weapons of war" and to break "the pride of princes" (verses 3, 12). God loves his church and delights in his people. Do you?

+++

God is honored in Judah; his name is great in Israel. (1)
Thank God for the church. It pleases him to be honored there. In fact, Christ's victory over sin and death was for that very purpose.

> God has put all things under the authority of Christ and has made him head over all things for the benefit of the church. And the church is his body; it is made full and complete by Christ, who fills all things everywhere with himself. (Ephesians 1:22-23)

From heaven you sentenced your enemies; the earth trembled and stood silent before you. You stand up to judge those who do evil, O God, and to rescue the oppressed of the earth. (8-9)
Roman Catholic liturgy has long included the reading of this psalm in connection with the earthquake that accompanied Christ's death on the cross and the opening of the graves of dead saints (Matthew 27:51-53). The earth shook because when Christ descended to the realm of the dead, he came not as a prisoner but as a conqueror, setting the prisoners free![165]

Thank God that even in death Jesus rules. Willingly or unwillingly, every knee must bow and every tongue confess that Jesus Christ is Lord.

Human defiance only enhances your glory, for you use it as a weapon. (10)
God is so great, his sovereign power so irresistible and comprehensive, that even raw human rebellion must finally serve his ultimate purposes. God made a hard-hearted Pharaoh's resistance serve his glory (Exodus 7:1-5; 9:16), and he "causes everything to work together for the good of those who love God and are called according to his purpose for them" (Romans 8:28). Praise God that the worst mere mortals can do is not only no match for his power but must ultimately show his glory.

Make vows to the LORD your God, and keep them. Let everyone bring tribute to the Awesome One. (11)
"Nothing ages faster than gratitude," says an old Russian proverb. Maybe that's why thankfulness was formalized in ancient Israel. Prayers

for deliverance were accompanied by vows to give public thanks, not as a kind of quid pro quo—"God, if you do this for me, then I'll do that for you"—but as a promise to do the right thing, to give credit where credit is due. Plus, to publicly give glory to God would bring the whole congregation into the blessing. And what better way to bless others than with your blessing.

When you ask God for something, include a promise to give some kind of public thanks when you receive his answer. Though God doesn't need you to do this, you and those who hear you do, and he most certainly deserves it!

PSALM 77

For Jeduthun, the choir director: A psalm of Asaph.

1 I cry out to God; yes, I shout.
Oh, that God would listen to me!
2 When I was in deep trouble,
I searched for the Lord.
All night long I prayed, with hands lifted toward heaven,
but my soul was not comforted.
3 I think of God, and I moan,
overwhelmed with longing for his help. *Interlude*

4 You don't let me sleep.
I am too distressed even to pray!
5 I think of the good old days,
long since ended,
6 when my nights were filled with joyful songs.
I search my soul and ponder the difference now.
7 Has the Lord rejected me forever?
Will he never again be kind to me?
8 Is his unfailing love gone forever?
Have his promises permanently failed?
9 Has God forgotten to be gracious?
Has he slammed the door on his compassion?
Interlude

10 And I said, "This is my fate;
the Most High has turned his hand against me."
11 But then I recall all you have done, O LORD;
I remember your wonderful deeds of long ago.
12 They are constantly in my thoughts.
I cannot stop thinking about your mighty works.

13 O God, your ways are holy.
Is there any god as mighty as you?
14 You are the God of great wonders!
You demonstrate your awesome power among the nations.

15 By your strong arm, you redeemed your people,
the descendants of Jacob and Joseph. *Interlude*

16 When the Red Sea saw you, O God,
its waters looked and trembled!
The sea quaked to its very depths.
17 The clouds poured down rain;
the thunder rumbled in the sky.
Your arrows of lightning flashed.
18 Your thunder roared from the whirlwind;
the lightning lit up the world!
The earth trembled and shook.
19 Your road led through the sea,
your pathway through the mighty waters—
a pathway no one knew was there!
20 You led your people along that road like a flock of sheep,
with Moses and Aaron as their shepherds.

And I said, "This is my fate; the Most High has turned his hand against me." But then I recall all you have done, O LORD; I remember your wonderful deeds of long ago. (10-11)

A most unusual Internet auction was held on eBay in September 2005. A fund-raiser for a nonprofit organization called the First Amendment Project, it offered to the highest bidder the opportunity to be written into a Stephen King novel—to be killed, actually. Billed as a gift for the "ultimate fan," the offer promised literary immortality for the highest bidder. After seventy-six bids were received, the winner paid $25,100 to see his name written into a Stephen King story.

Other authors offered their services too. John Grisham promised to write the highest bidder into one of his stories. That went for $12,100. Another bidder paid $6,350 to be mentioned in an "utterance" in Lemony Snicket's *Book the Thirteenth*.[166]

The idea piqued the interest of the 7-Eleven convenience store chain. In the fall of 2007, 7-Eleven conducted a nationwide contest in which the winner would be written into a *Simpsons* episode. What fun: Buy junk food at junk food central, enter the contest, and you might be written into a story alongside Homer Simpson, the ultimate junk food connoisseur.

The appeal of being written into a story bigger and better than the one we are living runs deep in our souls, especially if our personal stories are becoming increasingly tragic, like Asaph's in this psalm. His life seems doomed to end hopelessly and bitterly: "This my fate; the Most High has turned his hand against me." God is his opponent, and there's absolutely nothing he can do about it. Who could? He's in a fight he can't possibly win. There's no exit; it's fate.

But wait: Asaph remembers that his personal story is part of a Great Story that is bigger and better than his subjective experience can see. "But then I recall all you have done, O Lord; I remember your wonderful deeds of long ago" (verse 11). With just one word—*remember*—he moves from fate to hope. He remembers the Great Story that gathers up and redeems and protects his little story. He is relieved and comforted to remember that the big story is not about him and his struggles but about God and his faithfulness. And as he recounts the Great Story—how God has repeatedly saved his people throughout history—he can relax and be filled with the joy of knowing that God has written his little story into that big story.

Remember: Jesus assured us that the same God who created the heavens and the earth, who liberated the slaves in Egypt, doesn't miss it when a sparrow falls or a hair falls from your head (Matthew 10:29-31). Remember the price Christ paid to include you in his Great Story:

> You know that God paid a ransom to save you from the empty [fated!] life you inherited from your ancestors. And the ransom he paid was not mere gold or silver. It was the precious blood of Christ, the sinless, spotless Lamb of God. (1 Peter 1:18-19)

+++

I cry out to God; yes, I shout. **(1)**

Have you ever shouted to God? The psalms are filled with that kind of expression: shouts and cries and sobs and loud remonstrances. You don't have to do these things to show God that you mean what you say, but it may be helpful for *you* to let your emotions and words match up. As with any relationship, human or divine, feelings really matter, and letting your feelings out with volume can deepen your sense of God's presence. "The earnest prayer of a righteous person has great power and produces wonderful results" (James 5:16). "Let us knock loudly at the door of grace," wrote J. C. Ryle. "Let us settle it in our minds that cold prayers are a sacrifice without fire."[167]

You don't let me sleep. I am too distressed even to pray! (4)
Make good use of your insomnia. Pray when you can't sleep. I have a friend who kept asking God to help him wake up earlier so he could pray more. Part of his problem in getting up early was that he was so sleepy from waking up in the middle of the night. Then it occurred to him that maybe God's answer to his prayer for more time to pray was to wake him up. The last I heard, he was quite content with his nighttime prayer sessions.

Has the Lord rejected me forever? Will he never again be kind to me? (7)
That's how it can feel sometimes—that God has permanently turned his back on you. I call it myopia of the moment, the false conclusion that the way it is now is the way it always will be. It's not only illogical to think that way, it's flat-out wrong, because it's inconsistent with the character of God.

But go ahead and pray your bad conclusions. Tell God how things appear to you. He already knows how you feel, but if you tell him, your fear can create a bond between you, emotionally.

You led your people along that road like a flock of sheep, with Moses and Aaron as their shepherds. (20)
Remember your leaders with thanksgiving. Pray for them earnestly. God used his appointed leaders Moses and Aaron to lead Israel and to show them his faithfulness. These men were signs of his love, and so are the leaders God has given you and your church. Follow the command of Hebrews 13:17:

> Obey your spiritual leaders, and do what they say. Their work is to watch over your souls, and they are accountable to God. Give them reason to do this with joy and not with sorrow. That would certainly not be for your benefit.

PSALM 78

A psalm of Asaph.

1 O my people, listen to my instructions.
Open your ears to what I am saying,
2 for I will speak to you in a parable.
I will teach you hidden lessons from our past—
3 stories we have heard and known,
stories our ancestors handed down to us.
4 We will not hide these truths from our children;
we will tell the next generation
about the glorious deeds of the LORD,
about his power and his mighty wonders.
5 For he issued his laws to Jacob;
he gave his instructions to Israel.
He commanded our ancestors
to teach them to their children,
6 so the next generation might know them—
even the children not yet born—
and they in turn will teach their own children.
7 So each generation should set its hope anew on God,
not forgetting his glorious miracles
and obeying his commands.
8 Then they will not be like their ancestors—
stubborn, rebellious, and unfaithful,
refusing to give their hearts to God.

9 The warriors of Ephraim, though armed with bows,
turned their backs and fled on the day of battle.
10 They did not keep God's covenant
and refused to live by his instructions.
11 They forgot what he had done—
the great wonders he had shown them,
12 the miracles he did for their ancestors
on the plain of Zoan in the land of Egypt.

13 For he divided the sea and led them through,
making the water stand up like walls!
14 In the daytime he led them by a cloud,
and all night by a pillar of fire.
15 He split open the rocks in the wilderness
to give them water, as from a gushing spring.
16 He made streams pour from the rock,
making the waters flow down like a river!

17 Yet they kept on sinning against him,
rebelling against the Most High in the desert.
18 They stubbornly tested God in their hearts,
demanding the foods they craved.
19 They even spoke against God himself, saying,
"God can't give us food in the wilderness.
20 Yes, he can strike a rock so water gushes out,
but he can't give his people bread and meat."
21 When the LORD heard them, he was furious.
The fire of his wrath burned against Jacob.
Yes, his anger rose against Israel,
22 for they did not believe God
or trust him to care for them.
23 But he commanded the skies to open;
he opened the doors of heaven.
24 He rained down manna for them to eat;
he gave them bread from heaven.
25 They ate the food of angels!
God gave them all they could hold.
26 He released the east wind in the heavens
and guided the south wind by his mighty power.
27 He rained down meat as thick as dust—
birds as plentiful as the sand on the seashore!
28 He caused the birds to fall within their camp
and all around their tents.
29 The people ate their fill.
He gave them what they craved.

30 But before they satisfied their craving,
while the meat was yet in their mouths,
31 the anger of God rose against them,
and he killed their strongest men.
He struck down the finest of Israel's young men.

32 But in spite of this, the people kept sinning.
Despite his wonders, they refused to trust him.
33 So he ended their lives in failure,
their years in terror.
34 When God began killing them,
they finally sought him.
They repented and took God seriously.
35 Then they remembered that God was their rock,
that God Most High was their redeemer.
36 But all they gave him was lip service;
they lied to him with their tongues.
37 Their hearts were not loyal to him.
They did not keep his covenant.
38 Yet he was merciful and forgave their sins
and did not destroy them all.
Many times he held back his anger
and did not unleash his fury!
39 For he remembered that they were merely mortal,
gone like a breath of wind that never returns.

40 Oh, how often they rebelled against him in the
wilderness
and grieved his heart in that dry wasteland.
41 Again and again they tested God's patience
and provoked the Holy One of Israel.
42 They did not remember his power
and how he rescued them from their enemies.
43 They did not remember his miraculous signs in Egypt,
his wonders on the plain of Zoan.
44 For he turned their rivers into blood,
so no one could drink from the streams.

45 He sent vast swarms of flies to consume them
and hordes of frogs to ruin them.
46 He gave their crops to caterpillars;
their harvest was consumed by locusts.
47 He destroyed their grapevines with hail
and shattered their sycamore-figs with sleet.
48 He abandoned their cattle to the hail,
their livestock to bolts of lightning.
49 He loosed on them his fierce anger—
all his fury, rage, and hostility.
He dispatched against them
a band of destroying angels.
50 He turned his anger against them;
he did not spare the Egyptians' lives
but ravaged them with the plague.
51 He killed the oldest son in each Egyptian family,
the flower of youth throughout the land of Egypt.
52 But he led his own people like a flock of sheep,
guiding them safely through the wilderness.
53 He kept them safe so they were not afraid;
but the sea covered their enemies.
54 He brought them to the border of his holy land,
to this land of hills he had won for them.
55 He drove out the nations before them;
he gave them their inheritance by lot.
He settled the tribes of Israel into their homes.

56 But they kept testing and rebelling against God
Most High.
They did not obey his laws.
57 They turned back and were as faithless as their parents.
They were as undependable as a crooked bow.
58 They angered God by building shrines to other gods;
they made him jealous with their idols.
59 When God heard them, he was very angry,
and he completely rejected Israel.

60 Then he abandoned his dwelling at Shiloh,
the Tabernacle where he had lived among the people.
61 He allowed the Ark of his might to be captured;
he surrendered his glory into enemy hands.
62 He gave his people over to be butchered by the sword,
because he was so angry with his own people—his special possession.
63 Their young men were killed by fire;
their young women died before singing their wedding songs.
64 Their priests were slaughtered,
and their widows could not mourn their deaths.

65 Then the Lord rose up as though waking from sleep,
like a warrior aroused from a drunken stupor.
66 He routed his enemies
and sent them to eternal shame.
67 But he rejected Joseph's descendants;
he did not choose the tribe of Ephraim.
68 He chose instead the tribe of Judah,
and Mount Zion, which he loved.
69 There he built his sanctuary as high as the heavens,
as solid and enduring as the earth.
70 He chose his servant David,
calling him from the sheep pens.
71 He took David from tending the ewes and lambs
and made him the shepherd of Jacob's descendants—
God's own people, Israel.
72 He cared for them with a true heart
and led them with skillful hands.

He led his own people like a flock of sheep, guiding them safely through the wilderness. . . . But they kept testing and rebelling against God Most High. They did not obey his laws. (52, 56)

As shepherds outside of Gevas, Turkey, were eating breakfast one morning, they were surprised to see a sheep charge over the edge of a cliff and fall to its death. What followed took away their breath—and their appetite. Most of the remaining 1,500 sheep followed the first sheep and leaped over the same cliff. About 450 sheep died; the others survived only because as the corpses piled up at the bottom of the cliff, their falls were cushioned.[168]

That gives new meaning to the prophecy of Isaiah 53:6: "All of us, like sheep, have strayed away. We have left God's paths to follow our own." Sheep are dense and stupid; so are sinners. God, the Good Shepherd, has his hands full. It's a good thing he is patient, says this psalm.

Psalm 78 is long—seventy-two verses total. But it is shorter than the books whose history it summarizes: Exodus, Numbers, Deuteronomy, and even parts of Joshua, Judges, and 1 Samuel. It is a distillation of all that history down to one big lesson, summarized by the apostle Paul in Romans 5:8: "God showed his great love for us by sending Christ to die for us while we were still sinners."

The psalm also reminds us that there has been no golden age for the people of God. Hebrews 11 selects the great men and women of the Bible and parades them in a kind of hall of fame of faith. But most of our history is more like a hall of shame, redeemed only by the boundless mercy of God. We are supposed to learn from all this. Their story is our story, written to show us how not to live (1 Corinthians 10:1-13; Hebrews 3–4).

+++

We will not hide these truths from our children; we will tell the next generation about the glorious deeds of the LORD. . . . So each generation should set its hope anew on God, not forgetting his glorious miracles and obeying his commands. Then they will not be like their ancestors—stubborn, rebellious, and unfaithful, refusing to give their hearts to God. (4, 7-8)

Do you know the story Asaph is talking about? If not, will you make an effort to learn it? If you do, have you been diligent about passing it on to your children? You have no children, you say? Oh, but you do if you are in the church, the family of God. The next generation is everybody's responsibility.

These lines are a call for confession and commitment. Vow before the Lord to do all in your power to pass the story on.

Note the reason all must know the story: "Then they will not be like their ancestors—stubborn, rebellious, and unfaithful, refusing to give their hearts to God" (verse 8). Pray that your church will correct the ignorance that can doom another generation to be as bad as the ones before.

They stubbornly tested God in their hearts, demanding the foods they craved. (18)

A quick check of the foods they craved will show how selective their memories had become (see Numbers 11:4-6). They had been slaves in Egypt—no slave ate as well as they "remembered" they had. Ingratitude does that to us—it makes God look bad and life look better without him. Have you forgotten to be grateful? The more you find yourself grumbling, the more you can be sure you need to confess your ingratitude.

But in spite of this, the people kept sinning. Despite his wonders, they refused to trust him. . . . Yet he was merciful and forgave their sins and did not destroy them all. (32, 38)

This is the refrain that repeats itself throughout the psalm. It's a cycle—we sin, we suffer, we cry to God to save us, he answers, we forget and sin more, we suffer . . . and on and on. Does God ever tire of this? Is there a statute of limitations on his mercy? Your death is the outside limit.

But remember: His kindness is meant to lead you to repentance, not contempt and complacence (Romans 2:4). Pray that your heart will yield to his mercy.

He took David from tending the ewes and lambs and made him the shepherd of Jacob's descendants—God's own people, Israel. He cared for them with a true heart and led them with skillful hands. (71-72)

The psalm builds to a crescendo: one defection after another, one monumental act of divine mercy after another. Where sin abounded, grace abounded even more. God answers the stubborn rebellion of his unfaithful people by giving the greatest shepherd-king they ever had: David, whose lineage would include the Good Shepherd, the King of kings, Jesus.

Give thanks for this! Pray also that all who serve Jesus, and especially those who serve him as pastors, will be good and skilled in the ways of the Good Shepherd.

PSALM 83

A song. A psalm of Asaph.

1 O God, do not be silent!
Do not be deaf.
Do not be quiet, O God.
2 Don't you hear the uproar of your enemies?
Don't you see that your arrogant enemies are rising up?
3 They devise crafty schemes against your people;
they conspire against your precious ones.
4 "Come," they say, "let us wipe out Israel as a nation.
We will destroy the very memory of its existence."
5 Yes, this was their unanimous decision.
They signed a treaty as allies against you—
6 these Edomites and Ishmaelites;
Moabites and Hagrites;
7 Gebalites, Ammonites, and Amalekites;
and people from Philistia and Tyre.
8 Assyria has joined them, too,
and is allied with the descendants of Lot. *Interlude*

9 Do to them as you did to the Midianites
and as you did to Sisera and Jabin at the Kishon River.
10 They were destroyed at Endor,
and their decaying corpses fertilized the soil.
11 Let their mighty nobles die as Oreb and Zeeb did.
Let all their princes die like Zebah and Zalmunna,
12 for they said, "Let us seize for our own use
these pasturelands of God!"
13 O my God, scatter them like tumbleweed,
like chaff before the wind!
14 As a fire burns a forest
and as a flame sets mountains ablaze,
15 chase them with your fierce storm;
terrify them with your tempest.

16 **Utterly disgrace them**
until they submit to your name, O Lord.
17 **Let them be ashamed and terrified forever.**
Let them die in disgrace.
18 **Then they will learn that you alone are called the Lord,**
that you alone are the Most High,
supreme over all the earth.

Do to them as you did to the Midianites and as you did to Sisera and Jabin at the Kishon River. (9)

Do that to them?

Sisera was the army commander for Jabin, a king who had terrorized and oppressed Israel for twenty years. When God took up Israel's cause, he appointed the judge Deborah to lead the fight against this enemy. Her army crushed them in battle—ten thousand warriors and nine hundred iron chariots, all destroyed. Sisera ran for his life and found himself at the tent of a woman named Jael, whose husband's clan had been on good terms with his master, Jabin. Thinking he was safe with her, Sisera asked if he could hide there. Jael welcomed him into her tent; she even refreshed him with goat's milk, tucked him in for a much-needed nap, and promised to stand guard while he rested. When he was deeply asleep, she tiptoed to where he lay, holding a tent peg in one hand and a mallet in the other. With a few deft strokes, she drove the tent peg right through his temple and into the ground, leaving quite a mess, we can be sure.[169]

Treat the enemy that way, Asaph prayed.

Oreb and Zeeb, also very bad men, were beheaded by Gideon's troops and their heads brought to him as trophies. Do that kind of thing to our enemies, Asaph prayed; and likewise as you did with Zebah and Zalmunna, who were personally executed by Gideon.[170] Do that too, Lord.

This psalm is a call to pray as a warrior, fiercely. There are those out there who hate us Christians so much that if they had their way, they would wipe us out and destroy the very memory of our existence (verse 4). Pray to God that he do them in before they do us in.

In this psalm, Asaph lists an array of nations, most of which were in various combinations of military alliances against Israel at one time or another. We have no record in the Bible or outside the Bible, however, of the exact grand alliance Asaph mentions. Of particular note in this list is Tyre, since there is no mention anywhere of Israel ever fighting against her. However, Jezebel, the daughter of the king of Tyre and Sidon, married Israel's king Ahab and brought about one of the greatest crises of Israel's history. So these nations, Tyre included, represent all those who throughout history have devised "crafty schemes" against God's people, just as the serpent did against Adam and Eve. They are continuing the ancient and bitter conflict between the serpent's offspring and the woman's offspring.[171]

If that is the case, then these enemies are vile and to be treated with extreme malice. Tyre is especially evil, for from Tyre came Jezebel and Athaliah, and the idolatry and materialism that threatened Israel's very identity. Better the coercion of Assyria than the seduction of Tyre. Far worse than what the other nations would do to the body was what Tyre could do to the soul. Jesus said so.[172] The prophet Elijah's fight against this worst of all threats set him apart forever in Israel's mind as the prophet par excellence.[173]

Tyre represents what we now understand better from the New Testament—that the enemies Asaph prayed against are ultimately not human, flesh-and-blood enemies but spiritual ones. Our real fight is "against evil rulers and authorities of the unseen world, against mighty powers in this dark world, and against evil spirits in the heavenly places."[174]

Let this psalm teach you how to fight the good fight.

+++

Do not be quiet, O God. Don't you hear the uproar of your enemies? **(1-2)**

Pray for God to speak to you in the midst of the noise.

The world puffs itself up and makes a big show because it has so little substance. But sometimes it can get so loud that the voice of God cannot be heard. God's voice can and may thunder over the tumult, as in Psalm 29. But more often it whispers beneath the uproar, as in Elijah's experience on Mount Sinai.[175]

They devise crafty schemes against your people; they conspire against your precious ones. (3)
Pray for protection against the "crafty schemes" of the devil. Let Luther's great hymn "A Mighty Fortress Is Our God" help you, for the song expresses what Asaph knows about our enemy the devil:

> His craft and power are great,
> And, armed with cruel hate,
> On earth is not his equal.

That being the case, we must pray for God to act!

> Did we in our own strength confide,
> Our striving would be losing;
> Were not the right Man on our side,
> The Man of God's own choosing:
> Dost ask who that may be?
> Christ Jesus, it is He;
> Lord Sabaoth, His name,
> From age to age the same,
> And He must win the battle.

Pray to the "Lord Sabaoth," the "LORD of Heaven's Armies."

O my God, scatter them like tumbleweed, like chaff before the wind! (13)
Pray fiercely, like a warrior, with extreme malice against the demonic forces. Pray with the martyred saints in heaven for God to avenge their blood. Pray for Christ to return with the armies of heaven to "release the fierce wrath of God, the Almighty, like juice flowing from a winepress" on all that is wicked.[176]

Name this world's injustices—pray against abortion, war, and the exploitation of women and children. Cry out for God to bring down oppressive regimes.

PSALM 84

For the choir director: A psalm of the descendants of Korah, to be accompanied by a stringed instrument.

1 How lovely is your dwelling place,
O LORD of Heaven's Armies.
2 I long, yes, I faint with longing
to enter the courts of the LORD.
With my whole being, body and soul,
I will shout joyfully to the living God.
3 Even the sparrow finds a home,
and the swallow builds her nest and raises her young
at a place near your altar,
O LORD of Heaven's Armies, my King and my God!
4 What joy for those who can live in your house,
always singing your praises. *Interlude*

5 What joy for those whose strength comes from the LORD,
who have set their minds on a pilgrimage to Jerusalem.
6 When they walk through the Valley of Weeping,
it will become a place of refreshing springs.
The autumn rains will clothe it with blessings.
7 They will continue to grow stronger,
and each of them will appear before God in Jerusalem.

8 O LORD God of Heaven's Armies, hear my prayer.
Listen, O God of Jacob. *Interlude*

9 O God, look with favor upon the king, our shield!
Show favor to the one you have anointed.

10 A single day in your courts
is better than a thousand anywhere else!
I would rather be a gatekeeper in the house of my God
than live the good life in the homes of the wicked.
11 For the LORD God is our sun and our shield.
He gives us grace and glory.

The LORD will withhold no good thing
from those who do what is right.
12 O LORD of Heaven's Armies,
what joy for those who trust in you.

What joy for those who can live in your house, always singing your praises. (4)

Question: What's a man looking for as he knocks on the door of a brothel in the red-light district of, say, Amsterdam? Sex, you say. Much more than sex, said G. K. Chesterton—much, much more: "Every man who knocks on the door of a brothel is looking for God." The only difference between that man and the person who kneels in a church to take Holy Communion is that the former is looking for gratification in the wrong place. He doesn't know that it's really God he's looking for. The thirst, the hunger, the satisfaction he's craving in sex can be quenched only by God. And if he keeps looking for God in sex, it will kill him.

It's the same with all our appetites and longings. "Lust is the craving for salt of a man dying of thirst," wrote Frederick Buechner. "A glutton is one who raids the icebox for a cure for spiritual malnutrition."[177] It's good to be hungry if there's real food to eat; terrible if what you eat only makes you hungrier—and starves you to death as it does.

It seems we humans have this infernal habit of mistaking the things God gives for the God who gives them, of worshiping the things he makes instead of their Maker. "They traded the truth about God for a lie. So they worshiped and served the things God created instead of the Creator himself, who is worthy of eternal praise!"[178]

But the purpose for which God made everything was for his glory, to show off his greatness. For a human, it would be egotistical. For God it is truthful. We need him to do this. His glory puts everything else in perspective. "For you are the fountain of life, the light by which we see."[179]

Everything God creates and gives is meant to be a sign pointing back to God—our true home, our true destination. Sin is making the sign home, worshiping the things God created instead of the Creator himself. The writer of this psalm knew that. He was physically away from home and achingly homesick. But he knew his longings were signposts to deeper things. His prayer is a prayer of hunger and thirst for God, of longing and homesickness for the only One who can satisfy him. How happy he would be if he could be at home with God—what joy!

+++

What joy for those who can live in your house, always singing your praises. (4)
For the writer of this psalm, God's house is the Temple in Jerusalem. But it is much more—it is the symbol of his presence with his people. The building, though important, isn't really the point; it is the God the psalmist encounters in the building that matters. For the Christian, this is even more true, for God's "house" is Christ himself,[180] and Christ's Body, the church.[181] Pray that the life of your church will embody the joy of those who always sing God's praises.

What joy for those whose strength comes from the LORD, who have set their minds on a pilgrimage to Jerusalem. (5)
We are pilgrims in the world. We are not yet home; we're passing through, looking forward to "a city with eternal foundations, a city designed and built by God."[182]

Pray to hold thankfully, but lightly, all that you have in this world.

Ask God to deliver you from the tyranny of the trivial and to help you "set your sights on the realities of heaven."[183]

Pray that the journey will be joyful even when it is hard. Pray that the "Valley of Weeping" will become "a place of refreshing springs" (verse 6) for all who suffer in this world.

LORD of Heaven's Armies, what joy for those who trust in you. (12)
Pray that you will experience not only joy in the journey but a contentedness with what God gives you and where he has you. This tranquility comes only when we trust the Good Shepherd's wisdom and love. Pray for greater trust in Jesus, the *Lord of Heaven's Armies*.

PSALM 87

A song. A psalm of the descendants of Korah.

1 On the holy mountain
stands the city founded by the LORD.
2 He loves the city of Jerusalem
more than any other city in Israel.
3 O city of God,
what glorious things are said of you! *Interlude*

4 I will count Egypt and Babylon among those who know me—
also Philistia and Tyre, and even distant Ethiopia.
They have all become citizens of Jerusalem!
5 Regarding Jerusalem it will be said,
"Everyone enjoys the rights of citizenship there."
And the Most High will personally bless this city.
6 When the LORD registers the nations, he will say,
"They have all become citizens of Jerusalem."
Interlude

7 The people will play flutes and sing,
"The source of my life springs from Jerusalem!"

> Regarding Jerusalem it will be said, "Everyone enjoys the rights of citizenship there." And the Most High will personally bless this city. (5)

Since 1886, the Statue of Liberty has greeted thousands of immigrants into the mouth of the Hudson River, the New York Harbor, and a new life in the United States. Inside the statue's pedestal is a bronze plaque with a poem by Emma Lazarus, "The New Colossus." Unlike the old Colossus of Rhodes, which stood for the power of conquest, this new Colossus, in Lazarus's metaphor, goes out to invite all who would come to freedom and a new life:

> Give me your tired, your poor,
> Your huddled masses yearning to breathe free,
> The wretched refuse of your teeming shore.
> Send these, the homeless, tempest-tost to me,
> I lift my lamp beside the golden door!

Psalm 87 celebrates a far greater prospect: All the peoples of the earth streaming into Jerusalem—not unwillingly as the vanquished or desperate as exiles, but joyfully as the redeemed. When the Kingdom comes and God's rule is complete, whatever was once written on their old birth certificates—Egyptian, Babylonian, Ethiopian—will be null and void. The new reality will be the joy of new birth and new life in God's Holy City.

The message of the Kingdom of God has always been rigorously exclusive: one Lord, one faith, one baptism, one God and Father.[184] But the invitation to believe and enjoy the blessings of God is thoroughly inclusive: All who will believe may come—and many have come, from east and west and north and south,[185] and from every tribe and language and people and nation.[186] And as Paul put it, all who have faith in Christ are citizens of the heavenly Jerusalem.[187]

This is a happy psalm! It takes all narrow identities and connects them to the whole world, God's world.

Examples of its universality abound—and are delightful. Over the years, Christians have found literally thousands of ways to give the same answer to Jesus' question "Who do you say I am?" The distinguished historian of Christian doctrine Jaroslav Pelikan has written about several hundred of these statements of faith. One that originated in Africa is the Masai Creed, a Christian confession proclaiming that Jesus "was always on safari doing good." It also affirms that after Jesus had been "tortured and nailed hands and feet to a cross, and died, he lay buried in the grave, but the hyenas did not touch him, and on the third day, he rose from the grave. He ascended unto the skies. He is the Lord."

Pelikan first heard of this creed from one of his students, a woman who had served as a member of a religious order in a hospital in East Nigeria. When he first heard it, he was thrilled. He said, "And so she brought it to me, and I just got shivers. Just the thought, you know, the hyenas did not touch him, and the act of defiance—God lives even in spite of the hyenas."[188]

What an interesting place the Kingdom of God will be. No earthly city has ever seen such richly textured diversity and color—and yet been so unified. I want to be there one day with my Masai kindred and rejoice that the hyenas couldn't touch Jesus.

+++

On the holy mountain stands the city founded by the LORD. He loves the city of Jerusalem more than any other city in Israel. O city of God, what glorious things are said of you! (1-3)

Praise God for the church, the people of God.

John Newton took this psalm as a jumping-off place for his hymn "Glorious Things of Thee Are Spoken." Let its words be your prayer of praise.

Glorious things of Thee are spoken,
Zion, city of our God!
He, whose word cannot be broken,
Form'd Thee for His own abode. . . .

Bless'd inhabitants of Zion,
Wash'd in the Redeemer's blood!
Jesus, whom their souls rely on,
Makes them kings and priests to God.
'Tis His love His people raises
Over self to reign as kings,
And as priests, His solemn praises
Each for a thank-off'ring brings.

Saviour, if of Zion's city
I through grace a member am,
Let the world deride or pity,
I will glory in Thy name:
Fading is the worldling's pleasure,
All his boasted pomp and show:
Solid joys and lasting treasure,
None but Zion's children know.

When the LORD registers the nations, he will say, "They have all become citizens of Jerusalem." (6)
Pray for the nations of the earth to come to Christ. Pray that the mission-zeal of your church be white hot "to bring the nations into the white-hot enjoyment of God's glory."[189]

The people will play flutes and sing, "The source of my life springs from Jerusalem!" (7)
Pray for the spiritual revival of your church. Ask the Spirit of God to move his people to drink more deeply from the spring of living water,[190] and say with joy, "The source of my life springs from Jerusalem."

PSALM 88

For the choir director: A psalm of the descendants of Korah. A song to be sung to the tune "The Suffering of Affliction." A psalm of Heman the Ezrahite.

1 O Lord, God of my salvation,
I cry out to you by day.
I come to you at night.
2 Now hear my prayer;
listen to my cry.
3 For my life is full of troubles,
and death draws near.
4 I am as good as dead,
like a strong man with no strength left.
5 They have left me among the dead,
and I lie like a corpse in a grave.
I am forgotten,
cut off from your care.
6 You have thrown me into the lowest pit,
into the darkest depths.
7 Your anger weighs me down;
with wave after wave you have engulfed me.
Interlude

8 You have driven my friends away
by making me repulsive to them.
I am in a trap with no way of escape.
9 My eyes are blinded by my tears.
Each day I beg for your help, O Lord;
I lift my hands to you for mercy.
10 Are your wonderful deeds of any use to the dead?
Do the dead rise up and praise you? *Interlude*

11 Can those in the grave declare your unfailing love?
Can they proclaim your faithfulness in the place of destruction?

12 Can the darkness speak of your wonderful deeds?
Can anyone in the land of forgetfulness talk about your righteousness?
13 O LORD, I cry out to you.
I will keep on pleading day by day.
14 O LORD, why do you reject me?
Why do you turn your face from me?

15 I have been sick and close to death since my youth.
I stand helpless and desperate before your terrors.
16 Your fierce anger has overwhelmed me.
Your terrors have paralyzed me.
17 They swirl around me like floodwaters all day long.
They have engulfed me completely.
18 You have taken away my companions and loved ones.
Darkness is my closest friend.

O LORD, why do you reject me? Why do you turn your face from me? (14)

I'll never forget the look on my eighteen-month-old son Danny's face when I had to restrain him as a lab technician pricked his little finger for a blood sample. His screams were awful for this dad to hear. But harder than the screams and the panicked squirming of his little body was the look in his eyes. They searched my face in terror and confusion. His daddy was helping this cruel stranger hurt him! How could that be? If he had had the language and self-awareness of a grown-up, he might have said that the greater pain, far greater than the pain of the needle, was the pain of doubting my love for him, my good intentions. Had his daddy ceased to be his daddy and abandoned him?

But he held on to me tightly.

This roughly is what Heman the Ezrahite is doing as he pours out his pain to God in this darkest and bleakest of all psalms. He is holding on tightly to a God he no longer understands and whom he fears no longer loves him. From where he stands, it appears that God has

> forgotten him
> and cut him off from his care;
> thrown him into the lowest pit,
> the darkest depths;
> crushed and
> drowned him in his anger;
> driven his friends away,
> made him repulsive to them;

rejected him
and hidden his face from him;
paralyzed him with his terrors;
robbed him of his closest friends,
and left him with only darkness for company.

That's what God looks like to him. Has he ever looked that way to you? Or to someone you know?

But what makes this prayer so remarkable is just that: It is a prayer. He holds on to God as tightly as he can. He doesn't fall into a sullen silence; rather, he keeps the conversation going, even if it seems to him to be maddeningly one sided.

Heman has much to teach about how to pray in dark times.

+++

LORD, God of my salvation . . . (1)
Keep hoping, even when all you feel is hopelessness. It's significant that Heman still addresses this God who has him so confused as "God of my salvation." The hope in his address is subtle but real. Language matters when we speak to God; just learning to habitually say the right things about God can keep hope alive. Keep clinging and calling to Daddy.

You have thrown me into the lowest pit, into the darkest depths. Your anger weighs me down; with wave after wave you have engulfed me. (6-7)
Don't be afraid to be honest, even wrong, about God. It's better to be transparent in doubt than theologically correct in unbelief.

Surely Heman must have been taught in synagogue school that God doesn't just arbitrarily allow his people to suffer like this. Or maybe not. But the important thing is that he doesn't try to qualify or moderate the expression of his experience. He just says what's on his mind. God loves that. It allows what has been a barrier to become a bridge.

I am as good as dead, like a strong man with no strength left. (4)
Death is a very bad thing, but a very good thing to keep before you when you pray. Which is what Heman does. In the Orthodox tradition, Psalm 88 is one of six psalms (the *Hexapsalmos*) prescribed for Matins,

the earliest hour of prayer each day.[191] The intent is to keep the reality of death before the believer daily. Otherwise the gospel loses its full weight. Christ's cross and resurrection were more than vivid examples of self-giving love; they were the conquest of our greatest enemy, death. The celebration of the gospel against the background of death will keep one thankful, sober, and alert.

LORD, I cry out to you. I will keep on pleading day by day. (13)
Persistence may be the most underrated virtue in prayer. Three times Heman declares his persistence (verses 1, 9, 13). It's hard to persist when things seem so dark. But Jesus, who was better acquainted with darkness than anyone else, assures us that God is responsive to persistent praying.[192] Remember, on the cross he cried out a prayer very much like Heman's:

> My God, my God, why have you abandoned me? Why are you so far away when I groan for help? Every day I call to you, my God, but you do not answer. Every night you hear my voice, but I find no relief.[193]

You have driven my friends away by making me repulsive to them. (8)
Learn to pray as a companion of the Hemans of this world. Saying this psalm regularly will teach you how to pray empathetically. And who knows, one day it may help you speak to God when things are unspeakably dark for you.

PSALM 90

A prayer of Moses, the man of God.

1 Lord, through all the generations
you have been our home!
2 Before the mountains were born,
before you gave birth to the earth and the world,
from beginning to end, you are God.

3 You turn people back to dust, saying,
"Return to dust, you mortals!"
4 For you, a thousand years are as a passing day,
as brief as a few night hours.
5 You sweep people away like dreams that disappear.
They are like grass that springs up in the morning.
6 In the morning it blooms and flourishes,
but by evening it is dry and withered.
7 We wither beneath your anger;
we are overwhelmed by your fury.
8 You spread out our sins before you—
our secret sins—and you see them all.
9 We live our lives beneath your wrath,
ending our years with a groan.

10 Seventy years are given to us!
Some even live to eighty.
But even the best years are filled with pain and trouble;
soon they disappear, and we fly away.
11 Who can comprehend the power of your anger?
Your wrath is as awesome as the fear you deserve.
12 Teach us to realize the brevity of life,
so that we may grow in wisdom.

13 O LORD, come back to us!
How long will you delay?
Take pity on your servants!

14 Satisfy us each morning with your unfailing love,
so we may sing for joy to the end of our lives.
15 Give us gladness in proportion to our former misery!
Replace the evil years with good.
16 Let us, your servants, see you work again;
let our children see your glory.
17 And may the Lord our God show us his approval
and make our efforts successful.
Yes, make our efforts successful!

Lord, through all the generations you have been our home! Before the mountains were born, before you gave birth to the earth and the world, from beginning to end, you are God. (1-2)

The Cathedral of Milan has three doorways, each spanned by a magnificent arch. Inscribed over the arch on one side is, "All that pleases is but for a moment." Carved underneath is a beautiful wreath of roses. Inscribed over the arch on the opposite side is, "All that which troubles is but for a moment." Carved beneath is a cross. The inscription over the arch in the central doorway is, "That only is important which is eternal." Two arches are about mere moments in time; the central arch is about eternity. But all three touch on the themes of Psalm 90: God alone is eternal, he alone is permanent, he is our only home. Everything else is momentary, ephemeral, passing away.

That's the good news. Now for the bad news, without which the good news wouldn't be good news: Life is hard and then we die—and it's our fault. Many of us never enter the cathedral, not because we can't, but because we won't. Stubborn sin keeps us out.

> You spread out our sins before you—our secret sins—and you see them all. We live our lives beneath your wrath, ending our years with a groan. Seventy years are given to us! Some even live to eighty. But even the best years are filled with pain and trouble; soon they disappear, and we fly away. (verses 8-10)

"The wages of sin is death, but the free gift of God is eternal life through Christ Jesus our Lord" is the apostle Paul's way of saying the same thing.[194] The hardness of life and the grimness of death are the visible manifestations of the deep, inner truth that because of our sin, we live our lives beneath God's wrath. Our only hope is that God show us mercy instead of wrath.

Psalm 90 is the cry of a man who knows all this. Read the first ten verses slowly and meditate on life beneath God's wrath. Let the bad news sink in so you may pray for the Good News, the gospel.

+++

Who can comprehend the power of your anger? Your wrath is as awesome as the fear you deserve. (11)
Pray that you would be more deeply convinced of the great wickedness of your sin—that God is absolutely just in his wrath and that the measure of his anger is the reverence he deserves, but has not received, from us.

Teach us to realize the brevity of life, so that we may grow in wisdom. (12)
We live in a culture that is in deep denial about the reality of death. Pascal's observations of his contemporaries in seventeenth-century France apply equally to us:

> The last act is bloody, however fine the rest of the play. They throw earth over your head and it is finished forever. . . . We run heedlessly into the abyss after putting something in front of us to stop us seeing it.[195]

Pray that you would be sober and realistic about your mortality. Earlier generations of Christians were more willing than ours to face the reality of death. It was once common to read this psalm in tandem with Paul's great resurrection manifesto in 1 Corinthians 15. Neither text makes sense, or gives us any hope, without the other. Read 1 Corinthians 15 ("But thank God! He gives us victory over sin and death through our Lord Jesus Christ") after you have read Psalm 90.

LORD, come back to us! How long will you delay? Take pity on your servants! (13)
This is the essence of prayer: Help, Lord! Have mercy, Lord! Really, we cannot say these words too often. Pray them frequently.

Satisfy us each morning with your unfailing love, so we may sing for joy to the end of our lives. (14)
Pray that God would end the dark night of sin and guilt. Pray that the sun of his love would rise on you and everyone else in darkness.

Give us gladness in proportion to our former misery! Replace the evil years with good. (15)
This is a bold prayer: that we would get not the great punishment we deserve but a great mercy we don't deserve—that God would give us such blessing that the good he gives would actually match the punishment he gave and cancel it out! Ask God to treat you better than you deserve.

Let us, your servants, see you work again; let our children see your glory. (16)
What do you pray for the next generation, for your children and their children? That they make a lot of money and acquire a lot of stuff, or achieve much worldly success? How about this: that they see the glory of God? The flickering light of a candle is swallowed up in the blazing light of the midday sun. So it is with the best this world has to offer. Pray that this, and the next, generation would see the glory of God.

And may the Lord our God show us his approval and make our efforts successful. Yes, make our efforts successful! (17)
Seeing the inevitability of death, some people despair of their lives and their work ever having any meaning. This psalm offers a better response: Without God, nothing can succeed, so we pray, "God make it succeed!" The prayer is repeated twice, which is a Hebrew way of saying, "God, make our work succeed a lot!" Pray that your work would succeed a lot, to the glory of God.

PSALM 91

1 Those who live in the shelter of the Most High
will find rest in the shadow of the Almighty.
2 This I declare about the LORD:
He alone is my refuge, my place of safety;
he is my God, and I trust him.
3 For he will rescue you from every trap
and protect you from deadly disease.
4 He will cover you with his feathers.
He will shelter you with his wings.
His faithful promises are your armor and protection.
5 Do not be afraid of the terrors of the night,
nor the arrow that flies in the day.
6 Do not dread the disease that stalks in darkness,
nor the disaster that strikes at midday.
7 Though a thousand fall at your side,
though ten thousand are dying around you,
these evils will not touch you.
8 Just open your eyes,
and see how the wicked are punished.

9 If you make the LORD your refuge,
if you make the Most High your shelter,
10 no evil will conquer you;
no plague will come near your home.
11 For he will order his angels
to protect you wherever you go.
12 They will hold you up with their hands
so you won't even hurt your foot on a stone.
13 You will trample upon lions and cobras;
you will crush fierce lions and serpents under
your feet!

14 The LORD says, "I will rescue those who love me.
I will protect those who trust in my name.

15 When they call on me, I will answer;
I will be with them in trouble.
I will rescue and honor them.
16 I will reward them with a long life
and give them my salvation."

Those who live in the shelter of the Most High will find rest in the shadow of the Almighty. (1)

*H*ow sneaky of Satan to use this psalm to tempt Jesus in the wilderness! He took the Lord to the Holy City, to Jerusalem, to the highest point atop the Temple, and challenged him to prove his faith and his Sonship by jumping off. He appealed to Holy Scripture as justification, quoting Psalm 91:11-12:

> If you are the Son of God, jump off! For the Scriptures say,
> "He will order his angels to protect you.
> And they will hold you up with their hands
> so you won't even hurt your foot on a stone."

It's worth noting that the devil knows the Bible better than most. That being the case, we should recognize the limitations of mere Bible knowledge, content without understanding and humility. Cults have been birthed by people sitting alone with their Bible and a concordance. It's sobering to see the way the Liar can weave truths into fiction.

Jesus knows his Bible too, and he responded with understanding and humility.

> The Scriptures also say, "You must not test the LORD your God."[196]

The promises of Psalm 91 are meant to engender trust, not presumption. Like all genuine prayer, their purpose is not for us to get God to give us what we want but for us to trust him to give us what he wants—and in the manner he wants to give. Those who trust the Lord will be cared for in all the ways the psalm says, but not always in the ways we think. His ways are not our ways.[197]

Jesus knew this. So he went to the cross "because of the joy awaiting him."[198] Yes, the joy! Ahead of him would be everything the psalm says God would protect him from: traps, diseases, terrors of the night, arrows in the day, and evil mobs. He would be crucified, humiliated, and crushed. But God would nevertheless be his refuge and safety; he would still reward him with long life. The weight of glory would totally outweigh the burden of suffering. In fact, the victory would be greater, not in spite of the apparent defeat, but because of it. For the devil, the great serpent, the fierce lion, would slam the Son of God with all the evil he had, gnaw and chew on him every way he knew how, and still come up empty and impotent.

Elisabeth Elliot knew this because she learned it from Jesus. In 1956 her husband, Jim, was murdered, along with four other young missionaries—killed by the very people they came to tell the Good News of Jesus. She was a young wife and a new mother, and now she was a widow. Could she still trust the promises of Psalm 91? When she wrote Jim Elliot's biography a few years later, the title she gave it answered this question. It came from Psalm 91:1—*Shadow of the Almighty*.

+++

He will cover you with his feathers. He will shelter you with his wings. His faithful promises are your armor and protection. (4)
Just to know that God is faithful, no matter what happens, is armor and protection enough. Pray that faith and hope will grow strong in your heart. Know that your true life is hidden in Christ, covered with his feathers, sheltered with his wings.

> You died to this life, and your real life is hidden with Christ in God. And when Christ, who is your life, is revealed to the whole world, you will share in all his glory.[199]

> Happy and strong and brave shall we be—able to endure all things, and to do all things—if we believe that every day, every hour, every moment of our life is in God's hands.[200]

Do not be afraid of the terrors of the night, nor the arrow that flies in the day. Do not dread the disease that stalks in darkness, nor the disaster that strikes at midday. (5-6)
Pray this psalm a lot. It's a great way to pray what our Lord told us to pray: "Lead us not into temptation, but deliver us from the evil one."

From the earliest days of the church, Psalm 91 was one of a very few psalms almost all agreed should be prayed every day. The only question was when. In the East it was typically prayed at midday, in response to its mention of "the disaster that strikes at midday." The thought was that the evil of midday was like the way some of us feel after lunch: slothful and dull. Spiritual weariness was the great temptation. In the West, this psalm typically has been prayed in the evening, against "the terrors of the night," the power of death and fear.

Psalm 91 is also an appropriate psalm to be prayed at a funeral service.

You will trample upon lions and cobras; you will crush fierce lions and serpents under your feet! (13)
Pray against the demonic powers by claiming God's promise to protect you from them. Scholars may argue whether the psalmist had demonic powers in mind when he wrote it. But we know from the larger witness of Scripture that it is the demonic powers against which we contend.[201] The devil is like a lion; he is also like a serpent, in fact, he is the great serpent of the book of Revelation.[202]

Rather than fearing the evil spiritual powers, we can pray against them. David gave us a wonderful prayer in Psalm 35:

> O LORD, oppose those who oppose me.
> Fight those who fight against me.
> Put on your armor, and take up your shield.
> Prepare for battle, and come to my aid.
> Lift up your spear and javelin
> against those who pursue me.
> Let me hear you say,
> "I will give you victory!" (verses 1-3)

Saint Patrick is credited with writing a classic prayer for divine protection, which others amended over the centuries. In 1889, the dean of the Chapel Royal at Dublin Castle asked Cecil Alexander to adapt the words so that "Saint Patrick's Lorica" (or breastplate) could be included in the Irish hymnal. Her words are still rich with meaning today:

Against the demon snares of sin,
The vice that gives temptation force,
The natural lusts that war within,
The hostile men that mar my course;
Or few or many, far or nigh,
In every place and in all hours,
Against their fierce hostility
I bind to me these holy powers.

Against all Satan's spells and wiles,
Against false words of heresy,
Against the knowledge that defiles,
Against the heart's idolatry,
Against the wizard's evil craft,
Against the death wound and the burning,
The choking wave, the poisoned shaft,
Protect me, Christ, till Thy returning.

PSALM 96

1 Sing a new song to the LORD!
Let the whole earth sing to the LORD!
2 Sing to the LORD; praise his name.
Each day proclaim the good news that he saves.
3 Publish his glorious deeds among the nations.
Tell everyone about the amazing things he does.
4 Great is the LORD! He is most worthy of praise!
He is to be feared above all gods.
5 The gods of other nations are mere idols,
but the LORD made the heavens!
6 Honor and majesty surround him;
strength and beauty fill his sanctuary.

7 O nations of the world, recognize the LORD;
recognize that the LORD is glorious and strong.
8 Give to the LORD the glory he deserves!
Bring your offering and come into his courts.
9 Worship the LORD in all his holy splendor.
Let all the earth tremble before him.
10 Tell all the nations, "The LORD reigns!"
The world stands firm and cannot be shaken.
He will judge all peoples fairly.

11 Let the heavens be glad, and the earth rejoice!
Let the sea and everything in it shout his praise!
12 Let the fields and their crops burst out with joy!
Let the trees of the forest rustle with praise
13 before the LORD, for he is coming!
He is coming to judge the earth.
He will judge the world with justice,
and the nations with his truth.

Sing a new song to the LORD! Let the whole earth sing to the LORD! (1)

Why do people climb mountains?" The most famous answer to that question is George Mallory's. When asked why he climbed the Matterhorn, he replied, "Because it is there!" Willi Unsoeld, a mountaineer and a philosopher, didn't like that answer. He thought there was a deeper reason: "People climb mountains because of a universal desire to find the point of convergence."[203] That is what it feels like on a mountaintop. One looks at the complexity of all the geography below, the cities and forests and rivers and hills, and has the sensation that all their lines come together and converge at the peak.

If only there were a place to stand where all the complexity of life truly came together the way landscape seems to on a mountaintop! There is such a place: It is where all the peoples of the earth stand together, united in the worship of God.

Has there been such a time? Not yet. But there will be, and we are to pray and work toward that great day when Jesus Christ is elevated to the place of highest honor and every knee bows and every tongue confesses that he is Lord, to the glory of God the Father.[204] That is the hope, command, and prayer of Psalm 96.

+++

Publish his glorious deeds among the nations. Tell everyone about the amazing things he does. Great is the LORD! He is most worthy of praise! He is to be feared above all gods. (3-4)

Pray for missions and all who work to publish God's glorious deeds. Pray for opportunities for you to "tell everyone about the amazing things he does." Pray, remembering that, as John Piper puts it,

> Missions begins and ends in worship. . . . When the flame of worship burns with the heat of God's true worth, the light of missions will shine to the darkest peoples on earth. . . . Where passion for God is weak, zeal for missions will be weak. Churches that are not centered on the exaltation of the majesty and beauty of God will scarcely kindle a fervent desire to "declare *his glory* among the nations" (Ps. 96:3). . . . How can people who are not stunned by the greatness of God be sent with the ringing message, "*Great* is the LORD and greatly to be praised; he is to be feared above all gods"? (Ps. 96:4). Missions is not first and ultimate; God is. . . . Thousands . . . have been moved and carried by the vision of a great and triumphant God. That vision must come first. Savoring it in worship precedes spreading it in missions.[205]

Pray that the worship of your congregation be fuel for missions.

O nations of the world, recognize the LORD; recognize that the LORD is glorious and strong. Give to the LORD the glory he deserves! Bring your offering and come into his courts. Worship the LORD in all his holy splendor. (7-9)

This psalm marvelously engages the praying imagination.[206] Picture this: The peoples of the earth, every tribe and language and ethnicity, all gathered in one great mass at the gates of the Holy City, the new Jerusalem, to do something the creation has yet to see in its fullness: "Give to the LORD the glory he deserves!" (verse 8). They've all come with their offerings. And what might those offerings be? The vision in Revelation gives a clue: Kings and peoples will bring their glory and honor into the city (Revelation 21:24, 26). Surely this glory-offering must have something to do with who they are as a people—as Masai or French or Chinese or Mexican. I imagine it as their music and dance, their food and their stories. See them carry trays of fried rice and tacos and honey to the sounds of drums, accordions, flutes, and tubas. They're wearing straw hats and sarongs, cowboy boots and

Italian loafers. Maybe I'm off, but I'm off in a good way. Can you think of something better?

You imagine, too, and pray, saying of every nation you can think of—"O nations of the world [fill in the blank], recognize the LORD."

Let the heavens be glad, and the earth rejoice! Let the sea and everything in it shout his praise! Let the fields and their crops burst out with joy! Let the trees of the forest rustle with praise before the LORD, for he is coming! (11-13)

Then there is the created order. This psalm commands the heavens, the earth, the sea, the fields, and the trees of the forest to join in and add their own unique voices to the joyful praise.

Imagine and pray for pines and myrtle and barley and whales and anemones—whatever you can think of—to "give to the LORD the glory he deserves!" (verse 8).

When the Lord comes in glory, we will see the whole creation celebrate his greatness. For now we have a unique role to play in the world. The poet George Herbert wrote that when we use human language to praise God, we act as "the world's high Priest" presenting "the sacrifice for all" the rest. For us to refrain from praise is not to refrain unto ourselves alone but to render mute the rest of creation and to "commit a world of sin in one."[207] So don't hold back:

Sing to the LORD; praise his name. Each day proclaim the good news that he saves. Publish his glorious deeds among the nations. Tell everyone about the amazing things he does. (2-3)

Few psalms, or any passages of Scripture, span and unify so much of the Bible the way Psalm 96 does. It reaches back to the purpose for which God created a people, by calling Abram and promising that "all the families on earth will be blessed through you" (see Genesis 12:1-3). It is strengthened by Jesus' command to "make disciples of all the nations" (see Matthew 28:18-20). It is fulfilled finally in heaven, when "the kings of the world will enter the city in all their glory" (Revelation 21:24). To pray for missions is to pray from the heart of God and his Bible.

PSALM 100

A psalm of thanksgiving.

1 Shout with joy to the LORD, all the earth!
2 Worship the LORD with gladness.
Come before him, singing with joy.
3 Acknowledge that the LORD is God!
He made us, and we are his.
We are his people, the sheep of his pasture.
4 Enter his gates with thanksgiving;
go into his courts with praise.
Give thanks to him and praise his name.
5 For the LORD is good.
His unfailing love continues forever,
and his faithfulness continues to each generation.

Shout with joy to the LORD, all the earth! (1)

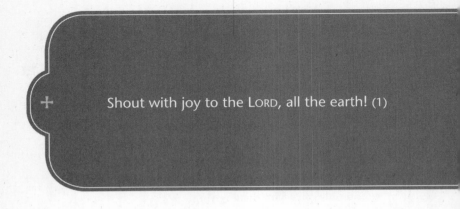

The real difference between Christians, says Brennan Manning, is not what one might think—liberal or conservative, Protestant or Catholic, fundamentalist or charismatic, Democrat or Republican. The real difference is between the aware and the unaware.

Aware of what? The love of God. "When somebody is aware of that love—the same love that the Father has for Jesus—that person is just spontaneously grateful. Cries of thankfulness become the dominant characteristic of the interior life, and the by-product of gratitude is joy."[208]

Another way of saying the same thing is that the real difference is between those who will obey the command of this psalm and those who won't. "Shout with joy to the LORD, all the earth! Worship the LORD with gladness. Come before him, singing with joy."

But that raises a big question: If gratitude and joy are spontaneous, why are they *commanded*? Shouldn't they just spring up in people who are awake to the goodness of God? The truth is, gratitude and joy are often what wake us up. They are choices. Remember: Gratitude and joy are organs of perception; we don't see in order to give thanks and rejoice, we give thanks and rejoice in order to see. Do you see no reason to be joyful and grateful? Rejoice and give thanks so you will! "Thanksgiving is not the result of perception; thanksgiving is the access to perception."[209]

+++

Enter his gates with thanksgiving. (4)
So just do it. Obey the command: Give thanks and rejoice. In *The Message*, Eugene Peterson's paraphrase of verse 4 is "Enter with the password: 'Thank you!'" The way into the presence of God is to give praise and thanks.

He made us, and we are his. We are his people, the sheep of his pasture. (3)
A big reason to be grateful is found in verse 3: "He made us, and we are his." Here the possibilities for insightful joy abound.

Thank God for the way he made you. Mother Teresa said God's "first word" to us is the fact that he made us. "This is the gift of ourselves to ourselves: our existence, our nature, our personal history, our uniqueness, our identity. . . . Our very existence is one of the unique and never-to-be-repeated ways God has chosen to express himself in space and time."[210]

Thank God that he makes saints out of sinners, enemies into beloved children. "God is a potter; he works in mud."[211]

Thank God for his people, the church, "the sheep of his pasture." This is the main meaning of the psalm. No Christian is an only child.

His unfailing love continues forever, and his faithfulness continues to each generation. (5)
Thank God, and claim the promise of his love for you and for all who will come after you. If you are a parent, you may resonate with the saying "No parent is happier than his or her least happy child."[212] Give thanks that God loves your children—and your children's children—more than you do.

Pray for the fulfillment of the command in verse 1: "Shout with joy to the LORD, all the earth!" The goodness of God extends through time from one generation to another and through space to all the peoples of the earth. God's love is wider than we can imagine—but we should try! Whenever we gather to praise God, we should have in view the hope that all the world will one day join us.

PSALM 102

A prayer of one overwhelmed with trouble, pouring out problems before the* L*ORD.

1 Lord, hear my prayer!
Listen to my plea!
2 Don't turn away from me
in my time of distress.
Bend down to listen,
and answer me quickly when I call to you.
3 For my days disappear like smoke,
and my bones burn like red-hot coals.
4 My heart is sick, withered like grass,
and I have lost my appetite.
5 Because of my groaning,
I am reduced to skin and bones.
6 I am like an owl in the desert,
like a little owl in a far-off wilderness.
7 I lie awake,
lonely as a solitary bird on the roof.
8 My enemies taunt me day after day.
They mock and curse me.
9 I eat ashes for food.
My tears run down into my drink
10 because of your anger and wrath.
For you have picked me up and thrown
me out.
11 My life passes as swiftly as the evening shadows.
I am withering away like grass.

12 But you, O Lord, will sit on your throne forever.
Your fame will endure to every generation.
13 You will arise and have mercy on Jerusalem—
and now is the time to pity her,
now is the time you promised to help.

14 For your people love every stone in her walls
and cherish even the dust in her streets.
15 Then the nations will tremble before the LORD.
The kings of the earth will tremble before his glory.
16 For the LORD will rebuild Jerusalem.
He will appear in his glory.
17 He will listen to the prayers of the destitute.
He will not reject their pleas.

18 Let this be recorded for future generations,
so that a people not yet born will praise the LORD.
19 Tell them the LORD looked down
from his heavenly sanctuary.
He looked down to earth from heaven
20 to hear the groans of the prisoners,
to release those condemned to die.
21 And so the LORD's fame will be celebrated in Zion,
his praises in Jerusalem,
22 when multitudes gather together
and kingdoms come to worship the LORD.

23 He broke my strength in midlife,
cutting short my days.
24 But I cried to him, "O my God, who lives forever,
don't take my life while I am so young!
25 Long ago you laid the foundation of the earth
and made the heavens with your hands.
26 They will perish, but you remain forever;
they will wear out like old clothing.
You will change them like a garment
and discard them.
27 But you are always the same;
you will live forever.
28 The children of your people
will live in security.
Their children's children
will thrive in your presence."

But you, O LORD, will sit on your throne forever.
Your fame will endure to every generation. (12)

*B*ruce Larson had an unusual way of convincing people to turn their lives over to Jesus Christ. When he was working in New York City, he would walk a man or woman downtown to the front of the RCA building on Fifth Avenue. In front of the building was a gigantic statue of a massively proportioned, magnificently muscled Atlas, the world resting on his shoulders. As powerfully built as he is, he is straining under the weight, barely able to stand. Larson would say, "That's one way to live, trying to carry the world on your shoulders. But now come across the street with me."

Then he'd walk the person over to St. Patrick's Cathedral. There behind the altar is a little shrine of the boy Jesus. He appears to be no more than eight or nine years old. As little and as frail as he looks, he is holding the world in one hand, as if it were a tennis ball! Then Larson would say, "We have a choice. We can carry the world on our shoulders, or we can say, 'I give up, Lord; here's my life. I give you my world, the whole world.'"[213]

This is the Lord we confidently pray to in the worst of times.

+++

I eat ashes for food. My tears run down into my drink because of your anger and wrath. For you have picked me up and thrown me out. . . . He broke my strength in midlife, cutting short my days. (9-10, 23)

May you never have to suffer in the ways described in verses 3-11. But many have and many do, even this very moment. Maybe you do too. Jesus did. Take these words and pray them as your own, either to express what you feel or to identify with the sufferings of God's people and God's Son. Say them slowly and repeatedly.

But you, O LORD, will sit on your throne forever. Your fame will endure to every generation. (12)
Count the personal pronouns in verses 1-11. You'll find *I*, *me*, or *my* mentioned twenty-five times in just eleven verses. There's nothing wrong with that; pain will do that to anyone. It's not self-absorption; it's just that the self can be swallowed up in the suffering. Pain confines.

That's why the words "But *you*, O LORD" are so liberating. They are like a fresh breeze in a stale sickroom. The loving, sovereign God who rules forever from his throne in heaven puts everything in perspective; for it is from his throne that he "causes everything to work together for the good of those who love God and are called according to his purpose for them" (Romans 8:28).

Look at all the things that trouble you, name them before God, and then add, "But you, O LORD, will sit on your throne forever."

Let this be recorded for future generations, so that a people not yet born will praise the LORD. (18)
The sovereign Lord lifts our eyes up, and then out into the future, to coming generations. Pray that God will answer your prayers and the prayers of all who suffer in such a way that generations yet unborn will hear of it and worship the Lord.

Then the nations will tremble before the LORD. The kings of the earth will tremble before his glory. . . . And so the LORD's fame will be celebrated in Zion, his praises in Jerusalem, when multitudes gather together and kingdoms come to worship the LORD. (15, 21-22)
Let the same expansion of your prayer-vision spread from yourself to God to all who are to come, and then to all "the nations . . . [and] kings of the earth." Jesus was thinking this way when he prayed from Psalm 22 on the cross. What begins with, "My God, my God, why have you abandoned me?" in verse 1 leads to, "The whole earth will acknowledge the LORD and return to him. All the families of the nations will bow down before him" in Psalm 22:27.

Pray for God to work this same happy ending through all suffering, yours and others'.

Long ago you laid the foundation of the earth and made the heavens with your hands. They will perish, but you remain forever; they will wear out like old clothing. You will change them like a garment and discard them. But you are always the same; you will live forever. The children of your people will live in security. Their children's children will thrive in your presence. (25-28)
Nothing lasts forever, not even the heavens and the earth. "They will wear out like old clothing," says the psalm. The Lord will "change them like a garment and discard them" (verse 26). Only God—and his people—are forever. His followers and their children will thrive in his presence. The church is the only permanent institution in history.

Do you value the church as highly as God does? Pray for grace to love the church as Christ does, for it is his own Body, his bride. Pray for your own local congregation to flourish in this hope.

PSALM 103

A psalm of David.

1 Let all that I am praise the LORD;
with my whole heart, I will praise his holy name.
2 Let all that I am praise the LORD;
may I never forget the good things he does for me.
3 He forgives all my sins
and heals all my diseases.
4 He redeems me from death
and crowns me with love and tender mercies.
5 He fills my life with good things.
My youth is renewed like the eagle's!

6 The LORD gives righteousness
and justice to all who are treated unfairly.

7 He revealed his character to Moses
and his deeds to the people of Israel.
8 The LORD is compassionate and merciful,
slow to get angry and filled with unfailing love.
9 He will not constantly accuse us,
nor remain angry forever.
10 He does not punish us for all our sins;
he does not deal harshly with us, as we deserve.
11 For his unfailing love toward those who fear him
is as great as the height of the heavens above the earth.
12 He has removed our sins as far from us
as the east is from the west.
13 The LORD is like a father to his children,
tender and compassionate to those who fear him.
14 For he knows how weak we are;
he remembers we are only dust.
15 Our days on earth are like grass;
like wildflowers, we bloom and die.

16 The wind blows, and we are gone—
as though we had never been here.
17 But the love of the LORD remains forever
with those who fear him.
His salvation extends to the children's children
18 of those who are faithful to his covenant,
of those who obey his commandments!

19 The LORD has made the heavens his throne;
from there he rules over everything.

20 Praise the LORD, you angels,
you mighty ones who carry out his plans,
listening for each of his commands.
21 Yes, praise the LORD, you armies of angels
who serve him and do his will!
22 Praise the LORD, everything he has created,
everything in all his kingdom.

Let all that I am praise the LORD.

Let all that I am praise the LORD; with my whole heart, I will praise his holy name. (1)

Frederick Lehman's hymn "The Love of God" expresses with gratefulness the impossibility of ever adequately describing the love of God:

> Could we with ink the ocean fill,
> And were the skies of parchment made;
> Were every stalk on earth a quill,
> And every man a scribe by trade;
> To write the love of God above
> Would drain the ocean dry,
> Nor could the scroll contain the whole,
> Though stretched from sky to sky.
>
> O love of God, how rich and pure!
> How measureless and strong!
> It shall forevermore endure,
> The saints' and angels' song.

Yet unfathomable as his love is, we must keep attempting to sing of it. Psalm 103 offers one of the best ways to try. Using its words and structure as a guide, pray through four stages.

+++

Let all that I am praise the LORD; may I never forget the good things he does for me. (2)

Praise the Lord for what he has done for you personally (verses 1-5):

What has God been to you? He forgives, heals, redeems, crowns, and satisfies—list the ways you have known him to do this. Praise him that he loves you from youth to old age, even renewing your youth like the eagle's (see also Psalm 92:14; Isaiah 40:30-31).

The LORD is compassionate and merciful, slow to get angry and filled with unfailing love. (8)
Praise him for his patient love for his people (verses 6-14): Maybe you've never thought to do this before, but it will greatly deepen your appreciation of the love of God. Use what you know of biblical history, or church history, and do what David does: think of God's patience with a people who have never distinguished themselves by their faithfulness—and of a God who has nevertheless. Their story is our story too. "Nevertheless" is a great grace word!

There is a line in this section of the psalm that could not be fully understood until Jesus came:

The LORD is like a father to his children, tender and compassionate to those who fear him. (13)
David said God is *like* a father. Jesus said God *is* the Father and that his very mission was to make the Father known (Matthew 11:27). If you think about it, the great love that this psalm celebrates makes better sense when you know that it is the love of a God who is the great Father, the Father of the fatherless.

John Fountain, a professor of journalism at the University of Illinois at Urbana-Champaign, lost his father at age four, when his dad was led away from his apartment in handcuffs, leaving his family in poverty. But in the years that followed, John discovered the God of this psalm, a God he came "to know as father, as Abba—Daddy."

He gave his testimony in the NPR series *This I Believe*:

> I believe in God. Not that cosmic, intangible spirit-in-the-sky that Mama told me as a little boy "always was and always will be." But the God who embraced me when Daddy disappeared from our lives. . . .
>
> The God who held my hand when I witnessed boys in my 'hood swallowed by the elements, by death, and by hopelessness;

who claimed me when I felt like "no-man's son," amid the absence of any man to wrap his arms around me and tell me, "everything's going to be okay," to speak proudly of me, to call me son.

I believe in God, God the Father, embodied in his Son Jesus Christ. The God who allowed me to feel his presence—whether by the warmth that filled my belly like hot chocolate on a cold afternoon, or that voice, whenever I found myself in the tempest of life's storms, telling me (even when I was told I was "nothing") that I was *something*, that I was his, and that even amid the desertion of the man who gave me his name and DNA and little else, I might find in him sustenance.[214]

But the love of the LORD remains forever with those who fear him. (17)

Praise God for his faithfulness in death (verses 15-18). Remember that life is short and your only firm hope is in the eternal Father, who made you and sympathizes with your frailty. The idea here is not to be somber but sober enough to understand freshly your hope in God's love.

The LORD has made the heavens his throne; from there he rules over everything. . . . Praise the LORD, everything he has created, everything in all his kingdom. (19, 22)

Praise God with the whole created order (verses 19-22): Actually, pray in such a way that the exhortations of verses 20-22 become your exhortations. Tell the angels to praise God. Tell creatures and plants and mountains and bodies of water to praise God! David did. So did Saint Francis. Address them by name: "Azaleas and whales, Gobi Desert and Lake Michigan—praise the Lord!"

PSALM 119

(selected verses)

Beth

9 How can a young person stay pure?
By obeying your word.
10 I have tried hard to find you—
don't let me wander from your commands.
11 I have hidden your word in my heart,
that I might not sin against you.
12 I praise you, O LORD;
teach me your decrees.
13 I have recited aloud
all the regulations you have given us.
14 I have rejoiced in your laws
as much as in riches.
15 I will study your commandments
and reflect on your ways.
16 I will delight in your decrees
and not forget your word.

Gimel

17 Be good to your servant,
that I may live and obey your word.
18 Open my eyes to see
the wonderful truths in your instructions.
19 I am only a foreigner in the land.
Don't hide your commands from me!
20 I am always overwhelmed
with a desire for your regulations.
21 You rebuke the arrogant;
those who wander from your commands are cursed.
22 Don't let them scorn and insult me,
for I have obeyed your laws.
23 Even princes sit and speak against me,
but I will meditate on your decrees.

24 Your laws please me;
they give me wise advice. . . .

He

33 Teach me your decrees, O LORD;
I will keep them to the end.
34 Give me understanding and I will obey your
instructions;
I will put them into practice with all my heart.
35 Make me walk along the path of your commands,
for that is where my happiness is found.
36 Give me an eagerness for your laws
rather than a love for money!
37 Turn my eyes from worthless things,
and give me life through your word.
38 Reassure me of your promise,
made to those who fear you.
39 Help me abandon my shameful ways;
for your regulations are good.
40 I long to obey your commandments!
Renew my life with your goodness.

Waw

41 LORD, give me your unfailing love,
the salvation that you promised me.
42 Then I can answer those who taunt me,
for I trust in your word.
43 Do not snatch your word of truth from me,
for your regulations are my only hope.
44 I will keep on obeying your instructions
forever and ever.
45 I will walk in freedom,
for I have devoted myself to your commandments.
46 I will speak to kings about your laws,
and I will not be ashamed.
47 How I delight in your commands!
How I love them!

48 I honor and love your commands.
I meditate on your decrees. . . .

Mem

97 Oh, how I love your instructions!
I think about them all day long.
98 Your commands make me wiser than my enemies,
for they are my constant guide.
99 Yes, I have more insight than my teachers,
for I am always thinking of your laws.
100 I am even wiser than my elders,
for I have kept your commandments.
101 I have refused to walk on any evil path,
so that I may remain obedient to your word.
102 I haven't turned away from your regulations,
for you have taught me well.
103 How sweet your words taste to me;
they are sweeter than honey.
104 Your commandments give me understanding;
no wonder I hate every false way of life.

Nun

105 Your word is a lamp to guide my feet
and a light for my path.
106 I've promised it once, and I'll promise it again:
I will obey your righteous regulations.
107 I have suffered much, O Lord;
restore my life again as you promised.
108 Lord, accept my offering of praise,
and teach me your regulations.
109 My life constantly hangs in the balance,
but I will not stop obeying your instructions.
110 The wicked have set their traps for me,
but I will not turn from your commandments.
111 Your laws are my treasure;
they are my heart's delight.
112 I am determined to keep your decrees
to the very end. . . .

Tsadhe

137 O LORD, you are righteous,
and your regulations are fair.
138 Your laws are perfect
and completely trustworthy.
139 I am overwhelmed with indignation,
for my enemies have disregarded your words.
140 Your promises have been thoroughly tested;
that is why I love them so much.
141 I am insignificant and despised,
but I don't forget your commandments.
142 Your justice is eternal,
and your instructions are perfectly true.
143 As pressure and stress bear down on me,
I find joy in your commands.
144 Your laws are always right;
help me to understand them so I may live.

> How I delight in your commands! How I love them! I honor and love your commands. I meditate on your decrees. (47-48)

Frederick Buechner writes, "To read the Bible as literature is like reading *Moby Dick* as a whaling manual or *The Brothers Karamazov* for its punctuation."[215] That's true enough. But Psalm 119 is a rather astonishing work of poetic literature whose message is powerfully advanced by the poetic form it takes.

Psalm 119 is an acrostic poem, meaning that each of its twenty-two stanzas bears the title of one of the twenty-two letters of the Hebrew alphabet in succession, and each of the eight lines of every stanza begins with that letter. So the title of the first stanza is *aleph*, the first letter of the Hebrew alphabet, and each of that stanza's eight lines begins with the letter *aleph*; and so on with *beth*, *gimel*, and *daleth*, to the end of the alphabet and the psalm. This is hard to do! And to make it even harder, one of the letters, *waw*, is never used in Hebrew as the first letter of a word. No words begin with *waw*! So the clever poet used *waw* as a prefix, meaning something like "and."

What's the point? The whole psalm is about the Law, the Torah, the Word of God. Using the alphabet this way points to an intimate, inner connection between human language and God's speech: It says that the basis of human language, its essence and character, is rooted in God's Word. We speak because God first speaks. Our words find their origin in God's Word. Thus the purpose of language is not merely to communicate one's point of view but to convey truth and ultimately to point back to the God who is both the truth and the origin of language.[216]

It's against the rich background of Psalm 119 that Jesus prayed for his disciples: "Make them holy by your truth; teach them your word, which is truth."[217] And so we pray also. The longest book in the Bible, the Psalms, is a book of prayers. The longest chapter in this book of prayers is a psalm celebrating the Law, the Word of God. Bonhoeffer saw this as "pure grace," that God, who gives the gift of language, would also give us the language of prayer.[218] The mystery that the Word of God may also become the words of humans is second only to the mystery of the Incarnation.

Charles Vaughn tells the story of a grandfather walking through his yard and hearing his little granddaughter repeat the words of the alphabet in a tone of voice that sounded like prayer. He asked her what she was doing. She explained: "I'm praying, but I can't think of exactly the right words, so I'm just saying all the letters, and God will put them together for me, because he knows what I'm thinking."[219] She wasn't far off. The God who gave her the letters of the alphabet and the gift of language will listen. Words matter to God, and they should matter to us—especially his words about his Word.

For purely practical reasons, the great length of Psalm 119 has forced many to pray it in "bite-size" chunks. Actually *bite-size* is a good term, because it suggests meditation, the careful, thoughtful chewing on the truth that is at the heart of prayer. God's Word is not fast food. What follows are some highlights and recurring themes from this psalm on the Word of God. Use them as material for praise, confession, and petition.

Don't worship the Bible but the God of the Bible. Let the words and commands of the Bible lead you to the God of the Bible. Pray the way the psalmist prayed, linking obedience to God's commands to the knowledge of God.

+++

I have tried hard to find you—don't let me wander from your commands. **(10)**
Pray that the Holy Spirit will give you understanding when you read the Scriptures.

Open my eyes to see the wonderful truths in your instructions. **(18)**
The Word of God shows the way of freedom. Pray that the power of the Word will make you free.

I will pursue your commands, for you expand my understanding. . . . I will walk in freedom, for I have devoted myself to your commandments. (32, 45)
Praise God that his Word is absolutely faithful.

Your promises have been thoroughly tested; that is why I love them so much. (140)
Pray that the Word of God will keep you from sin. There is an old saying: "This book will keep you from sin, and sin will keep you from this book."

I have hidden your word in my heart, that I might not sin against you. (11)
Pray that the Word of God will make you wise.

I am even wiser than my elders, for I have kept your commandments. (100)
Pray that the Word of God will guide you.

Your word is a lamp to guide my feet and a light for my path. (105)
Pray that the Spirit would use his words to illuminate your way—today and every day.

PSALM 120

A song for pilgrims ascending to Jerusalem.

1 I took my troubles to the LORD;
I cried out to him, and he answered my prayer.
2 Rescue me, O LORD, from liars
and from all deceitful people.
3 O deceptive tongue, what will God do to you?
How will he increase your punishment?
4 You will be pierced with sharp arrows
and burned with glowing coals.

5 How I suffer in far-off Meshech.
It pains me to live in distant Kedar.
6 I am tired of living
among people who hate peace.
7 I search for peace;
but when I speak of peace, they want war!

Rescue me, O LORD, from liars and from all deceitful people. (2)

*H*uman history as we know it began with a lie, the Big Lie.

> "You won't die!" the serpent replied to the woman. "God knows that your eyes will be opened as soon as you eat it, and you will be like God, knowing both good and evil."[220]

That's what the serpent said to the first humans about God's command and his intentions for us—that God is a liar and that all he wants to do with his command is to keep us down, dumb, and ignorant. We've been dying ever since we believed that first, big lie. And every other lie that has been told since is a variation on the first.

The Lord Jesus underlined the lying perverseness of the devil when he linked Satan's love of lies to his thirst for human blood:

> He was a murderer from the beginning. He has always hated the truth, because there is no truth in him. When he lies, it is consistent with his character; for he is a liar and the father of lies.[221]

The devil lies that he may murder. Behind his flattering smile are the jaws of a predator.

The problem is, something in us likes to be lied to. In Calvin Miller's mythic retelling of the New Testament story, the Singer Trilogy, the devil is portrayed as the "Prince of Mirrors." He will show you yourself from a thousand different angles, all at once, in dizzying confusion. Every look has an element of truth in it, but taken together, they all add up to the Big Lie, the inflated, overblown notion that we are gods, immortal and invincible, clever and wise.

Who, in their right mind, would be crazy enough to look into those deadly mirrors? Only those who are already fascinated with themselves. According to the Bible, that's all of us, each and every one. Our greatest fascination is our gravest danger. Apart from the mercy of God, we're all crazy and stupid.

So we pray for mercy.

+++

I took my troubles to the LORD; I cried out to him, and he answered my prayer. (1)
That's prayer reduced to its bare essentials:

> I have troubles,
> God has help,
> I cry out,
> God answers me.

What a deal! Who could pass it up? Only those who believe the Lie. If you have any sense at all, you will pray right now, this very moment, "Lord, help! Save me from the Lie. Save me from my fascination with the Lie. Lead me not into temptation. Deliver me from the evil one."

O deceptive tongue, what will God do to you? How will he increase your punishment? (3)
Pray for God to punish lies and the Liar—and all who serve him—in this life and the next.

How I suffer in far-off Meshech. It pains me to live in distant Kedar. (5)
Geographically, it's impossible to be in both Meshech and Kedar at the same time. Meshech was a hostile tribe located thousands of miles to the north of Israel, in what is now southern Russia. Kedar was a Bedouin tribe that moved along Israel's borders, and it had a reputation for violence and barbarism.

It's impossible to be in both places at once physically, but not spiritually. Meshech and Kedar stand for a hostile world, a world ruled by the murderous lies of the father of lies. It's the same world that hated Jesus and that Jesus said would hate us.[222]

Ask God to open the eyes of your heart to really see where you live—the culture and values you are immersed in and, to some degree, have embraced.

I am tired of living among people who hate peace. (6)
We can't leave the world, but we can pray to be kept safe in it. When we pray this way, we pray with Jesus himself, who prayed to his Father for us:

> I'm not asking you to take them out of the world, but to keep them safe from the evil one. They do not belong to this world any more than I do.[223]

Pray to be kept safe in the world.

We can also repent of the ways we have bought into the world's lies and its hatred of peace. To be tired of living among people who hate peace is to be weary of the things in yourself that have also hated peace.

Renounce anything in your heart and actions that doesn't love peace—the "residents" of Meshech and Kedar who may have moved in. Pray the old Puritan prayer that God destroy "the dark guest within whose hidden presence" makes life unbearable.[224]

PSALM 121

A song for pilgrims ascending to Jerusalem.

1 I look up to the mountains—
does my help come from there?
2 My help comes from the LORD,
who made heaven and earth!

3 He will not let you stumble;
the one who watches over you will not slumber.
4 Indeed, he who watches over Israel
never slumbers or sleeps.

5 The LORD himself watches over you!
The LORD stands beside you as your protective shade.
6 The sun will not harm you by day,
nor the moon at night.

7 The LORD keeps you from all harm
and watches over your life.
8 The LORD keeps watch over you as you come and go,
both now and forever.

I look up to the mountains—does my help come from there? (1)

I commented to a friend that the beautiful Pacific Northwest is the least churched region in the United States. He thought for a moment before he responded, imagining majestic scenes from the Cascade Mountains, I guess. Then he said, "It's so pretty up there, people don't need to go to church to feel close to God. All they need to do is go outside."

His theology came straight from any number of greeting cards I have seen. There is a picture of a mountain and a lake and a piercingly blue sky, with the first verse of this psalm printed below. Usually it comes from an older version of the Bible, something like,

> I will lift up my eyes to the hills—from whence comes my help?

The thought seems to be, *My help comes from the God who's up there on that beautiful mountain or at least is closer to those who get up there.*

My friend's theology was also thoroughly pagan. The mountains this psalm refers to are the mountains an Israelite would encounter on his pilgrimage to Jerusalem. They were often the places where the Canaanites—nature worshipers—would build shrines to their fertility gods: Baal and his female consort, Ashtoreth. The mountain peaks were places of debased idolatry, of drunken orgies and human sacrifice, where lies and depravity were canonized.

So the worshiper of the true and living God would pass the places of these pagan frauds on his way to the Temple and breathe a prayer of thanksgiving as he asked himself rhetorically, *I look up to the mountains—does my help come from there?* He would rejoice that his help did not come from the gods up on the mountains but from the God who made the mountains.

Look around you. What can you see of the false gods of our age? An hour spent watching television ads would more than suffice. In fact, you could turn your time before a television screen into an alternate form of worship:[225] After each ad say, "I look up to [say the name of the product being peddled]. Does my help come from [say it again]?" Then snort a sardonic chuckle, and say, "No way. My help comes from the LORD, who made heaven and earth!" Make it a tradition; pass it on to your children.

+++

My help comes from the LORD, who made heaven and earth! (2)
Praise God that this is so, that the power of the Creator is wielded by a Savior, the Lord of love.

> Look up into the heavens. Who created all the stars? He brings them out like an army, one after another, calling each by its name. Because of his great power and incomparable strength, not a single one is missing. O Jacob, how can you say the LORD does not see your troubles? O Israel, how can you say God ignores your rights?[226]

He will not let you stumble; the one who watches over you will not slumber. Indeed, he who watches over Israel never slumbers or sleeps. (3-4)
Pray your anxiety to God.

List some of the things that can keep you awake at night, worrying. Maybe you have children who keep you awake. Perhaps it's your health or money or a harsh word spoken to you.

Then thank God that each of these is in his care and that while you sleep, he can take care of them. You may slumber because God doesn't slumber. Truth be told, if he can persuade you to sleep, then he can do his good work with one less hindrance—you.

The LORD himself watches over you! The LORD stands beside you as your protective shade. The sun will not harm you by day, nor the moon at night. (5-6)

Circle all the words and phrases in this psalm that speak of God's protection and care. Say them to yourself through the day. Pray them before and as you enter a tense situation. Say them to the Lord when you are faced with a big decision.

PSALM 122

A song for pilgrims ascending to Jerusalem. A psalm of David.

1 I was glad when they said to me,
"Let us go to the house of the LORD."
2 And now here we are,
standing inside your gates, O Jerusalem.
3 Jerusalem is a well-built city;
its seamless walls cannot be breached.
4 All the tribes of Israel—the LORD's people—
make their pilgrimage here.
They come to give thanks to the name of the LORD,
as the law requires of Israel.
5 Here stand the thrones where judgment is given,
the thrones of the dynasty of David.

6 Pray for peace in Jerusalem.
May all who love this city prosper.
7 O Jerusalem, may there be peace within your walls
and prosperity in your palaces.
8 For the sake of my family and friends, I will say,
"May you have peace."
9 For the sake of the house of the LORD our God,
I will seek what is best for you, O Jerusalem.

I was glad when they said to me, "Let us go to the house of the LORD." (1)

I most definitely was not glad when I heard that enthusiastic invitation from under the covers of my bed on a Sunday morning. My mom was summoning me to get up and get ready to go to church, but the bed was warm and I was in junior high school—which meant the services at the little church we attended were boring to my pubescent tastes.

My problem with worship services grew worse as I got older and began to read my Bible more, especially as I read the book of Revelation. For it seemed to me that life in heaven was going to be nothing but an eternal worship service, an interminable performance of Handel's *Messiah* with a choir of billions. I remember asking my Sunday school teacher rather indignantly, "Is this all heaven is? Is this the reward I get for following Jesus—Sunday service every day, forever?" The teacher said something cryptic about it all being symbolic, which seemed to mean that whatever heaven was, it would be better than a worship service.

What I have since come to understand is that not only will heaven and its worship be better than I can possibly think but I will be too. The problem with our worship services now is not only that they are not as good as they one day will be but that we aren't either. We are on a journey to glory, to the eternal household of God, the new Jerusalem, being made more glorious as we go. In Christ, the "veil" has been removed, and as we gaze on Christ, we reflect his glory and are being transformed into his likeness.[227]

So worship now is practice, an exercise in the expansion of our capacity for adoration. But it points to what will be. C. S. Lewis borrowed an image from John Donne—"tuning our instruments"—to describe the relationship between the present and the future of worship.

> The tuning up of the orchestra can be itself delightful, but only to those who can, in some measure, however little, anticipate the symphony. . . . Even our most sacred rites, as they occur in human experience, are, like tuning, promise, not performance. Hence, like the tuning, they may have in them much duty and little delight; or none. But the duty exists for the delight. When we carry out our "religious duties" we are like people digging channels in a waterless land, in order that, when at last the water comes, it may find them ready. I mean, for the most part. There are happy moments, even now, when a trickle creeps along the dry beds; and happy the soul to whom this happens often.[228]

The pilgrims described in this psalm are us! To belong to Christ is to belong to his people, his church, and to be glad, very glad, to be traveling to the land of our true citizenship,[229] the new Jerusalem. To live in this hope is to worship in this hope—to be glad, very glad, that we are summoned "to go to the house of the LORD."

+++

All the tribes of Israel—the LORD's people—make their pilgrimage here. They come to give thanks to the name of the LORD, as the law requires of Israel. (4)

Pray that the Holy Spirit will expand your hope and turn your present duty to worship into a greater delight in worship.

Pray also that you will recognize and celebrate the grand diversity of the Body of Christ—that though we are one people, we have many tribes, traditions, and ways of doing things. Pray for a greater appreciation of the variety of ways we may worship God in spirit and in truth.

Confess the ways you might have dampened God's praise by a superior or hypercritical attitude toward the worship of your congregation.

Here stand the thrones where judgment is given, the thrones of the dynasty of David. (5)

The people of God live under the authority of the King—the greater

Son of David's dynasty. Life among the people of Christ should reflect our submission to him in the way we submit to each other in love. Nothing can kill the vitality of worship in a church more quickly than dissension and gossip.

Pray that the authority of Christ over his church will be expressed in the human authorities he establishes in his church. Pray also that just as the church needs good leaders, it needs good followers, humble men and women who will receive leadership, especially in worship.

Pray against the so-called worship wars that are such a blight on the modern American church. Ask God to get us out of ourselves and to save us from the delusion that our taste in music and liturgy is better than someone else's taste.

Pray for peace in Jerusalem. May all who love this city prosper. (6) Pray for the peace of heaven to come down on the people of God. Jerusalem's very name means "peace," *shalom*. Ask God to prosper his church and to bless richly those who love the church.

PSALM 123

A song for pilgrims ascending to Jerusalem.

1 I lift my eyes to you,
O God, enthroned in heaven.
2 We keep looking to the LORD our God for his mercy,
just as servants keep their eyes on their master,
as a slave girl watches her mistress for the slightest signal.
3 Have mercy on us, LORD, have mercy,
for we have had our fill of contempt.
4 We have had more than our fill of the scoffing of the proud
and the contempt of the arrogant.

We keep looking to the LORD our God for his mercy, just as servants keep their eyes on their master, as a slave girl watches her mistress for the slightest signal. (2)

In the Old Testament there is no finer picture of a servant at prayer than what is pictured in this psalm. In the culture of the ancient Near East, a master spoke to a slave as little as possible, especially during a meal. A good servant learned to watch the master closely, with complete, rapt attention. All that should ever be required was a nod of the head from the master, a look, the slightest hand gesture. If the master was forced to speak, the servant had already failed.

A good servant had learned to know the mind of the master.

That's the way the psalmist waits on God: single of mind, not looking to the left or the right, not distracted—just relentlessly attentive to the master's will.

When a massive army made its move toward Jerusalem to conquer and destroy it, Jehoshaphat prayed to the Lord, his Master:

> O our God, won't you stop them? We are powerless against this mighty army that is about to attack us. We do not know what to do, but we are looking to you for help.[230]

There it is again, the posture of a praying servant: We do not know what to do, but we are looking to you for help.

So what do we do when we don't know what to do? We keep watching and waiting on the Lord. Of course we act and decide as the situation demands, but we do so in the full knowledge that everything we do, we do before the Lord, and we are accountable to him.

The first church I served in called me back to preach twenty-five years after I left. On my way to the church that Sunday morning I remembered how foolish and brash I was when they had me as an assistant pastor. The saying "Seldom right, never in doubt" fit me pretty well then. I thanked God for his and their patience with me. I thanked him that he somehow managed to use me. I said to the Lord, "I was really in over my head then, wasn't I?" I distinctly heard the Lord answer, "So what makes you think you're in your depth now?"

It will always be the same: I am a servant of the Lord, and if I am a wise servant I will fix my eyes on him, "just as servants keep their eyes on their master." I will meditate on his Word and pray it back to him. To do the will of the Lord, I need to know the will of the Lord. I must soak in Scripture to know the mind of my master.

+++

I lift my eyes to you, O God, enthroned in heaven. (1)
Perspective is everything. To pray is to open your eyes to something of God's perspective—enthroned as he is in heaven, ruling the universe. If sin and darkness do nothing more than to keep our eyes looking down, then they have done their worst.

Say these very words as you begin to pray. Sometimes you must praise God much before you make your requests. It helps your faith to remember the majesty of the One to whom you pray.

> Why let the nations say, "Where is their God?" Our God is in the heavens, and he does as he wishes.[231]

Have mercy on us, LORD, have mercy, for we have had our fill of contempt. (3)
Contempt and ridicule cut deep. They are a species of malice more vicious than murder. To have your fill of contempt is to feel the pains of hell itself.[232]

You may need to pray from this awful place yourself, but if you do not, there are many who do and who need your prayers. Pray for abused children. Pray for the persecuted and tortured of the world. Pray for the beaten down and scorned.

PSALM 127

A song for pilgrims ascending to Jerusalem. A psalm of Solomon.

1 Unless the LORD builds a house,
the work of the builders is wasted.
Unless the LORD protects a city,
guarding it with sentries will do no good.
2 It is useless for you to work so hard
from early morning until late at night,
anxiously working for food to eat;
for God gives rest to his loved ones.

3 Children are a gift from the LORD;
they are a reward from him.
4 Children born to a young man
are like arrows in a warrior's hands.
5 How joyful is the man whose quiver is full of them!
He will not be put to shame when he confronts his
accusers at the city gates.

Unless the LORD builds a house, the work of the builders is wasted. Unless the LORD protects a city, guarding it with sentries will do no good. (1)

The Greek myth of Sisyphus provides a kind of pagan commentary on Psalm 127. Sisyphus was a wily fellow who so angered the gods that he was condemned to an eternity of exhausting and useless labor. Specifically, his punishment was to strain and struggle to roll a very large boulder to the top of a hill, only to have it roll back to the bottom so that he had to start over again and again and again forever.

Work without God can be like that—just wasted, meaningless toil. Interestingly, Solomon, whose name is on this psalm, comes to the same conclusion in another book with his name on it, Ecclesiastes:

> So what do people get in this life for all their hard work and anxiety? Their days of labor are filled with pain and grief; even at night their minds cannot rest. It is all meaningless.[233]

It's like the sign that is reportedly on the Alaskan highway: "Choose your rut carefully—you'll be in it for the next two hundred miles." Without God's blessing, all we do is ultimately a long journey down an eternal rut, leading nowhere. Jesus delivered the same stark warning when he said, "Anyone who isn't with me opposes me, and anyone who isn't working with me is actually working against me."[234] Who would dare to work against God? Only a fool! It's a black or white proposition, a hard-edged either-or. Either you work with God or you work against God. Either you fail or you succeed; either you live or you die.

But build with God, work with God, and watch with God, and there will be great, eternal blessing. The promise in verse 2 is as sweet as the warning in verse 1 is bitter. It is also a summons to pray.

+++

It is useless for you to work so hard from early morning until late at night, anxiously working for food to eat; for God gives rest to his loved ones. (2)
Take your pick: Do you want useless, anxious work or rest? It's an easy choice, right? Maybe it's not so easy. Which do you find yourself most often falling into—peaceful sleep or worry, trust or anxiety?

Pray for God to increase your trust in his love for you, "for God gives rest to his loved ones." Confess your lack of trust.

Do you keep the Sabbath day holy, the day God commanded us to observe because we are no longer slaves to work?

> Remember that you were once slaves in Egypt, but the LORD your God brought you out with his strong hand and powerful arm. That is why the LORD your God has commanded you to rest on the Sabbath day.[235]

Pray for faith to stop working on the Sabbath. Pray for forgiveness if you have not used that day for rest and worship! It is, you know, one of the Ten Commandments. And it is a blessing for God's beloved.

Elizabeth Barrett Browning loved this psalm, and wrote,

> Of all the thoughts of God that are
> Borne inward into souls afar,
> Along the Psalmist's music deep,
> Now tell me if that any is,
> For gift or grace surpassing this—
> He giveth his beloved—sleep.[236]

Children are a gift from the LORD; they are a reward from him. (3)
Curiously, the contrast to anxious toil—and an abrupt one, at that—is the gift of rest, and children. The word translated "rest" in the New Living Translation is literally "sleep" in the Hebrew, which gives it a stronger association with a bed—the place where children are

commonly conceived. It's where people sleep and make love that some of God's greatest blessings come! Children are not God's only gift for trusting him. But they rank right up there with the best of his gifts.

The message is a strong one: If you want to build with God, it will be about people, not things. A mere house is not a home. Houses are supposed to house . . . households.

Does your work reflect God's priorities for people and families? Pray that it will.

Do you in any way sacrifice people on the altar of your career? Pray for forgiveness and the gift of repentance.

Children born to a young man are like arrows in a warrior's hands. How joyful is the man whose quiver is full of them! He will not be put to shame when he confronts his accusers at the city gates. (4-5)
Picture an arrow being shot toward a target in the distance. That is the vivid image of the future in the psalm. In the culture of Solomon's day, a large family (especially of sons) was a kind of insurance against poverty and exploitation in old age.

Again, God blesses his beloved with provision for the future. And again, it comes from the time we invest in people, not the money we put into retirement accounts.

Thank God for the people in your life. Pray for the wisdom and foresight to treat them as the blessings they are.

Pray for your children and the children of others. Their righteousness as adults will mean more for your future than you can know now. But live long enough and you'll see. It is God's promise.

PSALM 128

A song for pilgrims ascending to Jerusalem.

1 How joyful are those who fear the Lord—
all who follow his ways!
2 You will enjoy the fruit of your labor.
How joyful and prosperous you will be!
3 Your wife will be like a fruitful grapevine,
flourishing within your home.
Your children will be like vigorous young olive trees
as they sit around your table.
4 That is the Lord's blessing
for those who fear him.

5 May the Lord continually bless you from Zion.
May you see Jerusalem prosper as long as you live.
6 May you live to enjoy your grandchildren.
May Israel have peace!

Your wife will be like a fruitful grapevine, flourishing within your home. Your children will be like vigorous young olive trees as they sit around your table. (3)

I have a pair of photographs, faded a little, that I love. They are in what is called a diptych, two panels joined by hinges. On one side is a picture of my wife, Lauretta, and me on a pier at a beach in Southern California. We're kissing and laughing simultaneously, a rather messy but fun arrangement. We're young and exuberant and without children. The photo opposite it was taken about ten years later. There are four Pattersons in it now: Lauretta and me and two little boys, our first two children, Danny and Joel. The message is, see where all that kissing took us!

Lauretta gave me the diptych as a gift on our tenth wedding anniversary. Generous friends watched our boys so we could go away for a day and a night to celebrate. I unwrapped it over dinner. The next morning I got up to read Scripture and pray with the pair of photos in front of me. It "just so happened" that one of the appointed readings for that day was Psalm 127, with its line "Children are a gift from the Lord; they are a reward from him."[237] No one will ever be able to make me believe that was a mere coincidence.

It also "just so happened" that since Lauretta had been feeling a little "different" lately, we went to a pharmacy that day to purchase a pregnancy testing kit. Sure enough, we discovered she was pregnant. That pregnancy ended up bringing us Andy. No one will ever be able to convince me that was coincidence, either. I could go on about our fourth child, Mary, and the pregnancy that led to her birth. That's a great story too, and another no-way-it's-a-coincidence tale.

As I write this, all our kids are grown up, ranging in age from twenty-three to thirty-one. Two are married, and one has a very "special friend." Amazingly, we still live in the same town and get together a lot. Meals around the table are raucous and full of laughter and prayer. My wife and kids are some of the most interesting and funny people I have ever known. Lauretta never looked better to me.

I say all this with deep joy tinged with uneasiness. I fear my story may sadden those whose families have unraveled and depress those who wish they had a family but don't. We live in a fallen world, and things are sometimes not the way they are supposed to be. I fear that I may take pride in this singular gift from God and treat it as my own achievement, instead of the gracious gift it is. Most of all, I fear that I may forget to be thankful and give the glory to God.

But I will still say what I know and tell of what I have seen of God's promises. This psalm is to be prayed with a literal and dogged faith that will not let go of God until he does what he says he will do for those who fear him.

+++

How joyful are those who fear the LORD—all who follow his ways! . . . That is the LORD's blessing for those who fear him. (1, 4)

The fear of the Lord is the beginning of wisdom, which is the foundation of blessing.[238] You can read all about it in the book of Proverbs, whose themes echo throughout this psalm.

Pray that reverence for God's name be your first priority, that his Kingdom and reputation be the first concern of your life. Do as Jesus commanded, and expect to be blessed: "Seek the Kingdom of God above all else, and live righteously, and he will give you everything you need."[239]

You will enjoy the fruit of your labor. How joyful and prosperous you will be! (2)

When sin entered the world, work was cursed with frustration and futility. The ground Adam tilled for food became infested with thorns. From that time on, Adam and all his children would die trying to make a living. To fear the Lord is to undo in some measure the damage done when God was not feared.

Pray that God be honored in your work and that he bless you with a prosperity that points back to God as the giver of every good gift.

Your wife will be like a fruitful grapevine, flourishing within your home. (3)

That fruitful vine image can be taken two or three ways. It can be a picture of general fruitfulness, of sexual charms, or of festivity and celebration. Did I use the word *or*? I should have used the word *and*, for it can be all of the above.

Thank God for his promise to such a woman, and pray for its fulfillment in a blessed and joyful marriage.

Author Philip Yancey tells of an actor, a sex symbol, who was interviewed on the late-night David Letterman show. He was asked by Letterman how his escapades with gorgeous women on the screen compared to his real life off the screen.

The actor told Letterman that he had been happily married for twenty years. And he added, "Here's the difference in a nutshell. In the movies, life is mostly about sex and occasionally about children. Married life is mostly about children and occasionally about sex."[240]

Not true. Married life is mostly about sex *and* children. It's one piece, one big fabric of blessedness in marriage. Ask God to unify your view of sexual fulfillment with the joy of children. It's a very biblical prayer.

May the LORD continually bless you from Zion. May you see Jerusalem prosper as long as you live. May you live to enjoy your grandchildren. May Israel have peace! (5-6)

God's blessings on a family are not meant to be restricted to its members only. The blessing expands, in ever-widening circles, to include the nation and future generations.

God promised Abraham that the whole world would be blessed through his family.[241] As members of Abraham's family through faith in Christ, we should pray for the same kind of thing to happen through our families.

Be bold in this prayer. Ask God to bless the world and generations yet unborn, not only through your children, but through others' children also.

PSALM 131

A song for pilgrims ascending to Jerusalem. A psalm of David.

1 LORD, my heart is not proud;
my eyes are not haughty.
I don't concern myself with matters too great
or too awesome for me to grasp.
2 Instead, I have calmed and quieted myself,
like a weaned child who no longer cries for its mother's
milk.
Yes, like a weaned child is my soul within me.

3 O Israel, put your hope in the LORD—
now and always.

LORD, my heart is not proud; my eyes are not haughty. (1)

I love to tell this story because it changed my life. It's about how I lost my confidence in myself—a most happy event.

It came by way of two bulging discs in the lumbar region of my back. I needed six weeks of total bed rest, the doctor said. At the end of the rest, he'd determine whether I needed surgery. That wasn't good news, *But at least I will get a lot of reading done,* I thought. But the combination of pain, painkillers, and muscle relaxants nixed that notion. Plus, my bed was too soft for my back, so I spent the entire six weeks lying on the floor. The pain was humiliating: A trip to the restroom was a race between my capacity for pain and the capacity of my bladder. I often had to lie on the floor of the restroom to recover from the trip.

I was of no use to the church I was pastoring either, or so I thought. I couldn't do any of the things a pastor has to do to be a good pastor: preach, teach, make calls, lead meetings and worship. All I could do was pray, which didn't seem like much. So to make it seem more substantial, I decided to pray for every single person in my congregation every day. It took me two or three hours. Don't get me wrong: This wasn't piety; it was boredom and desperation. But very soon those times of prayer grew to be sweet.

Near the end of my convalescence, I had taken a walk and was back on the floor resting and thinking what it would be like to go back to work. I prayed, "Lord, these times of prayer have been sweet. It's too bad I won't have time to pray this much when I go back to work." The Lord answered me very clearly: He said, *Stupid.* Really. It was in a friendly tone, though. He continued, *You have the same twenty-four hours each day when you're well as when you're sick. The trouble with you, Ben, is when you're well you think you're in charge; when you're sick you know you're not.*

I am still far from where I want to be, but I'm not what I was. I want to be able to say with a full heart, "Yes, like a weaned child is my soul within me." Praying this psalm is a good way to get there.

+++

LORD, my heart is not proud; my eyes are not haughty. I don't concern myself with matters too great or too awesome for me to grasp. (1)

The twin sins of pride and presumption are renounced in this verse. They go together because pride undervalues other people and presumption overvalues oneself. Both look down on everyone and everything, including God. They manifest themselves in vaulting ambition and its flip sides, anxiety and the need to control.

Ask the Holy Spirit to give you as much insight into your life and its motives as you can bear. Repent of pride and presumption.

The opposite of pride is humility, or the first word of the psalm, *Lord.* That's it, *Lord.* Only the humble can address God this way. Say *Lord* over and over. Tell him you know he is sovereign and you are not. "Humility is the obverse side of confidence in God," said John Baillie, "whereas pride is the obverse side of confidence in self."

Instead, I have calmed and quieted myself, like a weaned child who no longer cries for its mother's milk. Yes, like a weaned child is my soul within me. (2)

In the culture of the Bible, weaning came much later in life than it usually does in ours. A child might have been six or seven before he or she was weaned. The contrast between a nursing child and a weaned child is profound. The nursing child expects food on demand and gets cranky when she doesn't get it. The weaned child is able to wait until Mom is ready, because she knows Mom can be trusted. The self is no longer the center of the universe. Mom is not a means but a person to know and love.

Ask yourself when you last felt truly contented and at peace. Then pray for this grace. Say to God, "Yes, like a weaned child is my soul within me." If you don't mean it, say it until you do. Tell him you want to trust him even when he's not doing what you'd like him to do. Tell him you'd rather know him better than have him fulfill all your demands.

PSALM 133

A song for pilgrims ascending to Jerusalem. A psalm of David.

1 How wonderful and pleasant it is
when brothers live together in harmony!
2 For harmony is as precious as the anointing oil
that was poured over Aaron's head,
that ran down his beard
and onto the border of his robe.
3 Harmony is as refreshing as the dew from Mount Hermon
that falls on the mountains of Zion.
And there the LORD has pronounced his blessing,
even life everlasting.

How wonderful and pleasant it is when brothers live together in harmony! (1)

I remember the moment I knew, for the first time, that God loved me. It was on a mild, sunny day in November 1963. I don't remember the exact date, but I remember everything else, like where I was walking (across the commons to my dorm room at what was then La Verne College) and even what I was wearing (blue jeans and a white T-shirt). As I walked along, it dawned on me that Jesus had been walking beside me, smiling and speaking of his deep affection for me. It felt something like what I imagined the disciples on the road to Emmaus felt when they realized that Jesus had been walking with them.

I had believed for a long time that God loved me in some broad and powerful way. After all, he had died on the cross for my sins. But I perceived no delight in the divine benevolence. I assumed that in his great love God had managed, with massive effort and a weary sigh, to overcome his disgust toward my lust, greed, and envy, and atone for my guilt. But now I knew and felt that he not only loved me, he actually liked me.

It startled me. As good as it felt, I wondered, *Why now, why here?* Before I got to my room, I knew why: For the past several weeks I had been experiencing the "wonderful and pleasant" harmony this psalm celebrates. My friends and I had been spending a lot of time talking into the wee hours of the morning about the kinds of things college students talk about. As the hours grew late and we got sleepy, our defenses would drop, and sometimes something very personal and intimate would slip out of our mouths, something we had never, ever shared with anyone. At first, whenever that happened to me, I would panic: *Oh no! What if they laugh at me or quietly get up and walk away in silence and disgust?* But that never happened. What usually happened was that someone would say, "You too? I thought I was the only one. . . ."

What had been happening to me was that as the real Ben stepped shyly into the public, he was being loved. Those conversations had been visible signs of God's invisible grace. They were samples of the blessing God pronounces when we live together in harmony.[242] God was loving me through his people.

It's a pleasure to pray this psalm.

+++

How wonderful and pleasant it is when brothers live together in harmony! (1)
This sounds so good. But do you pray for it to be so? Is it so in your church and in your relationships with other believers? Do you desire this the way Jesus does and as he prayed the night he was arrested to be crucified? "I pray that they will all be one, just as you and I are one—as you are in me, Father, and I am in you. And may they be in us so that the world will believe you sent me" (John 17:21).

Pray for harmony. Confess disharmony. Pray to love harmony as much as Jesus does.

For harmony is as precious as the anointing oil . . . (2)
The anointing oil was what consecrated and empowered the priests of the Old Testament. In Christ, the whole church is a holy nation, a priestly people. Harmony is to the church what the anointing oil was to the Aaronic priesthood. It sets us apart and empowers us.

Pray for the gospel to go out in the power of the Holy Spirit, through the church, as we live together as one in Christ.

. . . that was poured over Aaron's head, that ran down his beard and onto the border of his robe. (2)
This is a vivid picture of the work of intercessory prayer.

The phrase *Aaron's beard* was more than descriptive; it was prescriptive. A beard was a symbol of manhood and a requirement for a priest, since the crucial work of a priest was not for mere boys but for mature men. The precious oil poured on Aaron's head ran down and accumulated in a beard that covered his chest. Beneath his beard, on his chest, were twelve stones, one for each of the tribes of Israel. His people, then, were always on his heart as he carried out his priestly duties of prayer and sacrifice.

All believers are priests to one another. Let your prayers for others reflect this—may this anointing oil of the unity of the Holy Spirit move you to pray fervently and frequently for your brothers and sisters in Christ.

Harmony is as refreshing as the dew from Mount Hermon that falls on the mountains of Zion. (3)

The dew that fell on the usually parched and dry ground of Zion was a boon to the plant life there; it made things green and fresh. Harmony is to people what the dew is to plants.

Pray for the people of your church to be refreshed and to flourish in the love and harmony of the Holy Spirit.

And there the LORD has pronounced his blessing, even life everlasting. (3)

The word *there* is emphatic in the Hebrew. The blessing God pronounces is not a general blessing but specific to a place: wherever two or three are gathered together in the name of Christ.[243]

Again, remember the importance of prayers for the church, the Body of Christ. Pray and work for unity and harmony, not just as a pleasant "extra" in the Christian life, but as central to Christ's passion for his people.

PSALM 137

1 Beside the rivers of Babylon, we sat and wept
as we thought of Jerusalem.
2 We put away our harps,
hanging them on the branches of poplar trees.
3 For our captors demanded a song from us.
Our tormentors insisted on a joyful hymn:
"Sing us one of those songs of Jerusalem!"
4 But how can we sing the songs of the LORD
while in a pagan land?

5 If I forget you, O Jerusalem,
let my right hand forget how to play the harp.
6 May my tongue stick to the roof of my mouth
if I fail to remember you,
if I don't make Jerusalem my greatest joy.

7 O LORD, remember what the Edomites did
on the day the armies of Babylon captured Jerusalem.
"Destroy it!" they yelled.
"Level it to the ground!"
8 O Babylon, you will be destroyed.
Happy is the one who pays you back
for what you have done to us.
9 Happy is the one who takes your babies
and smashes them against the rocks!

Happy is the one who takes your babies and smashes them against the rocks! (9)

What on earth could ever make someone want to do *that*? Plenty. Things like tearing open pregnant women and smashing infants' heads against the rocks were but a few of many abuses in the ancient soldier's catalog of cruelties. Wait, correction: This kind of appalling atrocity is not confined to the ancient past. It has been as much a feature of warfare and violence in the twentieth and twenty-first centuries as it was in the sixth century BC. Read about Hitler's Germany, Stalin's Russia, Pol Pot's Cambodia, and Amin's Uganda for starters. Or check out Nanking, Darfur, Myanmar, Burundi, Rwanda, and Croatia. There are also plenty of pictures to look at, if you have the stomach for it.

What on earth could ever make someone want to do *that*? Someone doing it to you, that's what. If the Babylonians did this to Israel while the Edomites cheered them on, then it is understandable that an Israelite would wish the same thing on them.

It's understandable, but inexcusable. Nothing could be further from the teachings of our Lord and the gospel's message of reconciliation. So what are we to do with this psalm? The one thing we must not do is eliminate it, or worse, edit out the offensive part. Rather, let me suggest five perspectives that can help us to allow Psalm 137 to guide our prayers.[244]

+++

O Babylon, you will be destroyed. Happy is the one who pays you back for what you have done to us. (8)

Hear the heart of it. Listen to the whole person who utters it, not just the words spoken. God did this with Jeremiah and Job, whose use of hyperbole would shock us if we heard the kinds of things they said to God spoken in a church prayer meeting.[245] God doesn't buy everything they say and doesn't let them rave on indefinitely, but with a mixture of sympathy and rebuke, he lets them know he hears them.[246] The mere fact that they are speaking to God about God, and not about God to others, is enough for God. What God did with them, and the author of Psalm 137, we should do with others.

Pray that the Holy Spirit would teach you to listen to Scripture and to others the way God listens to you. Pray also that you yourself would not be afraid to speak to God with passion and hyperbole.

Let it affect you. Derek Kidner says this verse is like a raw wound thrust in your face. Smooth, facile answers—though true—don't come easily after we've really let a person's pain into our consciousness. Verses like Psalm 137:9 can be a way to work through the problem the gospel answers. "To cut this witness out of the Old Testament would be to impair its value as revelation, both of what is in man and of what the cross was required to achieve for our salvation."[247]

Pray the way Bob Pierce, the founder of World Vision, prayed: for a heart that can be broken by the things that break the heart of God.

Look at it through the lens of the Cross. The reconciling death of Christ on the cross created a new situation the psalmist knew nothing of. But we know, do we not? The purpose of Christ's death was to deal with the very evil that so consumed the psalmist and his enemies, because as Paul put it, "You were his enemies, separated from him by your evil thoughts and actions. Yet now he has reconciled you to himself through the death of Christ in his physical body."[248]

What the psalmist wished for his enemies, Jesus took on himself. "He was pierced for our rebellion, crushed for our sins. He was beaten so we could be whole. He was whipped so we could be healed."[249]

Pray that the forgiveness Christ has extended to you would extend through you to others.

Appreciate the spiritual realities behind Babylon and Edom. The book of Revelation portrays the ancient city of Babylon as a symbol and a spiritual reality—the same spiritual enemy Paul warns about in Ephesians 6:10-20.[250] In his vision, John sees Babylon as a great, vulgar whore, seducing the nations, drunk on ghastly things:

> In her hand she held a gold goblet full of obscenities and the impurities of her immorality. A mysterious name was written on her forehead: "Babylon the Great, Mother of All Prostitutes and Obscenities in the World." I could see that she was drunk—drunk with the blood of God's holy people who were witnesses for Jesus. I stared at her in complete amazement.[251]

Later in the revelation, God's wrath is seen to be no less than the wrath of the psalmist, as all heaven shouts with joy when this city is destroyed. This Babylon deserves our most extreme malice.

Pray to love what God loves and to hate what God hates: Hate the world, the flesh, and the devil.

Apply it personally. Someone said, "All man's Babylons seek but to impart the glories of his Babylonian heart." Michael Wilcock observes that it is a small step from hating the evil of the whore of Babylon to hating the demonic babies she has birthed in your own heart.[252] These babies must be dashed against the rocks! As C. S. Lewis wrote,

> I know things in the inner world which are like babies; the infantile beginnings of small indulgences, small resentments, which may one day become dipsomania or settled hatred but which woo us and wheedle us with special pleadings and seem so tiny, so helpless. . . . Against all such pretty infants (the dears have such winning ways) the advice of the Psalm is the best. Knock the little bastards' brains out. And "blessed" is he who can, for it's easier said than done.[253]

PSALM 139

For the choir director: A psalm of David.

1 O Lord, you have examined my heart
and know everything about me.
2 You know when I sit down or stand up.
You know my thoughts even when I'm far away.
3 You see me when I travel
and when I rest at home.
You know everything I do.
4 You know what I am going to say
even before I say it, Lord.
5 You go before me and follow me.
You place your hand of blessing on my head.
6 Such knowledge is too wonderful for me,
too great for me to understand!

7 I can never escape from your Spirit!
I can never get away from your presence!
8 If I go up to heaven, you are there;
if I go down to the grave, you are there.
9 If I ride the wings of the morning,
if I dwell by the farthest oceans,
10 even there your hand will guide me,
and your strength will support me.
11 I could ask the darkness to hide me
and the light around me to become night—
12 but even in darkness I cannot hide from you.
To you the night shines as bright as day.
Darkness and light are the same to you.

13 You made all the delicate, inner parts of my body
and knit me together in my mother's womb.
14 Thank you for making me so wonderfully complex!
Your workmanship is marvelous—how well
I know it.

15 You watched me as I was being formed in utter seclusion,
as I was woven together in the dark of the womb.
16 You saw me before I was born.
Every day of my life was recorded in your book.
Every moment was laid out
before a single day had passed.

17 How precious are your thoughts about me, O God.
They cannot be numbered!
18 I can't even count them;
they outnumber the grains of sand!
And when I wake up,
you are still with me!

19 O God, if only you would destroy the wicked!
Get out of my life, you murderers!
20 They blaspheme you;
your enemies misuse your name.
21 O LORD, shouldn't I hate those who hate you?
Shouldn't I despise those who oppose you?
22 Yes, I hate them with total hatred,
for your enemies are my enemies.

23 Search me, O God, and know my heart;
test me and know my anxious thoughts.
24 Point out anything in me that offends you,
and lead me along the path of everlasting life.

If I ride the wings of the morning, if I dwell by the farthest oceans, even there your hand will guide me, and your strength will support me. (9-10)

At the Museum of Modern Art in New York City, there is a sculpture of a hand by the French sculptor Auguste Rodin. Two clay figures of a man and a woman appear to be emerging out of its palm. It was one of Rodin's favorites; he and his students made many casts of it.

Rodin called his masterpiece *The Hand of God*. Picture that hand and know this: Before you cared one way or another, and whether or not you ever do, God has held you in his hand. That is the message of this psalm.

It's significant that the Scripture says he has held you in his hand, not his intellect. Surely his intellect, if one can call it that, comprehends us completely. But God's knowledge of us is not that of a scientist peering through a microscope but of a lover gazing at his beloved.

+++

O Lord, you have examined my heart and know everything about me. . . . You go before me and follow me. You place your hand of blessing on my head. Such knowledge is too wonderful for me, too great for me to understand! (1, 5-6)

His hand has held you not only by his knowledge of you, but also by his presence with you (verse 7). There is no place you can go where you won't find God there with you, ahead of you. A child was asked how she knew there was only one God. She answered, "Because he's so big there isn't room for anyone else." There is room for you, however. He is everywhere present, not just as a fact of his deity, but because of his love. Further, his hand has done more than hold you; he has shaped you by creating you, even knitting you together in your mother's womb. You are a marvel (verses 13-16).

You have been held not only in his hand but by his loving eye.

You watched me as I was being formed in utter seclusion, as I was woven together in the dark of the womb. You saw me before I was born. Every day of my life was recorded in your book. (15-16)

Parents can understand a little bit about this. When one of my sons was seven or eight years old, I took him on a camping trip to the Grand Canyon. Each evening we would watch yet another gorgeous sunset over the canyon and almost whisper in reverent awe our appreciation of God's work in that place. Each evening I was especially aware of his profile outlined against the setting sun. My precious son. So the last evening I said, "You know, there's something here more beautiful than what you're looking at."

He looked at me and said, "No way! What is it? Where is it?"

I said, "It's you. You are more lovely to God than this whole canyon. He made you in his image. He doesn't say that about anything else he made."

We sat together in silence for quite a while.

The wonderful upshot of thoughts like these for prayer is that your Father not only knows what you need before you ask,[254] but he is leaning close to hear you ask. If you bring some great and troubling situation to him, you need not worry that he will say, "Really? Oh, that's terrible. I had no idea. Let me think about what to do." He is master of the situation before you pray about it. In fact, you are praying about it because he has moved you to pray. So be at peace.

> How precious are your thoughts about me, O God. They cannot be numbered! (verse 17)

O LORD, you have examined my heart and know everything about me. (1)

It's a done deal. Complete. Full circle. The examination is over and thorough, and the data is in. The verdict?

> Lord, you know what I do and where I go. You see me when I'm in motion and when I sleep. You know what I think and what I will say. Lord, though you see me clearly and truly, you give me "blessing pats" on my head.[255]

Thank the Lord that his love is able to see you clearly and still affirm you and bless you. Might the Lord be calling you to love someone else so generously? Ask the Lord to fill you with himself that you may do so.

You go before me and follow me. You place your hand of blessing on my head. (5)
Stop a moment and physically place your hand on your head. Press down firmly. What if the blessing of the Good Shepherd were as tangible as the weight of your own hand?

Ask him to place a "hand of blessing" on your head—to palpably see you, know you, love you, and surround you behind and before.

God, if only you would destroy the wicked! Get out of my life, you murderers! . . . O LORD, shouldn't I hate those who hate you? Shouldn't I despise those who oppose you? (19, 21)
When enemies attack is not the time to roll over and play dead. Ask the Lord to fight against your enemies, and his. Join him in his opposition to them. It's nearly impossible to pray this psalm and not become acutely aware of the evil of the murder of the unborn. Pray that God would act to end the shame and scourge of abortion. After all, it's his battle, and it's his reputation that is at stake.

Search me, O God, and know my heart; test me and know my anxious thoughts. Point out anything in me that offends you, and lead me along the path of everlasting life. (23-24)
Happily, the psalm ends with a prayer for God to keep doing all the things the psalmist has thanked him for doing throughout his life. This prayer is a way of saying, "Do it some more, Lord!" Pray that God's love for you and those you love would continue in tangible ways.

PSALM 150

1 Praise the LORD!

Praise God in his sanctuary;
praise him in his mighty heaven!
2 Praise him for his mighty works;
praise his unequaled greatness!
3 Praise him with a blast of the ram's horn;
praise him with the lyre and harp!
4 Praise him with the tambourine and dancing;
praise him with strings and flutes!
5 Praise him with a clash of cymbals;
praise him with loud clanging cymbals.
6 Let everything that breathes sing praises to the LORD!

Praise the LORD!

Praise the LORD! Praise God in his sanctuary; praise him in his mighty heaven! (1)

Let's see if we can get our minds around this command to praise God in his mighty heaven. Philip Yancey offers some comparisons:

> If the Milky Way galaxy were the size of the entire continent of North America, our solar system would fit in a coffee cup. Even now, two Voyager spacecraft are hurtling toward the edge of the solar system at a rate of 100,000 miles per hour. For almost three decades they have been speeding away from earth, approaching a distance of 9 billion miles. When engineers beam a command to the spacecraft at the speed of light, it takes thirteen hours to arrive. Yet this vast neighborhood of our sun—in truth the size of a coffee cup—fits along with several hundred billion other stars and their minions in the Milky Way, one of perhaps 100 billion such galaxies in the universe. To send a light-speed message to the edge of that universe would take 15 billion years.[256]

Well, I guess we really can't get our minds around it. It's too big to think about—God being praised among all those spectacular things spread out across all those great distances. But we are commanded to praise him nevertheless—*everywhere*. God's mighty heaven is his sanctuary. Picture the sky as a huge, vaulted dome, and think of everywhere under that dome as the proper place for worship, and you get the picture of all of life as the arena, the sacred space for the adoration and praise of God. There is no such thing as secular under God. It's all his. So, though we may not be able to get our minds around what it means to worship God out in some distant galaxy, we can begin to get our minds around the command to worship God at home or at work. I have a little sign in my study that says, "My Work Is Part of My Worship." I saw another little sign over a kitchen sink that said, "Divine Services Conducted Here Every Day." Whoever thought of those sayings understands where God's sanctuary is, where he is to be worshiped.

Pray that this be so, everywhere and with everyone.

+++

Praise him for his mighty works; praise his unequaled greatness! (2) Why should we worship God everywhere? Do we even need to ask?

We praise God for the same reason we applaud a great performance. Philosopher George Santayana reportedly walked out of a classroom one fine spring day. Midsentence in a lecture he looked out the window at the beauty outside and said, "Gentlemen, I very much fear that sentence will never be completed. You see, I have an appointment with April."

I have a friend who, when she sees something beautiful in the world, likes to laugh and say of God, "Oh, there he goes, showing off again." Why should we adore God? Open your eyes, for heaven's sake!

But above all, greater than his works in creation, is what the *Book of Common Prayer* calls his "immeasurable love in the redemption of the world through our Lord Jesus Christ; for the means of grace and the hope of glory." Because of all that God made, and all that he saves, the prayer continues,

> And, we pray, give us such an awareness of your mercies, that our hearts may be sincerely thankful, and that we may show forth your praise not only with our lips, but in our lives, by giving up ourselves to your service, and by walking before you in holiness and righteousness all our days; through Jesus Christ our Lord, to whom, with you and the Holy Spirit, be honor and glory throughout all ages. Amen.

Pray this prayer for yourself and your church. And grow your capacity for worship by filling your mind and heart with Scripture that tells us of "his mighty works" and "unequaled greatness."

Praise him with a blast of the ram's horn; praise him with the lyre and harp! (3)

The psalm lists much more than a ram's horn, a lyre, and a harp. It goes on to include several other instruments—tambourine, dance, strings, flutes, and cymbals (verses 4-5). The point is, use every place, every expression, and every instrument and means at your disposal to praise God. He likes music, including percussion, apparently *loud* percussion, as in "loud clanging cymbals." Oh yes, God likes dance, too.

Pray that you and your church would experience and employ the breadth of ways that God likes to be praised.

Confess any cultural prejudice and temperamental limitations that may keep you and your church from the biblical fullness of adoration. Ask God to remove them.

Let everything that breathes sing praises to the LORD! Praise the LORD! (6)

Everything that breathes is everything that lives, especially human beings. When God breathed his breath into Adam, he became a living being.[257] In the introduction, I first quoted poet George Herbert's wonderful line about prayer, which he describes as "God's breath in man returning to his birth."[258] When we praise God, we give back to God something of what he gave to us when he gave us life. We breathe out and we breathe back in, for in praise, "God's mirth roars in our veins and we are alive and enlivened."[259] God's Spirit moves like oxygen in the bloodstream of our souls.

Pray that the command of this psalm be fulfilled so that everything that breathes will sing praise to the Lord. This is a petition for evangelism and disciple making,[260] so name nations and the names of people as you pray. John Piper urges us to remember that:

> Missions is not the ultimate goal of the church. Worship is. Missions exists because worship doesn't. Worship is ultimate, not missions, because God is ultimate, not man. . . . Worship, therefore, is the fuel and goal of missions. It's the goal of missions because in missions we simply aim to bring the nations into the white-hot enjoyment of God's glory. The goal of missions is the gladness of the peoples in the greatness of God. . . . But worship

is also the fuel of missions. Passion for God in worship precedes the offer of God in preaching. You can't commend what you don't cherish. Missionaries will never call out, "Let the nations be glad!" who cannot say from the heart, "I rejoice in the Lord. . . . I will be glad and exult in you, I will sing praise to your name, O Most High" (Psalm 104:34; 9:2). Missions begins and ends in worship.[261]

NOTES

1 James Boice, *Romans*, vol. 2, "The Reign of Grace," Romans 5–8 (Grand Rapids, MI: Baker Book House, 1992), 892.
2 John 1:1-4
3 1 John 4:19
4 Dietrich Bonhoeffer, *Psalms* (Minneapolis: Augsburg, 1974), 15.
5 Charles Spurgeon, *Spurgeon's Expository Encyclopedia*, vol. 4 (Grand Rapids, MI: Baker Book House, 1978), 329.
6 From Ben Patterson, *He Has Made Me Glad* (Downers Grove, IL: InterVarsity Press, 2005), 12. Isaac Loeb Peretz (1852–1915) was a Polish Jewish writer of great distinction in the late nineteenth and early twentieth centuries. The story, as I tell it, is embellished somewhat but faithful to the events as Peretz told him in his short story, originally titled "Bontsche Shveig."
7 I am indebted to W. Bingham Hunter for this insight in his fine little book on prayer, *The God Who Hears* (Downers Grove, IL: InterVarsity Press, 1986), 12.
8 C. S. Lewis, *The Weight of Glory* (New York: Touchstone, 1996), 26.
9 1 John 3:2
10 Augustine, *The Confessions* (Chicago: Houghton Mifflin Company, 1952), 1.
11 Hebrews 4:12
12 George Herbert, "Prayer" *The Complete English Works*, edited and introduced by Ann Pasternak Slater (London: David Campbell Publishers, Ltd., 1995), 49.
13 Quoted by Samuel Zwemer, *Taking Hold of God* (Grand Rapids, MI: Zondervan, 1936), 121.
14 Dante, *The Divine Comedy*, Canto 33 (Chicago: Houghton Mifflin Company, 1952), 157.
15 2 Corinthians 3:18
16 Zwemer, *Taking Hold of God*,121.
17 Eugene Peterson, *A Long Obedience in the Same Direction* (Downers Grove, IL: InterVarsity Press, 2000), 175.
18 P. T. Forsyth, *The Soul of Prayer* (London: Independent Press Ltd., 1954), 11.
19 Revelation 5:9
20 Cf. Matthew 22:31-32
21 Romans 12:15, NIV
22 Psalm 88:1-6
23 Romans 11:13-24
24 Rodney Clapp, *Tortured Wonders* (Grand Rapids, MI: Brazos Press, 2004), 173. Clapp uses these words to describe the whole of Christian spirituality: "In worship and through the sacraments, and in other practices of Christian spirituality, we learn the story of Christ. We are, as it were, written into it—body and soul. Participating in this story, hearing and imitating parts of it like a child learning how to read, we learn a vocabulary, a grammar, and a plot line not otherwise available to us."
25 Psalm 106:19-23
26 1 Corinthians 10:11
27 Psalm 106:47 (emphasis added)
28 1 Peter 2:5, 9
29 John 5:39
30 Cf. Matthew 5:17, where "accomplish their purpose" has the same meaning as "fulfill" in other translations.
31 Luke 24:27

32 Luke 24:44-45
33 Acts 2:25-28
34 Acts 2:29-31
35 A phrase taken from *The Jesus Storybook Bible*, written by Sally Lloyd-Jones and illustrated by Jago Silver (Grand Rapids, MI: Zondervan, 2007). A terrific book—theologically astute, even profound, and beautifully illustrated.
36 Bonhoeffer, *Psalms*, 15.
37 Hebrews 2:11
38 Blaise Pascal, *Pensées*, translated by A. J. Krailsheimer (New York: Penguin Books, 1966), 372.
39 Matthew 6:1-14; Romans 8:34; Hebrews 7:25
40 Romans 8:26-27
41 Eugene Peterson, *A Long Obedience*, 7.
42 Bonhoeffer, *Psalms*, 13–16.
43 Peter Kreeft, *The Fundamentals of the Faith* (San Francisco: Ignatius Press, 1988),191.
44 Spurgeon, *Spurgeon's Expository Encyclopedia*, vol. 4, 329.
45 Quoted by Eugene Peterson, *Answering God: The Psalms as Tools for Prayer* (San Francisco: HarperSanFrancisco, 1991), 142.
46 Erwin McManus, "Seizing Your Divine Moment," *Preaching Today* 25.
47 J. I. Packer, *Knowing God* (Downers Grove, IL: InterVarsity Press, 1973), 18–19.
48 Dietrich Bonhoeffer, *Meditating on the Word*, translated and edited by David Mel Gracie (Lanham, MD: Cowley Publications, 1986).
49 Psalm 1, in the original Hebrew, speaks literally of the joys of "the man" who delights in God's law. The translators of the New Living Translation render this in gender-inclusive language, as "those" and "they." But the Hebrew is emphatically masculine, indicating that what the psalm has primarily in mind is the Man of God, the Messiah, the Anointed One, the Christ. Psalm 2, then, is the continuation of Psalm 1, describing the hostility of the world toward God's chosen one, this Man who delights in God's law. But the gender-inclusive language is not a mistranslation as such; it is rather a translator's decision to connect the broader message of the psalm with the reader—that what is true of "the man" is true of all God's people.
50 Ephesians 6:12
51 Philippians 2:10-11
52 Revelation 2:26-28
53 Genesis 12:1-3
54 Patrick Henry Reardon, *Christ in the Psalms* (Ben Lomond, CA: Conciliar Press, 2000), 6.
55 Ephesians 6:12
56 1 Peter 2:11
57 Matthew 16:26
58 Ephesians 6:13-17
59 Ephesians 6:18
60 Matthew 10:28-31
61 1 Peter 2:23
62 Thomas à Kempis, *The Imitation of Christ*, quoted in *Christianity Today* 41, no. 1.
63 John 15:18
64 Psalm 127:2
65 George Herbert, "Even-song," *The Complete English Works*, 61.
66 John 7:38
67 An insight from Derek Kidner's excellent commentary on the Psalms, *The Tyndale Old Testament Commentary Series, Psalms 1–72* (Downers Grove, IL: InterVarsity Press, 1973), 58.
68 Romans 8:26
69 Psalm 16:11
70 Film producer Linda Obst (*Sleepless in Seattle* and *Contact*) said this of the culture of Hollywood. This was first reported in the *Los Angeles Times* (February 13, 2001); reprinted in *Citizen* magazine (May 2001), 9.
71 Reuters, on AOL News (September 8, 2005).
72 His condition: weak, hurting, sick at heart, dying, worn out, sobbing. weeping, grieving, fearful.

[73] His desires of the Lord: don't rebuke me; don't discipline me in your anger; have compassion; heal, restore, and rescue me; return to me; save me.
[74] About his enemies: go away, be disgraced and terrified, turn back in shame.
[75] Hebrews 12:7-11
[76] Psalm 40:2
[77] Reardon, *Christ in the Psalms*, 12.
[78] Romans 6:23
[79] 1 John 1:9
[80] 2 Samuel 16:8
[81] James 1:19-20
[82] 1 Peter 5:8
[83] Revelation 3:7
[84] Act II, Scene 2. Quoted in John Stott, *The Contemporary Christian* (Downers Grove, IL: InterVarsity Press, 1992), 40.
[85] Genesis 1:26
[86] Hebrews 2:8-9
[87] Quoted in Reardon, *Christ in the Psalms*, 16.
[88] Note how Jesus quotes this line in Matthew 21:16, using it as an indirect claim to his deity.
[89] John 5:17, 19
[90] Pascal, *Pensées*, number 739.
[91] Figures taken from J. R. Rozko, in "The Other Side of 'At-Risk': Freeing Youth from Suburban Oppression," *Theology News and Notes* (Fall 2007).
[92] Eugene Peterson, *Run with the Horses*, quoted in Howard Hendricks, "Beyond the Bottom Line," *Preaching Today*, tape no. 101.
[93] Habakkuk 1:13
[94] David Ian Miller, "Finding My Religion: Julia Sweeney Talks about How She Became an Atheist," August 15, 2005, *San Francisco Chronicle*, http://www.sfgate.com/cgi-bin/article.cgi?f=/g/a/2005/08/15/findrelig.DTL.
[95] Pascal, *Pensées*, 423.
[96] John Baillie, "Our Knowledge of God," *Christianity Today* 33, no. 14.
[97] Quoted in Phillip E. Howard, *The Life and Diary of David Brainerd*, ed. Jonathan Edwards (Grand Rapids, MI: Baker Books, 1989), 14, emphasis added.
[98] Peter quoted this passage in his Pentecost sermon and saw in it a prophecy of Christ's resurrection (Acts 2:25-31).
[99] John Piper, "Fireworks and Full Moon: A Parable," in *The Bethlehem Star*, newsletter of Bethlehem Baptist Church, July 7, 1993.
[100] *The Oxford Dictionary of Quotations* (Oxford: Oxford University Press, 1980), 256.
[101] Hebrews 10:19-22
[102] John 10:1-30
[103] Psalms 28:9; 79:13; 80:1; 95:7; 100:3
[104] John 10:11-14
[105] Matthew 10:29-31
[106] 2 Samuel 6:12-23
[107] Ephesians 1:19-23
[108] Bennett Cerf, "This Land Is God's Land," *Leadership Journal 1*, no. 2.
[109] Hebrews 4:14-16
[110] Matthew 28:18
[111] Romans 11:36, NIV
[112] Psalm 36:8
[113] Romans 8:31-39
[114] Luke 10:41-42
[115] Rubem Alves, *Tomorrow's Child* (New York: Harper and Row, 1972), 195.
[116] W. H. Auden, "For the Time Being: A Christmas Oratorio" (New York: Random House, 1944).
[117] Exodus 32:11-14
[118] Luke 23:46
[119] William Barclay, *The Gospel of Luke* (Philadelphia: The Westminster Press, 1956), 301–302.

120 Told by Henri Nouwen in *Sabbatical Journeys*, cited by John Ortberg, from the sermon "Waiting on God," *Preaching Today* no. 199.
121 John Stott, "The Contemporary Christian," *Christianity Today* 38, no. 7.
122 Perry D. LeFevre, ed., *The Prayers of Kierkegaard* (Chicago: The University of Chicago Press, 1956), 21.
123 C. S. Lewis, *The Great Divorce* (New York: The Macmillan Company, 1959), 126–127.
124 Scan the psalm to survey the many ways it speaks of the punishment of the wicked. They bring much of it upon themselves (for instance, verses 2, 9-10, 13), even stabbing themselves with their own swords (verse 15)!
125 Alexander MacLaren, *Expositions of Holy Scripture*, vol. 4, Psalm 37 (Grand Rapids, MI: Baker, 1977), 259.
126 Ezekiel 36:26-27
127 Hebrews 10:1-10
128 Mark 14:36; see also John 5:30; Philippians 2:8.
129 Reardon, *Christ in the Psalms*, 77–78.
130 Dora Greenwell, "I Am Not Skilled to Understand," *Hymns II* (Downers Grove, IL: InterVarsity Press, 1976), 101.
131 William Cowper, "God Moves in a Mysterious Way," *The Hymnal* (Philadelphia: Presbyterian Board of Christian Education, 1933), 103.
132 Quoted in John Piper, *The Roots of Endurance* (Wheaton, IL: Crossway, 2002), 57.
133 Told by Bob Russell, author and preaching minister, Southeast Christian Church, Louisville, KY, www.PreachingToday.com/illustrations.
134 Psalm 36:8
135 Mark 4:39
136 C. S. Lewis, "Is Christianity Hard or Easy?" *Mere Christianity* (New York: Macmillan, 1952), 154.
137 Frederick W. Faber (1814–1863).
138 Thus Patrick Henry Reardon argues in his insightful essay on this psalm in *Christ in the Psalms*, 101–102. At least Judas suffered some remorse for his actions. Doeg was as morally dull as a sack of nails.
139 The complete story is found in 1 Samuel 21–22.
140 Romans 3:12
141 P. T. Forsyth, *The Soul of Prayer* (London: Independent Press, 1954), 11.
142 See 2 Corinthians 3:18, 2 Peter 1:3-4, and 1 John 3:2.
143 Told by Vernon Grounds in *Leadership Journal* 8, no. 1.
144 This account is taken from a conversation I had with Helen Roseveare at a conference in Kenya in 1994 and a portion of Philip Ryken's book *The Message of Salvation* (Downers Grove, IL: InterVarsity Press, 2000).
145 Hebrews 5:7
146 2 Corinthians 5:21
147 John 2:17-22
148 Romans 15:3
149 Matthew 26:39
150 See Mark 10:38; Luke 12:50; Romans 6:3.
151 Matthew 26:40
152 Acts 1:20
153 John 15:18-20
154 *Traveling Mercies* (New York: Anchor Books, 2000).
155 Karl Barth, *Church Dogmatics 3*, part 4, 615.
156 Robertson McQuilkin, "Let Me Get Home before Dark," *A Promise Kept* (Carol Stream, IL: Tyndale House Publishers, 1998), 81–84.
157 Frederick Buechner, *Wishful Thinking: A Theological ABC* (New York: Harper and Row Publishers, 1973), 2.
158 Alexander Maclaren, *Expositions of Holy Scripture*, Psalm 73 (Grand Rapids, MI: Baker Book House, 1977), 104.
159 1 Corinthians 15:24-28
160 Revelation 6:10-11
161 William Norman Ewer (1885–1976) in *The Oxford Dictionary of Quotations*, 1980), 209.

162 As Eugene Peterson put it in his paraphrase of this verse in *The Message*.
163 Deuteronomy 7:7-8
164 A "Hebrew of Hebrews" (Philippians 3:5, NIV).
165 Reardon, *Christ in the Psalms*, 151–152.
166 First Amendment Project, eBay.com (September 26, 2005); submitted by Sam O'Neal, St. Charles, IL, in PreachingToday.com.
167 J. C. Ryle, *A Call to Prayer* (Laurel, MS: Audubon Press), 28.
168 "450 Sheep Jump to Their Deaths in Turkey," Associated Press, July 8, 2005, http://www.usatoday.com/news/offbeat/2005-07-08-sheep-suicide_x.htm; John Sturgis, "Sheep in Mass 'Ewe-icide,'" *The Sun Online* (July 8, 2005), http://www.thesun.co.uk/sol/homepage/news/article109700.ece.
169 Judges 4:14-21
170 Judges 7:25; 8:18-21
171 Genesis 3:1, 15
172 Luke 12:4-5
173 See 1 Kings 16:29–19:18
174 Ephesians 6:12
175 1 Kings 19:1-13
176 Revelation 6:10; 19:11-16
177 Buechner, *Wishful Thinking*, 31, 54.
178 Romans 1:25
179 Psalm 36:9
180 John 1:14; 2:21
181 2 Corinthians 6:16; Ephesians 2:19-22
182 Hebrews 11:10
183 Colossians 3:1
184 Ephesians 4:5-6
185 Luke 13:29
186 Revelation 5:9-10
187 Galatians 4:24-26
188 Timothy George, "Delighted by Doctrine," *Christian History & Biography* (Summer 2006).
189 This is John Piper's wonderful phrase.
190 John 4:14
191 Reardon, *Christ in the Psalms*, 173–174.
192 Luke 18:1-8; an insight of Derek Kidner, *Psalms 73–150: A Commentary* (Downers Grove, IL: InterVarsity Press, 1975), 317.
193 Psalm 22:1-2
194 Romans 6:23
195 Pascal, *Pensées*, no. 165–166.
196 Matthew 4:5-7
197 Isaiah 55:8-9
198 Hebrews 12:2
199 Colossians 3:3-4
200 Henry van Dyke, "The Upward Path," *Christianity Today* 40, no. 1.
201 Ephesians 6:10-20
202 1 Peter 5:8; Revelation 12:9; 20:2
203 Earl Palmer, *Alive from the Center* (Waco, TX: Word, 1982), 19.
204 Philippians 2:9-11
205 John Piper, *Let the Nations Be Glad!* (Grand Rapids, MI: Baker Book House, 2003), 11.
206 See Eugene Peterson's creative and utterly fascinating exploration of the idea of a praying imagination in *Reversed Thunder: The Revelation of John and the Praying Imagination* (San Francisco: Harper and Row, 1988).
207 George Herbert, "Providence," *The Complete English Works*, 113.
208 "The Dick Staub Interview: Brennan Manning on Ruthless Trust," ChristianityToday.com (December 10, 2002).
209 Virginia Stem Owens, *And the Trees Clap Their Hands*, quoted by Bob Benson and Michael W. Benson in *Disciplines for the Inner Life* (Waco, TX: Word Books, 1985), 334.
210 Quoted in *Leadership Journal* 10, no. 4.

211 Spoken by a character in Nikos Kazanzakis's novel *Christ Recrucified.*
212 Attributed to Chuck Swindoll.
213 Bruce Larson, *Leadership Journal 40* (Winter 1987).
214 Excerpted from "The God Who Embraced Me," *All Things Considered*, www.npr.org (posted November 28, 2005).
215 Buechner, *Wishful Thinking*, 6.
216 I owe a great debt to Patrick Henry Reardon and his comments in several places for these insights. See especially *Christ in the Psalms*, 237.
217 John 17:17
218 Dietrich Bonhoeffer, *Psalms: The Prayer Book of the Bible* (Minneapolis: Augsburg Fortress, 1970), 14–15.
219 Story taken from Ben Patterson, ed., *Prayer Devotional Bible* (Grand Rapids, MI: Zondervan, 2004), 1580.
220 Genesis 3:4-5
221 John 8:44
222 John 15:18-19
223 John 17:15-16
224 Arthur Bennett, ed., *The Valley of Vision: A Collection of Puritan Prayers and Devotions* (Edinburgh: Banner of Truth Trust, 2006), 127.
225 I say "alternate form of worship" because so many ads are in themselves worship of the false gods of our age.
226 Isaiah 40:26-27
227 2 Corinthians 3:18
228 C. S. Lewis, *Reflections on the Psalms* (New York: Harcourt, Brace, Jovanovich, 1964), 7.
229 Philippians 3:20; Galatians 4:26; Hebrews 12:22
230 2 Chronicles 20:12
231 Psalm 115:2-3
232 The words used for the shame and disgrace of hell in Daniel 12:2 carry the same idea.
233 Ecclesiastes 2:22-23
234 Luke 11:23
235 Deuteronomy 5:15
236 Quoted in Herbert Lockyer Sr., *Psalms: A Devotional Commentary* (Grand Rapids, MI: Kregel Publications, 1993), 654.
237 Psalm 127:3
238 Proverbs 1:7
239 Matthew 6:33
240 Philip Yancey, "Holy Sex: How It Ravishes Our Souls," *Christianity Today* (October 2003).
241 Genesis 12:1-3
242 Adapted from Patterson, *He Has Made Me Glad*, 96.
243 Matthew 18:20
244 The first three come from Derek Kidner's helpful commentary on this psalm: *Psalms 73–150: A Commentary on Books III–V of the Psalms* (Downers Grove, IL: InterVarsity Press, 1975), 461.
245 Jeremiah 20:15-17
246 For example, Jeremiah 12:5; 15:19 and Job 38:2; 42:7.
247 Kidner, *Psalms 73–150*, 461.
248 Colossians 1:21-22
249 Isaiah 53:5
250 Especially verse 12: "We are not fighting against flesh-and-blood enemies, but against evil rulers and authorities of the unseen world, against mighty powers in this dark world, and against evil spirits in the heavenly places."
251 Revelation 17:4-6
252 Michael Wilcock, *The Message of Psalms 73–150: The Bible Speaks Today* (Downers Grove, IL: InterVarsity Press, 2001), 256.
253 C. S. Lewis, *Reflections on the Psalms* (New York: Harcourt, Brace, Jovanovich, 1958), 136.
254 Matthew 6:8
255 My wife, Lauretta, came up with the "blessing pats" image, which I included in this prayer I wrote.

[256] Philip Yancey, *Prayer: Does It Make Any Difference?* (Grand Rapids, MI: Zondervan, 2006), 20.
[257] Genesis 2:7
[258] George Herbert, "Prayer," *The Complete English Works*, 49.
[259] Attributed to Theodore Jennings.
[260] Matthew 28:18-20
[261] Piper, *Let the Nations Be Glad!* 11.

PSALMS FOR SPECIFIC NEEDS

---

*While most of the psalms in this index are grouped according to specific occasions, this longest of the psalms provides an excellent tool for training your soul in the truth of God for all occasions. Read it slowly to meditate on the inexhaustibility of God and his truth. The great eighth-century Christian Alcuin said of this psalm that "there is no verse but that it contains either the way of God, the law of God, the commandment of God, the precept of God, his words, his judgments or his utterances. And so you have no need to spend your soul in the pursuit of all sorts of books."